ENVIRONMENT
UNDER FIRE

ENVIRONMENT UNDER FIRE

Imperialism and the Ecological Crisis in Central America

Daniel Faber

Monthly Review Press
New York

Library of Congress Cataloging-in-Publication Data
Faber, Daniel J.
    Environment under fire: imperialism and the ecological crisis in Central
America / Daniel Faber.
        p. cm.
    Includes bibliographical references and index.
    ISBN 0-85345-839-1 : $36.00. ISBN 0-85345-840-5 (pbk.) : $16.00
    1. Environmental policy—Central America. 2. Central America—Economic
conditions—1979- 3. Central America—Foreign economic
relations—United States. 4. United States—Foreign economic
relations—Central America. 5. Economic development—Environmental
aspects. I. Title.
HC141.Z9E54 1992
363.5'06'098—dc20   92-41825
                                                         CIP

Monthly Review Press
122 West 27th Street
New York NY 10001

Manufactured in the United States of America

10 9 8 7 6 5 4 3 2 1

For my loving father Charles F. Faber,
whose selfless and life-long dedication
to the betterment of humanity
has inspired me from the beginning.

CONTENTS

PREFACE

This book is the product of eight years of research, writing, and organizing around issues of U.S. foreign policy and the social and ecological crisis in Central America. Most of this work was carried out between 1985 and 1990 in my capacity as research director with the Environmental Project On Central America (EPOCA), an organization that brought together North Americans and Central Americans in common struggle against the exploitation of human and non-human nature in the region. Our educational and organizational efforts—including two major international environmental conferences in Nicaragua, material aid campaigns, lobbying and political mobilization projects, an award-winning video documentary, Green Paper reports, and sponsorship of ecological brigades and high-level environmental delegations—alerted tens of thousands to the root causes of war, poverty, and environmental destruction in Central America. And by forging links between the environmental and solidarity movements, it is my sincere belief that EPOCA helped broaden efforts to reverse the destructive path of U.S. foreign policy in Latin America as a whole.

I would like to express my sincere appreciation to the many friends and colleagues who contributed in different ways to my labor during this time. First and foremost, I would like to extend my deepest thanks to my dear friend James O'Connor, editor of *Capitalism, Nature, Socialism*. Without the intellectual stimulation and insights offered by his path-breaking work in the field of political economy and socialist ecology, I would have lacked the necessary theoretical tools for uncovering the systemic forces of destruction at work (and therefore the necessary political solutions) in Central America and the United States.

Secondly, I would like to offer my heartfelt gratitude to Josh Karliner, Dave Henson, Bill Hall, Florence Gardner, and Jane McAlevey, with whom I worked at the Environmental Project On Central America (EPOCA). Mere words cannot express the love and admiration I feel for each one of these dedicated activists—all of whom have made great personal sacrifices to advance the cause of social and ecological justice. Without their amazingly successful and tireless efforts, and the many others who worked with EPOCA, particularly Brad Erickson, Bonnie Souza, Robert Rice, Meg Ruby, Todd Steiner, Lisa Tweeten, Julie Sweig, and other members of the EPOCA collective, this book would not have been possible.

I would also like to thank Sean Swezey, Douglas Murray, Ethan Young, Michael Blim, Alan Klein, Mary Henderson, and Walter Gold-rank for their editorial and writing assistance with various parts of the manuscript and/or earlier versions of this work. All remaining logical errors, historical inaccuracies, and stylistic confusions are faults of my own making. A special thanks to Susan Lowes and Ethan Young at Monthly Review Press for their patience and kind support.

I extend my appreciation to EPOCA's many friends and associates in Central America—particularly Lorenzo Cardenal. I hope the book serves them well.

To my parents Chuck and Pat, as well Debbie, Jay, Zach, Kyffin, Mindy, Paul, Zane, Kendra, and Sue, and all other family members and friends who provided me with so many special moments over the years, I offer my eternal love. Thanks also to the whole Kurman gang extended.

Finally, my deepest appreciation and love go to my wife, Laura, for her tireless emotional and spiritual support, as well as her forbearance during my numerous absences, long sleepless nights, and other trying times that our relationship suffered while I was working on this book. May our baby daughter Emma Sophie have your sweet heart and soul.

INTRODUCTION:
ENVIRONMENT
UNDER FIRE

If there is a common element
which unites us on this earth,
it's precisely the natural environment
which we share
and which we all have to protect.
If we can't unite to protect
the environment,
then I don't think we can
save life on this planet.

Lorenzo Cardenal
National Parks Director, Nicaragua, 1985–1989

Central America is a region celebrated for its natural wealth and beauty. On the Pacific side, majestic volcanoes slope down to fertile checkerboard plains and rich coastal mangrove swamps. To the east, pine-covered mountains and cloud forests of the cooler interior highlands descend into dense tropical rainforests, sliced by steaming rivers headed for the sparkling warm waters of the Caribbean. Numerous freshwater lakes sit nestled in a rolling green landscape—an environment home to jaguars, monkeys, manatees, snakes, lizards, parrots, frogs, and other unique wildlife of almost infinite variety. North American songbirds such as the thrush, warbler, and flycatcher spend half the year in Central America's lush jungles and highlands. For eons this crumpled isthmus has served as a bridge and transition zone for tropical and temperate life-forms from North and South America and nurtured prosperous Indian civilizations for thousands of years. Medical and agricultural treasures lie hidden in the more than 1,000 species of plants found nowhere else on the globe.

But today, Central America's environment is under fire. Across the entire region, virtually every major ecosystem is rapidly being destroyed. The stark reality of this ecological devastation is shocking. More than two-thirds of the original tropical rainforests have been felled, with most of the deforestation taking place since 1950. At current rates of destruction the remaining forests will be gone in less than twenty years. Thousands of species of flora and fauna are in danger of extinction or have already been eliminated. Soil erosion is so bad that half of all farmland has been damaged, resulting in steady declines in agricultural productivity. The consequent destruction of major watersheds is responsible for the siltation of waterways, increased flooding and drought, and hundreds of millions of dollars in damage annually to the Central American economy.

The ecological crisis is also a matter of life and death for the region's small farmers and workers. Deadly pesticides banned in the United States are exported to Central America where they poison thousands of agricultural laborers each year. Much of the land, water table, and food chain along the Pacific coast is severely contaminated with these carcinogenic poisons. Unburdened by protective regulations, industries freely dump toxic chemicals into the environment. These chemical wastes have combined with agricultural residues and untreated sewage effluents to destroy water supplies. In El Salvador, only one

3

in ten people have access to safe drinking water, while in Honduras waterborne diseases annually account for 12 percent of all deaths.

The United States is also at war with nature in Central America. Over the last twelve years, the United States has supported brutal counterinsurgency campaigns and Vietnam-style "scorched earth" tactics, further devastating the forests and fields of Guatemala and El Salvador, while killing hundreds of thousands of people and displacing millions more. An undeclared economic and military war waged by the United States over the course of the 1980s against the Sandinista government also crippled many of Nicaragua's environmental and social programs, considered by many international environmentalists to be some of the most innovative and far-reaching measures ever undertaken by a poor third world country. And even now, as many of these wars have, for the moment, ended (with the important exception of Guatemala), the United States has failed to develop a coherent policy for the economic and ecological reconstruction of the region, let alone a comprehensive program that would address the root causes of poverty, war, and environmental destruction. As a result, Central America is now facing a social and ecological crisis unparalleled in its history.

Poverty, War, and Environmental Destruction: The Deadly Connections

The Spanish conquest planted the seeds that grew into today's Central American societies. The conquistadors imposed a political and economic system that benefited the Spanish Crown and local elites by extracting and exporting the region's natural resources. The Spanish massacred much of the local Indian population, while Old World diseases killed millions more. Others were enslaved and forced to service the colonial export system. Spanish colonialism reigned until roughly 1823, when the Monroe Doctrine staked out the Western Hemisphere as the domain of the United States. By the end of the nineteenth century, the U.S. had become the dominant economic and military power in Latin America. From then on, whenever nationalist movements threatened the "freedom" of U.S.-based multinational corporations and investors to exploit the land, natural resources, and labor of Central America, the U.S. government intervened, sending troops to the region thirty-six times between 1822 and 1964.

Since World War II, the United States has continued its role as an imperialist power in Central America by promoting a repressive and unequal development model that has further expanded, modernized, and diversified capitalist export-agriculture and industry. Today a capitalist export sector controlled by a small class of large landowners, or *latifundistas*, still holds power in Central America, and produces cotton, coffee, bananas, sugarcane, timber, beef, and various other fruits and vegetables for the world market. This export oligarchy monopolizes the best land and resources. They also receive the bulk of foreign development aid and financial credit to generate these cheap export commodities for the United States and other first world countries.

Laboring in service of this system, but receiving few of its benefits, Central America's majority, the poor peasant farmers and workers who make up the subsistence sector, struggle to survive by growing food on fragile land or by migrating to the cities in search of employment. The subsistence sector provides the capitalist export sector with an abundant source of extremely cheap labor for seasonal harvests. Thus, Central America's societies are deeply divided into two related sectors—one small and rich, the other vast and poor. This dichotomy has created an underdeveloped, two-tiered agricultural economy that leaves the majority of Central Americans little means to improve the quality of their lives. Land ownership patterns reveal the great inequities that characterize Central America. Half of all rural families in the region lack enough land to adequately support themselves.

With the assistance and intervention of the United States, the landed oligarchs manage to maintain this tremendous inequality by controlling the political and military power in their countries. Whether it be long lines of dictators or the newly elected governments in El Salvador, Guatemala, Honduras, and post-revolutionary Nicaragua, the export sector elite stays in charge.

Like human poverty, the environmental crisis now spreading through Central America stems from the unequal distribution of land and natural resources under this model of capitalist development. For the last four decades, large landowners have rapidly expanded their export-oriented holdings throughout the region. Forced off their lands by the *latifundistas*, tens of thousands of peasant families have moved into surrounding hillsides, clearing them of trees and planting food crops. However, most of the hillsides are of marginal quality and ill-suited for agriculture. As a result, soil erosion, habitat destruction, watershed deterioration, and flash floods torment the people and the land.

The disparity in control over natural resources also affects ecosystems surrounding Central America's major cities. Landless peasant families who migrate to the cities to find work often remain unemployed or underemployed. Governments in the region do not or cannot provide such basic services as water and electricity, forcing people to depend on outlying regions for food and firewood. Formerly forested areas surrounding cities such as Guatemala City, Managua, Panama City, San José, San Salvador, and Tegucigalpa are now barren and eroding.

Left with little means to improve the quality of their lives, Central America's poor have been forced to overexploit their natural resource base in order to survive. These survival strategies adopted by the peasantry in response to its impoverishment has resulted in the widespread degradation and ecological collapse of the subsistence sector. The development model is no longer viable, giving birth to popularly based movements for social and ecological justice. Only with significant agrarian and economic reforms, democratization of the state and political institutions, a respect for human rights, and a corresponding change in U.S. policy can the root causes of poverty and the ecological crisis in Central America be addressed.

In the United States, however, citizens, policymakers, and the press still tend to debate the social conflicts in Central America without addressing the profound environmental crisis now affecting the region. And when the U.S. environmental movement does try to raise issues concerning Central America, many groups too often neglect the political and economic roots of the crisis. Noticeable exceptions to this rule include Greenpeace, Earth Island Institute, National Toxics Campaign, Friends of the Earth, and the Highlander Institute. These organizations have actively opposed U.S. military intervention in Central America on both human rights and environmental grounds and worked to promote policy alternatives in the region.

Furthermore, although the ecological crisis of Central America has been the subject of considerable academic research, much of this work has failed to systematically examine the fundamental causes, manifestations, and impacts of ecological destruction from a political-economic (or class) perspective. Instead, these explanations emphasize oversimplified Malthusian notions of overpopulation, irrational and inefficient environmental planning, and/or the idea of "excessive demand" in the first world for environmentally destructive commodities (such as beef) from the third. Alone, these explanations are inadequate.

In this book, I hope to explain, in a theoretically sophisticated and empirically detailed fashion, the roots of Central America's current social and ecological crisis—a crisis grounded in decades of U.S.-promoted development policies that have favored production for export over production for local needs, the intensive exploitation of natural resources for profit over the sustainable use of these assets, and the interests of wealthy landowners and U.S.-based multinational corporations and banks over the interests of the popular classes that make up the majority of Central Americans. In doing so, I hope to demonstrate the responsibility that U.S. environmentalists must assume to help end the social and ecological devastation of Central America. By joining together with the solidarity and other movements, we can reverse U.S. policies and lead the way in promoting peace, justice, and environmental protection in not only Central America, but throughout the rest of the world as well.

Environmental Destruction in Central America

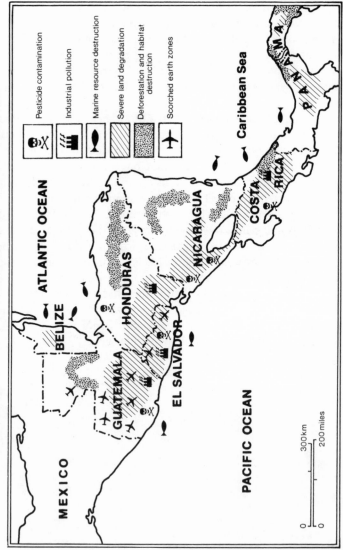

1
A LEGACY
OF ECOLOGICAL
IMPERIALISM

The day is not far distant when three Stars and Stripes at three equidistant points will mark our territory: one at the North Pole, another at the Panama Canal, and the third at the South Pole. The whole hemisphere will be ours in fact as, by virtue of our superiority of race, it already is ours morally.

U.S. President William H. Taft, 1912

Before the Spanish arrival, Central America was a land of dense ancient forests covering coastal lowlands and highland valleys alike, which contained tens of thousands of exotic plant and animal species. Nevertheless, it was a land that had been significantly transformed by human beings for over 20,000 years. The first inhabitants to "humanize nature" in the region were migratory hunters and gatherers from North America, arriving in what is now Guatemala and El Salvador during the late part of the last major continental icesheet, the Wisconsin glacial maximum, which ended 10,000 years ago. Agriculture-based Indian civilizations gradually developed over several millennia, supplemented by the gathering of wild plants and the hunting of small animals. By at least 1500 B.C., sedentary agriculture and permanent village life had become well established in much of Mesoamerica.[1]

Systems of permanent cropping or annual rotation and fallowing occurred in some localized areas, particularly along the more moist and fertile river bottoms. But most Indian plots cleared by fire were generally abandoned after a few short years, due to declining soil fertility and invasion by weeds and other unwanted plants. As a result, extensive areas of forests were cleared by Indian villagers to grow maize, beans, and other foods, but allowed to recuperate as secondary forests later on.[2]

These systems of communal agricultural production and hunting were ecologically sustainable. Consequently, Central America's indigenous peoples saw themselves and the natural world as in a state of harmony and highly spiritualized, where "the natural elements were personified, and people and gods were closely tied to animals, plants, and natural forces," as Robert M. Cormack describes.[3]

The "personified" natural world comprising Mesoamerica provided abundant means of subsistence for many thriving Indian civilizations. As the link between two great continents and two vast oceans, this land bridge served as a rich transition zone for a plethora of plants, animals, and insects unique to the region. It is today made up of the seven nations of Belize, Costa Rica, El Salvador, Guatemala, Honduras, Nicaragua, and Panama, stretching some 1,125 miles from the jungles of Mexico in North America to those of Colombia in South America. Together, these nations occupy some 210,840 square miles of territory.

11

The ponderous collisions of five tectonic plates that formed Central America created a marvelous variety of land forms and climatic zones. Today, these are some of the world's foremost storehouses of genetic wealth and biological diversity. There are at least twenty bioclimatically distinct life zones in Central America, with Costa Rica alone possessing twelve life zones.[4]

Blanketed in a protective cover of some 193,050 square miles of lush tropical forests, the region's indigenous peoples resided in a world containing about 20,000 species of vascular plants, or three times more than in all of the European continent. (It is estimated that scientists have defined and described less than half of Central America's flora.)[5] About the size of France, this area still ranks among the floristically richest on earth, comparable even to the Pleistocene refuge in Amazonia in its abundance and diversity of plant species.[6]

Three major geographical zones divided the region. In the rugged interior, the clash of uplifting geological forces created an imposing mountain spine, the *cordillera*, that stretched nearly 800 miles from what is now Guatemala to Panama. Closer to the Pacific than to the Atlantic and interspersed with majestic volcanic cones, the *cordillera* created cool and damp interior highlands of moderate rainfall and a mostly hilly and mountainous landscape, indented with intermontane plateaus (*mesetas*), valleys, and gorges formed by free-flowing streams and rivers. Hilly, mountainous, and highland valley zones comprised about three-fourths of the Central American landscape.[7] An oak-conifer natural forest complex covered the cooler highland zones from Mexico into Nicaragua, while an oak-laurel-myrtle complex thrived in the warmer and wetter mountains of Costa Rica and Panama.[8]

Across the higher mountain ranges stood cloud forests, home to the beautiful quetzal. These montane environments contained the greatest concentrations of Central America's endemic plants, species found nowhere else in the world. In mountainous sectors of Costa Rica, for instance, some 50 percent of the vascular plants were endemic, and up to 70 percent of the vascular plants are endemic in Guatemala.[9]

Throughout millennia, the numerous volcanoes lining the *cordillera* deposited layer after layer of volcanic ash, endowing Mesoamerica with some of the most fertile soils on earth.[10] The richly productive black-volcanic and alluvial river-basin type soils of the highland valleys supported dense Indian settlements for many thousands of years, particularly in Guatemala, Honduras, and El Salvador. There are several highland valleys where populations have been concentrated since pre-Colombian times. Guatemala City lies nearly 1,500 meters above sea level, and Tegucigalpa, the capital of Honduras, is situated at 900 meters. The central mesa, where most of Costa Rica's population lives, averages 1,000 meters.

Indigenous peoples cleared the richly forested valley basins for intensive irrigated cultivation, complemented by extensive migratory slash-and-burn cultivation of the surrounding highlands, creating *semi-natural* and *fully cultured landscapes*. Semi-natural landscapes or ecosystems contain largely spontaneous flora and fauna, but the vegetation structure has been altered by human activity so that it belongs to another structural formation type, such as a pasture. A fully cultured landscape or ecosystem is one in which the dominant flora and fauna have been replaced with other species under human direction.[11] David Browning describes how "forest and undergrowth were cleared by fire, the soil enriched by ash, the small maize field, the *milpa*, planted with a sharpened digging stick, the crop gathered, and a new site sought for clearance before the return of the rains."[12] Secondary forests would then rejuvenate to reclaim the land as a *subnatural landscape*, that is, one altered by human activity, but still belonging to the same structural formation type as the natural system from which it derives. (A *natural landscape* or ecosystem is one not altered by human activity.)[13]

To the northeast side of the region, the *cordillera* dropped toward the hot and humid lowlands stretching to the Caribbean coast. The lush lowlands enjoyed a nine-month rainy season, resulting from the warm, moisture-laden trade winds of the Caribbean, which moved across the cooler Central American landscape only to back up against the interior mountain walls of the *cordillera*, dumping huge amounts of rain. Here stood Central America's vast tropical lowland rainforests, home to the jaguar and other exotic animals. The constant rainfall and intense tropical sunlight accelerated evolutionary processes over millennia, making these forests some of the most biologically unique in the world.[14]

For centuries prior to the Spanish conquest in the sixteenth century, the lowland tropical forests of what is now the department of Petén in northern Guatemala were home to the thriving Mayan civilization, which reached from the Yucatán Peninsula in Mexico to El Salvador and northwestern Honduras.[15] Shifting agriculture and intensive terraced cultivation slowly thinned the forest, creating a variety of subnatural and semi-natural landscapes. By the time of the conquest, the original tree cover was greatly modified even though little of the forest was entirely removed. The remainder of the Caribbean lowlands beyond the boundaries of the Mayan Empire were occupied by only a few isolated Indian tribes, leaving the remainder of forests in completely natural or subnatural state.[16] To the southwest of the *cordillera*, the terrain dropped off from the steep bordering slopes of the western volcanic highlands to form the narrow Pacific coastal lowlands. Stretching from the Mexican border through Panama, the coastal plain spread up to twenty-five miles wide in Guatemala, while in parts of El Salvador and Costa Rica the western highland slopes virtually plummeted into the Pacific Ocean.[17] Insulated from the moisture-laden trade winds of the Caribbean by the *cordillera* for most of the year, the very hot littoral of mostly tropical dry and semi-deciduous forests possessed a short three-month season.

For many thousands of years, the Nahua-speaking Lenca, Pokoman, and Pipil Indians had been attracted to the Pacific lowlands of what is now El Salvador, with its fertile volcanic soils, favorable climate, and rich assemblage of flora and fauna. They called this area *Cuzcatlan*, or "land of richness." Like most other Indian tribes in Central America, they engaged in a combination of sustainable shifting agriculture, fishing, gathering, and hunting.[18]

Hidden amidst the crisscrossing ranges, steep mountain slopes, and intermontane valleys of Central America, lay a number of distinctive transisthmian depressions, such as the Motagua River Valley in Guatemala and Lake Nicaragua basin in Nicaragua. The steady precipitation of the highlands provided the region with an abundance of waterways out of the mountains, although most rivers were short and unnavigable, emptying into the lightly populated Caribbean lowlands. A bountiful number of lakes pocketed the landscape, the largest being Lago de Managua and Lago de Nicaragua, and perhaps the most beautiful, Lagos de Amatitlán and Atitlán in Guatemala.[19]

The region's coastal treasures included the coral reefs and offshore cays of Belize and Honduras; the black volcanic sand beaches of Guatemala and some of the world's longest uninterrupted beaches along the Pacific coast; and extensive coastal mangrove forests, grassbeds, marshes, swamps, lagoons, and other wetlands that provide nutrients and critical habitats for shrimp and numerous fish species. As described in Jeffrey Leonard's regional profile, Mesoamerica possessed "some of the most abundant, beautiful, and potentially productive coastal resources on earth."[20]

The Spanish Conquest of Nature

The assault on Central America's environment and indigenous peoples began with the Spanish arrival in Panama in 1509 and crossing of the isthmus in 1513 by Vasco Núñez de Balboa. During the early 1520s, Spanish expeditions ventured throughout the region from newly established Panama City, and from bases built by Hernán Cortés in Mexico.[21] This period marked the beginning of what would become almost five centuries of "old world" social and ecological imperialism in Latin America, or what Eduardo Galeano termed "the pillage of a continent."[22]

Ecological imperialism in Central America by the Spanish conquistadors assumed three distinct but interrelated dimensions. First, the initial purpose of the Spanish conquest was to extract the region's cultural and natural riches, particularly gold and silver, and enslave Indian labor to harvest this wealth. To appropriate the "new world's" natural resources, land, and labor-power for the Crown, required the military defeat of Indian cultures.

Thus, the second dimension of ecological imperialism involved the use of ecological-biological weapons, along with conventional ones, as instruments of mass murder and subjugation by the Spanish conquerors. The conquistadors utilized a divide-and-conquer approach by making alliances with certain Indian tribes to conquer others, then to cruelly subdue those former allies when they rebelled. (Many Indian communities, such as the Pipil of El Salvador and the Quiché of highland Guatemala, often engaged in fierce rivalries and conflicts with neighboring tribes before the Spanish arrival.)[23] In ecological terms, "old world" plants, animals, and diseases benefited the Spanish as biological allies in their defeat and demoralization of indigenous peoples.[24]

These conventional and biological weapons proved devastating. In Nicaragua, claimed by Fernández de Córdoba after bypassing the highlands of Costa Rica, a population of 825,000 Indians was reduced about 92 percent to between 50,000 and 65,000 by 1581.[25] Perhaps as many as one-half million Indians from Nicaragua and southern Honduras were captured, enslaved, and exported to Panama and Peru in the first decades of Spanish rule. Another 400,000 died of war and diseases like smallpox, resulting in a process of severe depopulation that did not stabilize until 1600. (It should be noted that in Honduras, the Indians proved more difficult to pacify and yielded smaller rewards in terms of the number of Indians taken, compared to the more sedentary Nicaraguan Indians. As a result, depopulation was certainly more devastating in Nicaragua.)[26]

In neighboring El Salvador and Guatemala, where Pedro de Alvarado led a number of military expeditions between 1524 and 1540, as many as five million Indians were killed.[27] By 1650, Central America's pre-conquest Indian population of between ten to thirteen million had been reduced to 540,000.[28]

Third, Spanish ecological imperialism had the effect of destroying communal modes of sustainable agricultural and hunting practices by those Indians who survived. The introduction of "old world" plants, animals, and invasive land uses undermined the viability of those remaining Indian villages, causing more enduring havoc on Indian life than was ever achieved by conventional war.

This destruction brought about the depopulation of existing settlements. Epidemic diseases combined with the slave trade to depopulate some areas of the Caribbean lowlands by as much as 90 percent within two generations. In these areas, land once cultivated by Indian communities reverted to subnatural landscapes of second-growth forests and often remained so for 300 years. Only after the slow recovery of the Indian population in the hills and highlands were second-growth woodlands gradually recleared.[29]

Half-wild herds of roaming cattle severely disrupted sedentary Indian practices, giving the Spaniards convenient excuses for claiming ownership to indigenous lands.[30] With traditional systems of communal land-use disrupted, the Spanish more easily subjugated Indian land and labor for extracting wealth for the Crown.[31] As one group of researchers summed up the difference between Indian and Spanish relations to the land,

> The indigenous relationship to nature can thus be described as one emphasizing sustainability and mutual interdependence, while the Spanish/European relationship was one of domination, exploitation and extraction. Even today, for many indigenous groups, land is a sacred trust. To be without land is to be torn from one's connection to nature. To work on the land for another who "owns" it is a repulsive, and perhaps sacrilegious, act.[32]

The Colonization of Nature

Ecological imperialism created the conditions for the Spanish colonization of Central America. In 1543, the Captaincy General of Guatemala was established, creating a governmental body for the Spanish to administer the region. (Panama eventually became part of the vice-royalty of Peru.) However, the Crown's economic ties to Central America were weak in comparison with those to mineral-rich Mexico and Peru. The silver reserves in Honduras, which in the early 1540s briefly represented the largest production in the Americas, soon petered out.[33] Many colonists began leaving the region for the mines in Mexico and Peru. Gradually, the Spanish realized that the value of Central America to the empire did not lie in its increasingly scarce mineral wealth, but rather in its potential agricultural wealth—the production of native plants for commercial ends.

Forced Indian labor became the means by which the Spanish could realize the value of their prize: the land. As one sociological study explains, "Land was to be awarded, bought and sold as just compensation for duty to one's king or as a tangible reward for one's nobility, Spanish birth, or social status."[34] Exploitation of the land became inseparable from the exploitation of the Indians. As historian David Browning explains, "to the Spaniard, the Indian was valuable not only because of his tribute, his labor and his soul for conversion, but because he was a cultivator who understood the land around him and was able to produce the plants the Spaniards required."[35]

Shattered by military conquest and ecological disruption, the Indian proved unable to resist the imposition of commercial export-agriculture for the benefit of the Spanish Crown. The decimation of

Indian populations by colonial war, disease, and famine created severe labor shortages in many areas. These labor shortages were overcome in other tropical countries through the importation of black African slaves, but not in Central America. (The African population of the Caribbean lowlands is made up mostly of descendants of runaway slaves from the Caribbean islands.)[36]

Cattle were introduced to the north coast of Honduras and Guatemala and quickly spread to the highland valleys.[37] Both cash crops and food crops were grown around the transisthmian routes that linked Spain with Peru. In particular, the Spanish expanded cacao and balsam production along the western slopes of the Soconusco coast of southern Mexico and Guatemala. (Prior to the conquest, Indians grew cacao on the southern slopes of the volcanic highlands.)[38] In areas where cacao and balsam were grown, the Spanish maintained existing patterns of land use and settlement but appropriated the crops from the Indians in the form of a tribute to the local Spanish authority, or *encomendero*.[39] The *encomiendas* were licenses compelling Indian labor into personal service of the *encomendero* in the name of collecting tribute for the Crown. This system was utilized until roughly 1720.[40]

By the mid-sixteenth century, the commercial production of indigo and sugar using slave labor began in the Pacific coastal areas and lower slopes of the volcanic axis in Guatemala, El Salvador, and Nicaragua. This development radically altered the cultural and natural landscape.[41]

Areas of primary and secondary forest, as well as brush, were cleared by axe and fire to plant the indigo shrub. (Indigo leaves are harvested for their pigment in the production of dye.) After three years, the land would usually be cleared once again and replanted or another fallow section would be fired and sown. Most of the indigo farmers used only a part of their property for planting of indigo. The rest lay as forest, unfenced grazing land, or milpa plots worked by sharecroppers, *colonos*, or tenant farmers.[42]

With the exception of sugar, neither indigo, balsam, nor cacao were grown and processed in such a way as to deforest significant areas, and they were often intercropped with a variety of subsistence crops.[43] In fact, with the decline of Spanish interest in cacao in the late sixteenth century, some Indian villages were able to regain their traditional language, customary forms of land tenure, and political independence. It is not accidental that these were the Indian communities at the center of the 1932 uprising against government land enclosures in El Salvador.[44]

The overall amount of land degradation for the production of these commercial exports proved minimal. In fact, the reversion of former Indian agricultural lands to second-growth forests and subnatural landscape was clearly far greater than the amount of woodlands cleared for these crops. From the early colonial period until the late seventeenth century, the massive Indian deaths resulting from Spanish imperialism allowed forest cover to advance onto large areas of abandoned agricultural land. In comparison with the region's original primary forests, the second-growth forests were biotically "underdeveloped" in terms of biomass, productivity, physiognomy, species composition, and community dynamics.[45]

During the period from 1516 to 1700, the Spanish Hapsburgs (in partnership with the Catholic Church) exercised loose control over Central America. In 1700, the Bourbon monarchs replaced the pre-Counter-Reformation Hapsburgs as the rulers of Spain. The Bourbons, guided by Enlightenment thought and the principles of French absolutism, initiated a series of political and economic reforms in an attempt to bolster the defense of the Spanish empire from growing foreign military interventions. The result was a stronger, more centralized administration over the colonies, a sharp reduction in the power of the Catholic Church, and the implementation of a developmentalist approach over the purely extractive orientation of the Hapburgs. The Bourbons wanted a strengthening of commercial agricultural trade not only between Spain and the colonies, but also within the colonies themselves.[46]

The Bourbon reforms spawned new social classes and modes of exploitation. The Hapsburg system of *encomienda*, in which a Spanish *encomendero* (commissioner) controlled vast expanses of land and the people living on it (but owned neither), was replaced by the *repartimiento* (apportionment) system of labor exploitation. Under *repartimiento*, Indian villages were required to give a certain number of days' labor per month to the *hacendado*, the new Spaniard owners of *hacienda* (plantation) land, in exchange for a modest fixed amount of money. *Repartimiento* became the principal form of Indian labor control until the end of the eighteenth century, when it was gradually replaced with debt peonage, vagrancy laws, and other coercive or "feudalistic" modes of labor exploitation.

Indian villages, particularly in the highlands of Guatemala, El Salvador, and northwestern Honduras, came under greater control of the Spanish, although disease and poverty continued to plague the available supply of Indian workers in the region. In areas of abundant labor, however, the exploitation of Indian communities for the benefit of the Crown changed the ecology of the terrain.

With the Bourbon reforms and expansion of commercial markets in western Europe, indigo became a leading export from the region, particularly El Salvador. Up to a half-million pounds of indigo were exported to Europe in peak years during the seventeenth century. This figure doubled during the eighteenth century, and indigo quickly became Central America's principal export, even after independence. The production of cochineal, a plant from which crimson dye is made, also expanded along with other crops like tobacco.

By 1800, some 300 to 400 *haciendas* devoted to cattle ranching, indigo, and other commercial crops (in addition to mining) had destroyed 30 percent of El Salvador's forests. Some parts of the country were devastated, particularly by mining operations in Morazán.[47] Timber production also took a toll on some areas, particularly the more accessible locations of dyewood along the Belize coast.[48] English loggers controlled these exports. When the dyewood export declined in the eighteenth century, it was replaced with the harvesting of mahogany for furniture production in Europe. Like the other crops, logging had little overall impact on the region's forest cover.[49]

By the early nineteenth century, the great European Napoleonic wars had crippled Spain's ability to administer its colonies. In 1821, Central America formed an alliance with Mexico and gained independence from Spain. Two years later on September 15, 1823, the region's provinces broke with Mexico to establish a loose federation. The indigo and cochineal dyes sought by English and other European textile manufacturers continued to be major exports. However, mass uprisings did allow many peasants to temporarily regain access to much of their land after independence.

The Central American provinces made numerous attempts to establish a stronger federation from 1825 to 1840, but the effort was wracked by a series of civil wars and conflicts between Liberal and

Conservative *caudillos*—the regional political bosses and large land-owners of Spanish descent. The Conservatives wanted to preserve traditional colonial institutions of the Hapsburgs (such as the traditional Catholic Church), while the Liberals advocated Bourbon-like reforms to promote capitalist development and create a progressive republic in the image of France, England, and the United States.[50]

As a result of these conflicts, the Hapsburgs emerged stronger than the Bourbons. In 1840, the Central American Federation dissolved, and each of the five provinces became a politically independent nation. The newly independent Central American countries quickly became dominated by agrarian *caudillos*, who created their own state structures, laws, and armies to guard and expand their family-based wealth and political power. In fact, having a private military force became a common way to hold political office. For example, an alliance between conservative castes of Indians and mestizos, conservative merchants, and agrarian landlords joined Rafael Carrera's peasant army to defeat the Liberals and rule Guatemala until 1865.

Harvesting Gold: The Rise of Capitalist Export-Agriculture

Following independence, Central America began experiencing growing economic stagnation as the European textile mills acquired new, cheaper synthetic chemical products and more reliable dye substitutes. Indigo and other natural dyes, which constituted the traditional exports of Conservative factions in Central America, became worthless commodities in the world market. By 1860, the market for Guatemalan cochineal had become paralyzed; and by 1878 to 1879, the Rotterdam and Liverpool markets for indigo had drastically shriveled.[51]

Liberal factions looking to encourage capitalist development and social modernization gradually rose to political power. The new Liberal *caudillos* sought to take advantage of the rapid capitalist industrial expansion sweeping Europe and the United States. To further profit from rising commodity prices, they opened their countries to foreign investment and expanded production of non-traditional exports such as coffee and bananas. Coffee was especially crucial. Although ownership of coffee production was overwhelmingly in the hands of

Central Americans (with the exception of Nicaragua and to a lesser degree Guatemala), there was substantial foreign investment in railroads, ports, roads, and banking—all necessary for coffee export.[52]

Coffee farms first appeared in Costa Rica in the 1830s; in the forests around San Salvador in El Salvador in the 1840s; along the Pacific slope of Guatemala in the late 1850s and 1860s (although the Liberals did not defeat Rafael Carrera's Conservative peasant army until 1865); and in the hilly regions of Matagalpa in Nicaragua during the 1850s. Although initially deterred by Conservative political and economic interests, coffee production accelerated greatly after the completion of the Panama Railway by U.S. investors in 1855. The railway made the "golden bean" much more accessible to European markets. Coffee farms quickly penetrated into the fertile highland forests. Panama and Honduras did not participate in the export coffee boom until after World War II.

The custom, according to David Browning, was "for workmen with axes to fell trees in order to clear ground for coffee plantings, with no thought for preserving the more useful and valuable timber." In some areas, such as on the slopes around the basin of Zapotitán west of San Salvador, the woodlands were cleared more rapidly with the use of fire, resulting in the destruction of large natural forests. Many landowners would only grant tenants the right to burn and till a piece of land rent-free for three years, on the condition that it be returned completely free of trees.[53]

Gradually, as most of the unclaimed national lands in El Salvador, Guatemala, and Nicaragua became planted in coffee groves, more and more growers began looking to the vast areas of fertile land in the central and western highlands for expanding their groves. However, the majority of tracts suitable for coffee production in these areas were controlled by Indian villages, the Catholic Church, and municipal and national governments. The ruling Liberals came to view the Indian *ejidos* (publicly owned lands) and *tierras comunales* (community held lands), as well as church- and state-owned lands, as barriers to the continued development of commercial coffee production, economic progress and the private accumulation of wealth, and began pressuring for their elimination.[54] To expand commercial coffee groves required nullification of pre-existing claims to ejidal (common public) lands attached to municipalities, communal lands attached to Indian communities, and lands belonging to the Catholic Church.[55]

By the 1870s, the Liberal *caudillos* of El Salvador, Guatemala, and Nicaragua had consolidated their hold on state power and began initiating a series of reforms aimed at creating the appropriate ecological and social conditions for the expansion of coffee production. The aim of these capitalist-oriented reforms included: (1) the commodifying of lands held by the Church, indigenous communities, and municipal and national governments (including the untitled holdings of individual peasants who had settled on national lands), for the purpose of their conversion into coffee-growing estates; (2) the creation of a cheap labor force (both "free" and coerced workers) for the planting, cultivation, and harvesting of coffee; and (3) the creation of public infrastructure and strengthening of state institutions necessary for the profitable production and marketing of coffee for export.

Absolute political control became crucial to the Liberal coffee growers. Control of land (rather than investment of capital), creation of a large semi-servile labor force, and development of a sophisticated infrastructure all required heavy state intervention into all spheres of social life.[56]

By the late 1870s and early 1880s, every Central American government had a titling law, granting Liberal coffee growers access to vast tracts of dense forests and agricultural land formerly held by Indian communities and the national government. Many of the estates also evolved out of the colonial *haciendas*.[57] In El Salvador, the state abolished all rights to ejidal and communal land holdings in 1881 through 1882, giving coffee growers control of 25 percent of the country's most desirable agricultural lands.[58]

In Guatemala, where private property became the only legally recognized form of land tenure, the state expropriated some 2.5 million acres of land formerly held by the Catholic Church and Indian villages between 1870 and 1920. Coffee exports jumped from 24,911,980 pounds in 1870 to some 186,658,850 pounds in 1915. Liberal government policies favoring immigrants resulted in German nationals owning 170 farms and producing more than half of the coffee exported in 1914.[59]

Likewise, the government of Nicaragua enacted an Agrarian Reform Law in 1877 that facilitated the privatization of the country's ejidal, communal, and undeveloped national lands for the purpose of expanding coffee production.[60] The coffee boom was ready to begin.

The Costs of the Coffee Boom

With the passage of these new "agrarian reform" laws, Central American governments played an active role in expropriating the vast forests and interspersed corn fields commonly held by sedentary Indian villages and municipal governments.[61] Despite a series of popular uprisings by dispossessed Indian communities from 1872 to 1898, which claimed thousands of lives regionwide, the Liberal reforms facilitated the conversion of the densely populated but richly forested western and central highlands into large coffee estates.

These estates, or *latifundios*, were owned predominantly by wealthy urban merchants anxious to profit from the booming international market, including German immigrants drawn by preferential offers of cheap land or outright grants. In Nicaragua, where coffee had become the principal export commodity, inequality of land ownership was less extreme than in neighboring Guatemala and El Salvador. According to John A. Booth, "the coffee producers included some creole *latifundists*, some small- and middle-sized farm owners, a segment of middle-class functionaries who took advantage of government stimuli to attain coffee holdings, and foreign (especially German and British) investors who eventually came to control coffee exporting and credit."[62]

To assist in the evictions and repression of peasant rebellions, governmental security forces were created, including a mounted police force in El Salvador in 1889. Security forces also guarded the newly established private coffee plantations from the Indians who had traditionally appropriated means of subsistence from the lands on which they were located.

The conservation and growth of woodlands along important watersheds were crucial to the economic health of the coffee plantations. Threats posed by fire and deforestation from slash-and-burn agriculture caused a number of protective measures to be passed to protect the plantations. In 1897, the Salvadoran government under pressure from the coffee oligarchy introduced a program to check deforestation. May 3 was declared *"Fiesta de Arboles,"* a day on which each person was required to plant a tree. Historian David Browning re-counts how security guards prevented "the firing of fields, the clear-ance of timber and undergrowth from the banks of rivers, unauthorized hunting and fowling, the use of barbasco poisons by freshwater fishermen, the building on or enclosure of public high-ways, the settlement, clearing, and burning of any land belonging to private estates."[63]

The repression and inequities accompanying the development of coffee production in El Salvador, Guatemala, and Nicaragua were not characteristic of every country in the region. In Costa Rica (despite its name "the Coast of Riches"), the first Spanish conquistadors found the country lacking in the two economic resources that they valued the most—Indians and precious minerals. The absence of these necessary conditions for agricultural plantation production or large-scale min-ing led to the creation of *minifundios,* or small family farms of colonial settlers oriented primarily to subsistence production as the foundation of the Costa Rican colonial economy.

Shortages of Indian labor-power limited economic development to such an extent that not a single large hacienda existed in Costa Rica prior to independence. Spanish settlers favored the mild climate and fertile volcanic soils of the central valley over the sweltering, jungle-cloaked Caribbean lowlands. At the time of independence, virtually the entire population, some 30,000 people, resided in the central valley, or *meseta.* Of these, 72 percent were of Spanish descent. The remaining 28 percent were Indians or mulattos.[64]

Following independence in 1823, the new Costa Rican government promoted coffee-export production as a means of economic develop-ment.[65] Costa Rica had no other important export crop and therefore no strongly entrenched Conservative interests to resist the developing coffee trade. Furthermore, the crop was ideally suited to the cool climate and ecological conditions of the *meseta.* The municipal govern-ment of San Jose began giving away large tracts of public land and supplying seeds to anyone willing to grow coffee, particularly the country's small family farmers. According to J. Edward Taylor, "In 1825 coffee was exempted from the 10 percent tax the Church collected from most agricultural products, and in 1831 the National Assembly declared that whoever cultivated coffee on public lands for a period of five years could claim the land as his own. In 1840 President Braulio Carrillo issued a decree ordering that all lands west of San José be planted in coffee."[66]

Trade in the "golden bean" grew rapidly over the next three decades, preserving existing *minifundios*, and advancing the formation of new ones into the lush woodlands of the central valley surrounding San José. The coffee trade expanded in 1849 when England emerged as a major buyer of Costa Rican coffee. But while the coffee bean brought prosperity to the country's small family farmers, it also unleashed a process of deforestation. In the words of two environmental historians, "As the plantations expanded, they moved up the hillsides, displacing some of the finest forests of the region, first in the areas of rich volcanic soil and subsequently in the adjacent darker alluvial soils as well." The relative simplicity of clearing the land of trees and growing coffee also led many small farmers to clear the richly forested state lands away from the center of the *meseta*.[67]

Despite the deforestation and rapid expansion of the *minifundio* coffee farms, little social conflict developed in the central valley. The Spanish conquest had decimated the already small population of indigenous people of Costa Rica. Thus the Costa Rican state did not require an elaborate repressive apparatus, such as a national guard, to convert woodlands into private property or control Indian labor; large-scale plantations did not exist.

The country's peasant families were allowed to peacefully establish *minifundios* on the vast public lands suitable for coffee production in the highlands around San José. With a mass base of relatively prosperous small farmers, Costa Rica could enjoy more democracy and less poverty and repression. As a result, political negotiation became institutionalized early on in Costa Rican society.

By the 1890s, high profits and prices on the world market for Central America's coffee growers created a frenzy of land speculation, Indian displacement, and deforestation—dramatically transforming the rich highland environments of every country in the region, including Costa Rica.

The most favorable altitudinal zone for coffee cultivation, 500 to 1,700 meters in elevation, conflicted with the existence of rich oak-pine forests and related woodlands throughout the region. El Salvador's oak-pine forests were endemic on the upper slopes of the south-central chain of interior volcanos and northern mountains bordering Honduras, extending from approximately 800 to 1,000 meters to about 2,000 meters in elevation. These forests were dominated by twelve species of *Quercus* and the ocote pine (*Pinus ocarpa*). Associated tree species included tixate, cedro, and zapotillor.[68]

The expansion of both minifundio and latifundio coffee estates devastated the sub-natural oak-pine forest complex and reconstructed the highland into fully cultured (or capitalized) landscapes. A newly distinctive and extensive two-story forest ecosystem was created on the ashes of the old-growth woodlands. The lower story was composed of coffee bushes (*coffee arabica*) about two meters in height and spaced in rows roughly two meters apart. The upper story was composed of shade trees, one of the principal species being madre de cacao (*cliricidia sepium*), a deciduous tree ten to fifteen meters in height. The crown formed a nearly closed canopy over the coffee bushes. Such phytophysiognomic modification also occurred with the development of secondary vegetation on extensive areas of abandoned peasant agricultural plots.[69]

In El Salvador, Guatemala, and Nicaragua, the confiscation of traditional communal lands also triggered massive migrations by displaced Indian villagers into the higher elevations of the central and western mountain slopes, resulting in the additional destruction of huge tracts of previously undisturbed oak-pine forests above the upper altitude limits for coffee production.[70] The coffee boom further displaced peasants onto other forested (but more ecologically fragile and marginal) agricultural lands, which they cleared for their own small subsistence plots.[71]

In El Salvador, many Indians moved to the rugged and inhospitable woodlands of the northern mountains. (In the present century, after decades of deforestation, misuse, exhaustion and erosion, the northern mountains gradually became El Salvador's poor, backward, and neglected *tierra olvidada* for peasant agriculture.)[72] Others took to the malaria-infested evergreen forests of the coastal Pacific lowlands, leading to widespread deforestation, erosion, and other environmental problems.[73]

The commercial privatization of the Nicaraguan and Guatemalan highlands by large coffee estates led to further ecological damage by disinherited Indian communities, although this process was much more gradual and less complete than in neighboring El Salvador. In many areas of Guatemala, communities retained *de facto* use of a portion of their traditional lands, although often without formal title, right up to the economic and political reform period of 1944 to 1954.[74]

Similar processes of ecological deterioration even began to occur in Costa Rica, as the equality of that society began to erode during the latter half of the nineteenth century. With the unhealthy reliance on increased borrowing from British bankers, land holdings became more concentrated as many small farmers went into debt and sold off their farms. In 1892, for instance, 11.1 percent of the value of all registered property in Costa Rica changed owners, the vast majority being coffee-growing estates.[75] Large landowners also continued to expand new coffee estates into the surrounding forests. Between 1883 and 1892, the number of large coffee haciendas increased 20 percent.[76]

Although most rural people in Costa Rica remained small landowners, the process of land concentration created a new class of landless wage laborers, and for the first time, the large *latifundio* existed side by side with the small farmer. Landless workers were an important source of seasonal wage labor for the coffee estates in the central valley, as well as for the construction of state roads, ports, railroads, the communication infrastructure, and other conditions of production for the coffee trade. Nevertheless, the labor market remained rather tight, resulting in higher wages and relatively equitable income distribution (despite growing inequities in land tenure). These labor shortages did retard a more extensive development of large *latifundio* coffee estates.

Growing landlessness exacerbated deforestation and habitat destruction, as many displaced farmers cleared public lands on the outer portions of the *meseta*, often at altitudes too low for coffee production. By the early 1900s, Costa Rica's richly diverse forests of oak, laurel, and myrtle, characteristic of the wetter and warmer highlands of southern Central America, had been extensively degraded. Most of the land ecologically suitable for coffee had been cleared and was producing sixteen million kilos annually, accounting for over 90 percent of the value of all exports.[77]

Ecological reconstruction of the highlands not only created the environmental conditions for coffee production, but also the social conditions for its planting and harvesting by a large work force of impoverished peasants and Indian laborers, particularly in those nations following the *latifundio* path. Robbed of their traditional lands, much of El Salvador's Indian peoples were converted into impoverished farmers or landless wanderers, whose desperation led them to serve as an important supply of cheap wage labor for the large coffee estates. In El Salvador and Costa Rica, capitalist relations of production dominated the coffee estates.

In Guatemala, however, the dominant social relations of production (or mode of labor exploitation) were feudal in character. To ensure an adequate supply of labor for the newly created coffee *latifundios*, debt bondage, vagrancy laws requiring peasants to have proof of employment, and other labor requirements were implemented by the Liberal government of Justino Rufino Barrios (1873–1885). The Guatemalan state intervened directly in the recruitment and control of workers, not only enforcing private debt contracts but also forcing increasing numbers of Indians into such labor debts.[78]

Labor shortages had always plagued Guatemala's coffee growers, particularly around Alta Verapaz, where the local Indian villagers had survived for centuries as subsistence producers. Large numbers of laborers were needed to cultivate and harvest the crop. Also, because of the unusually broken local terrain and absence (until the late 1870s) of a cart road to the river port of Panzós, laborers were also needed to carry the coffee to market and to return with imported goods.

In response to the labor shortages, the governor of Verapaz required towns in the northern half of the department to supply labor to new coffee estates being opened around Cobán in 1858. In 1876, Justino Rufino Barrios ordered departmental governors to begin supplying *mandamientos* (forced labor drafts) of workers to the coffee haciendas. This system, modeled on the colonial *repartimientos*, guaranteed the feudal-like *latifundio* coffee growers a labor force.[79] As historian David McCreery notes, semi-feudal modes of labor exploitation were utilized because the "cleverer landowners realized too that a free labor market, taken together with the sudden and continuing growth in demand for coffee workers, would lead to wage competition among employers, pushing up costs and squeezing profits."[80]

Coercive labor systems were required because most highland Indians were reluctant to seek work on the coffee haciendas as "free" wage laborers. The highland Indians dreaded the scorching hot and disease-ridden coastal zone and had little or no desire to work as wage laborers. Most could still adequately support themselves through subsistence agriculture, alone or in combination with petty commodity production and trade. A national army was created to expel Indians and to enforce the state's coercive labor requirements. With this more-or-less guaranteed labor supply, the state rapidly built roads, ports, and other infrastructural conditions of production necessary for commercial coffee agriculture.[81]

The Guatemalan state was reluctant to attempt wholesale dismantling of Indian subsistence patterns in the highlands to create a "free" wage labor force. Any such policy could have unleashed peasant rebellions not unlike those that had toppled the Liberals from power in the 1830s. Instead, traditional Guatemalan villages were maintained as labor reserves for the four to six months of the year when large numbers of workers were needed to clear the groves of weeds and later to harvest the beans. Coffee growers in need of labor would apply to the departmental governor, who would then order a village to supply the workers, set the length of their service, and sometimes their wage.[82] Caught in this squeeze, many Indians chose to be indebted to the haciendas, rather than risk being impressed on short notice and sent to work in possibly unhealthy and dangerous areas. When all other forms of resistance to labor impressment failed, entire families fled into unsettled areas such as the north of El Quiché or into the wooded mountains of Izabal.[83]

These systems of labor coercion began processes of environmental degradation of Indian lands in the highlands, placing great hardships on the villagers. Multitudes of highland Indians journeyed to the coast and back several times a year, often becoming infected with deadly diseases brought by the Spanish colonists. While plantation owners took better care of the debt peons who returned yearly to the same estates, victims of *mandamientos* were sent into new and unfamiliar areas. *Latifundistas* expressed little concern for their health, and provided brutal working and living conditions.[84] According to McCreery, "for real or imagined transgressions, laborers spent days clamped in stocks, exposed to rain, sun, and insects; they reported being beaten with machetes and kept days without food or water."[85]

Survivors of the *mandamientos* returned to their villages exhausted by overwork, malaria, intestinal parasites, and chest infections. Many were too weak to work their subsistence plots or undertake the long journeys necessary for trade. This bleeding of Indian labor crippled the highland communities and resulted in cultural despair and impoverishment and environmental decay. Forced labor migrations to the coast occurred during critical periods in the corn cycle. Peasant producers could not weed or harvest their fields on time or make improvements or repair damage to their fields. The declining productivity of peasant agriculture corresponded to the rise of coffee plantations. Eventually, the supply of highland labor became affected by acute food shortages resulting from the declining productivity of their land.[86] So, although the mode of exploitation was somewhat different in Guatemala, the results were similar to those in El Salvador—misery, repression, and environmental devastation for the Indian.

In Nicaragua, the Liberal José Santos Zelaya assumed the presidency in 1893. He immediately initiated a series of policies which, like those in Guatemala, tied more and more peasants to the plantations by means of a labor draft, and accelerated the further destruction of communal lands.[87] However, Nicaragua's coffee oligarchy was less powerful than its Salvadoran and Guatemalan counterparts. It remained subordinate to U.S. foreign policy interests because of the country's strategic location for a potential transisthmian canal.[88]

In the early 1900s, the U.S. examined the possibility of constructing a transit route using the natural waterways of the San Juan River and Lake Nicaragua connected by a short canal. But in negotiations with Washington, Zelaya refused to grant full legal control over the proposed canal to the United States. This act of "national sovereignty" led Washington to orchestrate Panama's secession from Colombia in 1903, under the threat of U.S. intervention, and the canal was eventually built through Panama.[89] Zelaya had further angered the U.S. by taking a number of actions in violation of the Monroe Doctrine of 1823, which staked out the Western Hemisphere as the domain of the United States. These included opening negotiations with Japan on constructing a Nicaraguan canal route, military interventions into Honduras and Guatemala, contraction of a loan from European banks for railway construction, and the canceling of special economic concessions for U.S. mining interests.

In 1909, the U.S. backed a Conservative coup by landing troops in the Atlantic port of Bluefields to overthrow Zelaya, thereby deterring the continued expansion of coffee production. From 1909 to 1933, U.S. Marines spent over twenty years in Nicaragua attempting to impose imperialist control over a nation unwilling to play the role of a client state.[90] In fact, the occupation of Nicaragua signaled the rise of a new imperialist power in Central America—the United States—willing to use military intervention to protect its economic interest over the land, labor, and natural resources of the region. Since 1905, U.S. troops have occupied Honduras five times, Panama three, and Nicaragua twice.[91] Despite growing U.S. intervention, by the early part of the twentieth century the expansion of coffee and other export crops, as well as commercial mining operations and displacement of traditional Indian villages, had dramatically transformed the Central American landscape.

In El Salvador, where deforestation was most extensive, less than 10 percent of the country's original forest formations remained. The expansion of other export crops, such as sugar in the Zapotitlán basin, and the utilization of firewood for mining, also contributed to the clearance of woodlands. By 1983 all of the mines except one had been forced to close because of the total lack of firewood. The northern portions of San Miguel, Morazán, and La Unión—the principal mining region of El Salvador during the nineteenth century—were described by one observer in the 1890s as "a barren and scrub-covered area." In fact, mining operations had already destroyed most of the forests of central Morazán by 1800.[92]

As one national publication celebrated in 1916,

> One of the great obstacles that our agriculture was confronted with was the deplorable system under which the national land was divided into *ejidos* and *tierras communales*, which caused land and labor to remain unused ... now the landscape presents to the traveler a scene similar to a vast chessboard where the various products of the fertile land may be admired; from the highest peaks to the beautiful valleys and plains, Salvador presents a view that reminds us of a large and well-kept garden, with every available piece of land, even at the highest levels, being under cultivation.[93]

The expansion of commercial coffee production and resulting destruction of animal habitat had seriously reduced a number of wildlife populations in that country, as well. According to the environmental historian Howard Daugherty, "most seriously affected were dwellers of the coastal evergreen forests, most of which had been cleared for agriculture or converted into park-like savannas." These animals included the tapir, brocket deer, porcupine, gray fox, weasel, and howler monkey, all of which had become rare by 1880. Due to hunting and habitat destruction, mountain lions and other American cats began to decline rapidly during this same period and were found only in areas that remained heavily forested. (Because of the expansion of secondary brush vegetation and livestock as prey, the coyote and white-tailed deer remained very abundant despite heavy exploitation.)[94]

Despite the enormous destruction of oak-pine forest and wildlife habitat, the coffee *Gliricidia* formation (and others) proved ecologically well suited to the steep terrain and local climatic conditions in the highlands. The interplanting of shade trees among young coffee bushes protected the soil from wind erosion, heavy rain, and the direct rays of the sun. While the madre cacao was planted at lower levels as a shade tree in El Salvador, the indigenous pepeto tree, pine, cypress, and several types of hardwood were often planted higher up and helped retain much of the original forest cover.[95]

Although accelerated erosion occurred on the steepest slopes, coffee groves generally provided the most stable and least eroded agricultural land in the country.[96] Almost any other type of conventional agriculture over a comparable period of time would long since have wasted the natural fertility of the soil.[97]

A relatively stable and productive ecosystem, coffee nevertheless formed an important aspect of the overall social and ecological crisis in Central America. Daugherty describes how ownership by a few landholders of the most fertile and productive agricultural land "forced the bulk of the population to subsist on marginal slope land ... [which could not] withstand continual cropping without permanent damage."[98]

By abolishing communal forms of property in favor of *latifundio* coffee estates, the Guatemalan, Nicaraguan, and Salvadoran governments effectively closed off the potentiality for a more democratic, egalitarian, and ecologically friendly path to capitalist development based, as in Canada or much of the United States, on widespread access to income earning property in rural areas.[99] Instead, the coffee oligarchs became kings of Central America.

"Banana Republics": The Plantation Road

The coffee boom expanded throughout the highlands of every Spanish Central America country (except Honduras) during the late nineteenth and early twentieth centuries. Occupied by numerous Indian communities, the rugged mountain terrain and poor public infrastructure in Honduras served as formidable barriers to the development of commercial coffee production. These obstacles would deter the development of a Costa Rica-style coffee sector until the 1940s.[100]

Lacking a powerful coffee oligarchy, Honduran politics became dominated by merchants and traditional landholders, most of whom tended to be large ranchers who remained untied to the international market.[101] With the country lacking a powerful agrarian capitalist class but holding an abundance of extremely poor subsistence farmers, the Honduran government looked to foreign interests for stimulating economic development. British, German, and U.S. capital were all drawn in by attractive mining concessions. By the end of the nineteenth century, silver accounted for 50 percent of the value of all exports.[102]

Hoping to attract further investments that would benefit the nation as a whole, the Honduran government extended generous concessions to U.S.-based banana companies. Beginning in the 1890s, several multinational companies began producing bananas in Honduras for the U.S. market.[103] The railroads built by these companies led directly from the coastal ports to the banana plantations and failed to integrate the rest of the country.[104]

Along the rich northern coast, around the more eastern port of La Ceiba, the Vaccaro Brothers (who later became Standard Fruit) created vast monocultural plantation estates out of the lowland tropical forests. Along the banks of the Cuyamel River near the more western port of Tela, Samuel Zemurray (commonly known as "Sam the banana man") set up the Cuyamel Fruit Company. By 1914, yet another corporation, the United Fruit Company and its major rivals controlled nearly one million acres of Honduras. By then, bananas accounted for

roughly 66 percent of the country's total exports.[105] Additional purchases were made after World War I, eventually swallowing
Zemurray's creation in 1929.[106]

These developments were mirrored in Costa Rica, where bananas
were first exported commercially in the 1880s. In 1884, the railroad
baron Minor C. Keith (later to become founder of the United Fruit
Company in 1899) reached an agreement with the Costa Rican government to complete a national railroad, from San José in the central
valley to Limón along the Atlantic coast. In exchange, Keith received
land grants equal to 7 percent of Costa Rica's national territory, in
addition to the land on which the railroad was constructed, as well as
large parcels for the building of piers, ports, and warehouses.[107]

Unlike the nationally owned coffee industry, however, Costa Rica's
banana industry functioned as an export enclave for the growing
economic interests of the United States, and contributed little to the
social development of the country. While the government initially
retained one-third of the shares in the railroad, they were given to
Keith in exchange for his assumption of the country's large debts
incurred in the earlier construction of part of the rail line. United Fruit
quickly established a shipping monopoly and charged exploitative
commercial rates. Although banana exports totaled millions of dollars
a year, not a single cent of tax was paid by United Fruit to the Costa
Rican government.

According to the historian Mitchell Seligson, "even the wages paid
to the workers did not enter the economy, because most of this money
went back to the *frutera* through its company stores, whose stock was
imported duty-free."[108] Costa Rica's experiences with United Fruit
revealed a pattern of economic dependency and exploitation by U.S.
corporations, a pattern that would be repeated in the region's more
repressive countries as well. During a guerrilla war against U.S.
occupation in Nicaragua (1927–1933), a peasant army led by rebel
officer Augusto César Sandino frequently raided the properties of
Standard Fruit and other Atlantic coast banana companies.[109]

Despite the ravages of the severe fungae Sigatoka and Panama
disease on banana trees, which compelled the plantations to move to
virgin soil after eight to ten years, planting continued to expand at the
expense of the Caribbean lowland tropical forests in Costa Rica,
Honduras, Guatemala, and Nicaragua.[110] In 1906, United Fruit re-

ceived a grant of 170,000 acres of land in the Atlantic coastal department of Izabal in Guatemala.[111]

In Nicaragua, both Cuyamel and the Atlantic Fruit Company owned plantations larger than 100,000 acres, although the largest was the Vaccaro Brothers (Standard Fruit), which accounted for 50 percent of all the country's banana exports at the end of the 1920s. Although United Fruit had huge holdings in Nicaragua, they were never extensively developed. The only export of any economic significance in Nicaragua, other than coffee and bananas, was timber from the Atlantic coast region, which accounted for about 10 percent of the country's exports in the late 1920s.[112]

In Honduras, 75 percent of the banana lands were owned by only three companies in 1918.[113] The United Fruit Company (UFCO) alone had 87,808 acres under cultivation by 1924, although the uncultivated area under its control was several times larger.[114] By then, internal Honduran politics had become virtually indistinguishable from the fruit companies' economic interests. In fact, U.S. control of Central America's entire banana industry was virtually complete.

U.S. Imperialism and the Rise of Caudillismo

By the 1920s, the development of commercial export agriculture had fully integrated Central America into the capitalist world economy. However, the region's narrow economic reliance on coffee and bananas as export commodities posed new dangers to the Central American people and environment. With the collapse of export-led growth in the wake of the 1929 world economic depression, the social and ecological dangers posed by this highly unequal system of *latifundia* agriculture and dependency on the United States and Europe erupted.

Wage workers, tenant farmers, and merchants were hit hardest by the economic crisis.[115] Regionwide, large coffee growers and the banana companies responded to falling world market prices by laying off workers and lowering money wages, which before the depression averaged twenty-five to thirty cents per day. After 1929, wages were reduced to around fifteen cents, sparking worker unrest and frequent clashes with the armed forces.[116] In response to growing worker unrest, the oligarchies turned to authoritarian *caudillismo*, the use of increased repression by military strongmen to safeguard the owners' class privileges and interests.

In Nicaragua, where the expansion of large-scale coffee estates during the 1920s had been much stronger than in other Central America countries, these conflicts were particularly pronounced. By 1928, Sandino's army of small peasant farmers, whose untitled lands had been stolen during the coffee boom, were fighting Nicaragua's client government of U.S. military occupation.[117]

In response to falling coffee prices between 1929 and 1933, large growers rapidly planted more coffee in hopes of recouping lost income by increasing volume. This process displaced thousands of small family farmers into the swelling ranks of the unemployed agricultural proletariat (including banana and sugar workers) and urban migrants.[118] Labor and peasant unrest increased, strengthening the Sandinista insurrection. With Sandino's army defending peasants against the National Guard and U.S. Marines (who would remain until 1933), many displaced and unemployed families began moving onto idle coffee estates during the depression to grow their own food.

Greatly alarmed by the strength of the peasant movement, some leaders of both the Conservative and Liberal parties backed the unseating of President Juan Bautista Sacasa, despite the U.S. military withdrawal and peace accords reached between Sandino and Sacasa. In February 1934, Sandino was assassinated by National Guard chief Anastasio Somoza García, who then launched a brutal counterinsurgency sweep of north-central Nicaragua. Somoza evicted peasants from coffee estates and conducted massacres of whole villages in the areas where support for Sandino had been strong. Much of the newly expropriated land fell into the hands of General Somoza and officers in the National Guard. In June 1936, Somoza pressured President Sacasa (his uncle) into resigning. On January 1, 1937, he assumed the presidency.[119] With the transition to authoritarian *caudillismo* complete, the Somoza family dictatorship would rule Nicaragua for over four decades with a favorable eye toward Washington and an iron fist for its enemies—the country's popular classes.

An even more brutal response to the economic crisis occurred in El Salvador in the early 1930s, where large coffee estates occupied over 261,820 acres, some 37 percent of all agricultural land in the country.[120]

Robbed of their homelands, hundreds of thousands of poor Indians were directly dependent on wage labor jobs on the coffee plantations for their survival. In 1930, some 309,000 agricultural wage-laborers out of a total population of approximately 1.5 million were directly employed in the coffee sector, meaning that during the dry season almost every laboring family in the nation was employed in the coffee harvest.[121]

When the depression hit and coffee growers decided not to harvest their crops, these peasants, having already lost their land, also lost their opportunity to work—even if it had been for minimal wages and under poor conditions. By 1930, unemployment reached well over 40 percent of the adult male population in the countryside.[122]

Backed by increasingly militant workers, Arturo Araujo of the Labor Party was elected President, taking office on March 1, 1931. Within a year, a military coup backed by the coffee oligarchy placed General Maximiliano Hernández Martínez in control of the government, ending any possibility for a democratic alternative to the crisis.

By 1932, a widespread peasant revolt erupted in the coffee producing areas of the western and central highlands. The government's response was swift and brutal. In what Salvadorans still refer to as *la matanza* (the massacre), the National Guard and "White Guards" of the oligarchy killed more than 30,000 people, virtually wiping out traditional Indian culture.[123] Leaders of popular peasant and worker organizations, including Communist Party leader Agustín Farabundo Martí, were arrested and executed.[124] A permanent system of repression became institutionalized within the state.

Authoritarian *caudillismo* also arose in Honduras. In the early 1930s, the depression led to increased worker militancy on the banana plantations. By 1932, a major strike of banana workers organized by the Honduran Union Federation (FSH), along with other labor unrest, was suppressed by the jailing and execution of labor leaders under the government of Tiburcio Andino Carías. With the support of the U.S. banana companies and numerous high government officials (many of whom were on the UFCO payroll), Carías eventually suspended the 1933 elections and appointed himself president till 1948.[125]

One of the notable exceptions to this political response to the depression took place in Costa Rica, even though the country had become thoroughly linked to the capitalist world economy through its dependency on coffee exports for foreign exchange. Between the 1928–1929 and the 1930–1931 growing seasons, coffee export earnings dropped by more than half, from $9.8 million to only $4.3 million. (Coffee still accounted for 70 to 80 percent of Costa Rica's export earnings after the crash.)[126] By then Costa Rica's small coffee oligarchy was politically dominant, even though the state remained responsive to the country's broad base of small family farmers (along with United Fruit).[127]

As in other Central American countries, large coffee growers and United Fruit responded to the economic crisis by cutting wages and laying off workers, triggering a series of strikes and actions by workers. In 1936, the *Frutera* abandoned its Atlantic coast plantations, due to labor strikes by its mostly Jamaican workers, and to infestations of Sigatoka disease. At least 17,290 acres of virgin land along the Pacific coast were developed as UFCO shifted its operations from the Atlantic region during the 1930s.[128]

Unlike its neighboring countries, however, the Costa Rican government was unwilling to use strong repressive measures against its popular classes. Instead, legislation that allowed the settlement of public lands by unemployed workers was passed. The rich forests of the surrounding lowlands became the government's escape valve, a means for displacing the social crisis to nature. Droves of landless and unemployed workers left the Meseta Central to become subsistence farmers in the Pacific forest plain and rainforests of the Atlantic lowlands. Between 1916 and 1936, the population increased 63.8 percent in the Pacific lowlands and 49.3 percent in the Atlantic lowlands. By 1936, 23.5 percent of all Costa Ricans resided in the lowlands, compared to 13.4 percent in 1883 and 7.6 percent at the beginning of the coffee boom in 1844.[129]

This political solution initiated a new cycle of environmental degradation and economic inequality. Isolated from the developed infrastructure of the central valley, limited by the poor agricultural soils of the tropical lowlands, and denied access to fertilizers, these subsistence farmers became forced to continually deforest and cultivate new lands as the productivity of their farms declined. Wealthy coffee growers from the central valley also participated in the land grabs, amassing thousands of acres in direct violation of the 740-acre limit set by the law.[130]

By the 1940s, Costa Rica saw continued worker militancy—especially on the part of those organized into labor unions on banana plantations—and the growing strength of the Communist party, the *Vanguardia Popular*. In response, presidents Rafael Angel Calderón and Teodoro Picada initiated a series of progressive reforms, including an advanced social security system and labor code. This led to an anticommunist uprising in 1948 against Calderón's party by José "Pepe" Figueres, with the support of an increasingly alarmed coffee oligarchy and the United States. By incorporating broad sectors of the urban middle class into the political power structure, Figueres and the National Liberation Party (PLN) quickly moved against organized labor and outlawed the Communist party, but he also abolished the army and left many of the reforms intact.

Costa Rica was able to avoid *caudillismo* in favor of a relatively more democratic path, characterized by a form of state-sponsored capitalist development with substantial social welfare protections for workers and the small farmers.[131]

In Guatemala, social unrest during the depression was contained by the regime of General Jorge Ubico (1931–1944), the first *caudillo* to emerge out of the depression.[132] During his rule, some 100 opposition labor, student, and political leaders were executed.[133] Labor unions were repressed, coffee estates and banana plantations were guarded by the military against land invasions, and anti-vagrancy laws (1934) replaced long-term debt servitude as a means for insuring adequate labor supplies.[134]

To fight the economic crisis and attract foreign investment, the Ubico government also made extensive land grants to UFCO on the Pacific coast in exchange for the construction of a Pacific coast port. Although the port was never built, the company acquired a plantation that covered much of the southern half of the department of Escuintla, making it the nation's largest landowner, with some 555,000 acres. Much of this land was dedicated to livestock production, although some 85 percent of the land was uncultivated reserve held against banana disease.[135]

During the 1940s, U.S. government pressure against German export houses and estates weakened much of Guatemala's coffee oligarchy. In 1944, after a long series of strikes, protests, and rebellions, Ubico was ousted from power, creating the opportunity for a more democratic politics to emerge. The administrations of Juan José Arévalo and Colonel Jacobo Arbenz passed progressive new labor codes and social legislation, designed to encourage labor organizing for better wages and working conditions, land redistribution, and other reforms that challenged the privileges of the coffee oligarchy and UFCO. Guatemala was embarking on a more populist path of national capitalist development.[136]

In 1952, conflicts between the U.S. and Guatemalan governments escalated with the passage of the agrarian reform law. In the words of Amnesty International researcher Michael McClintock,

> The agrarian reform law provided for the expropriation of idle or under-exploited land; such as the vast tracts held as "reserves" by United Fruit, much of them prime agricultural land turned over to cattle ranching or just left fallow. By June 1954, expropriation order(s) had been issued affecting 1,002 plantations, totalling 2.7 million acres. About half of the land was actually handed over to peasant cooperatives and small holders, with the estimates of the number of beneficiaries ranging up to 100,000 peasant families. Decrees to expropriate 387,000 acres from UFCO holdings on two coasts were issued; they offered compensation based on the company's own tax declaration of the value of the land: $1.18 million. The United Fruit company and the U.S. government denounced the offer and demanded $16 million in compensation.[137]

In June of 1954, the democratically elected government of Jacobo Arbenz fell to a CIA-organized operation, which included the bombing of Guatemala City on June 18 by U.S. Air Force planes out of Nicaragua. Arbenz resigned, and was eventually replaced with Colonel Carlos Castillo Armas. Existing political parties and labor unions were quickly dissolved; the 1952 Agrarian Reform Law was repealed; 99.6 percent of all expropriated land was returned to its former owners, including UFCO; all beneficiaries of the agrarian reform were dispossessed; and up to 9,000 Guatemalans were detained, many of them tortured and held without trial for several years. Another 8,000 to 10,000 people fled into exile.[138]

For the next three decades, Guatemala's brutal military dictatorship repressively ruled the country in the interests of the coffee oligarchy and multinational capital, and for their own personal economic interests as well.[139]

Conclusion

The natural history of Central America, like its political history, is a story of conquest and foreign domination. This history of social and ecological imperialism begins with the Spanish "explorers" in the sixteenth century. The Conquistadors imposed an exploitative and political system that served the Spanish Crown and local ruling elites by extracting and exporting the region's rich natural resources. Millions of local Indians were massacred by military expeditions and Old World diseases. Those who survived were enslaved and forced to serve the colonial export system.

Over the following centuries, Spanish colonists ensured their access to indigenous land and labor through a variety of repressive policies. Countless Indians died under the harsh working and living conditions imposed by the colonizers. Pushed to the brink, they rebelled in intermittent uprisings from the early sixteenth century onward and were vigorously crushed. The Spanish encouraged the rise of local economic and political elites to maintain internal order and the uninterrupted supply of labor and natural resources.

These local elites won independence from Spanish colonialism in the early nineteenth century and embarked their newly formed nations on a path of export-led commercial development. By the late 1800s, coffee plantations had expanded throughout the region, destroying vast tracts of ancient forests, displacing Indian communities to marginal lands, leaving soil vulnerable to rain and wind and initiating a cycle of erosion and flooding. In El Salvador, Guatemala, and to a lesser degree Nicaragua, the expansion of commercial coffee farms went along a *latifundio* road of capitalist development—the forceful and repressive consolidation of large-scale coffee estates by a powerful coffee oligarchy. Built on colonial-produced institutions and landscapes inherited from the past, the conversion of pristine oak-pine ecosystems into vast coffee estates represented the first wave of *capitalist* ecological transformation in Central America and would lay the political-economic groundwork for more extensive capitalist development in the twentieth century.

By the turn of the century, vast estates, including huge U.S.-owned banana plantations, controlled by a wealthy few, grew crops for foreign consumers (particularly U.S. citizens), while impoverished small farms struggled to raise food for domestic consumption. Under the guise of the Monroe Doctrine, the so-called coffee and banana republics of Central America had become subsumed by a new imperialist power—the United States. As demonstrated by the CIA-sponsored coup in Guatemala, any local or foreign government which threatened U.S. access to the cheap natural resources and workers in its own "backyard" would be met with gunboat diplomacy.

As will be discussed in Chapter 2, U.S. domination of the region continues. Today a capitalist export sector controlled by a few large landowners, or *latifundistas*, still holds power in Central America, and produces beef, cotton, coffee, bananas, sugarcane, timber, and other fruits and vegetables. This export elite monopolizes the most valuable lands and natural resources. They also receive U.S. economic and military assistance to generate these export commodities. On the other hand, the vast majority of Central America's workers and peasants in the subsistence sector struggle to survive by growing food on marginal land neglected by the export sector, or by migrating to the cities and plantations in search of employment. Thus, Central America's societies are deeply divided into two related sectors—one small and rich, the other vast and poor.

This dichotomy has created an underdeveloped, two-tiered agricultural economy that leaves the majority of Central Americans little means to improve the quality of their lives. And like human poverty, the environmental crisis spreading through Central America stems from unequal distribution of land and natural resources. That environmental destruction should parallel the destruction of human lives is not coincidental: they are two faces of a single process in which Central America has been trapped since the first days of its conquest by the Spanish.

As we shall see, the basic features that characterized Central America centuries ago—foreign domination, political repression, immense poverty and inequality, murder of indigenous peoples, popular rebellion, forced removal of people from their land, ecological deterioration and the massive extraction and export of resources, and the subordination of sustainable subsistence food production to plantation agriculture for the needs of foreign markets—are still present today. In this sense, the current social and ecological crisis must be regarded as the logical outcome of 500 years of imperialist domination by the Spaniards, and now the United States, over the people and environment of Central America.

2
POVERTY, INJUSTICE,
AND THE
ECOLOGICAL CRISIS

45

Our labor is every day more harshly exploited on the coffee farms, the cotton plantations, and sugar estates. We need land to sow. In other places they threaten us, and they expel us from land won through the sweat of our brows. . . . They even take from us the water, to make a profit from it. They exploit our forests, leaving our lands dry like deserts. For the workers of the countryside there are no roads, no medicines, no decent housing, no possibility of education, or rest. The wealth we produce serves to fatten our own enemies, to build a new military academy, to buy new and murderous arms. For us the repression is abundant. They kidnap our sons to take them as soldiers. When we demand our rights, when we demand part of all this wealth we produce they pursue us, torture us, and murder us. Not even in our own communities can we walk freely, but we must defend ourselves from the police, the army, the detectives, the Treasury Guard, and the bands of gunmen of the estate owners who have us in a constant state of siege.

Committee for Peasant Unity leaflet, 1978[1]

Central America's ecological and cultural diversity rivals any in the world. Along the Pacific littoral, once home to the Pipil and other Indian tribes, towering volcanos guard fertile coastal plains that turn white with cotton in the late spring. In the interior highlands, coffee trees and small peasant farms cover the mountain valleys and hillsides. To the east, montane cloud forests descend toward the Caribbean, turning into the largest pristine lowland tropical rainforests north of the Amazon basin, where ancient Mayan temples still stand.

From the iridescent blue flashes of the *morpho* butterfly in the Caribbean rainforests, to the transparent waters of Lago de Atitlán, which Aldous Huxley called the most beautiful place in the world, to the rare and misty shadow of the legendary quetzal, Guatemala's "bird of life, bird of death," Central America's natural wonders have dazzled generations of naturalists.[2]

Today, virtually every major ecosystem in the region has been severely degraded or destroyed. Pesticide pollution, deforestation, soil erosion, industrial contamination, and "scorched earth" military campaigns have besieged the region's economically impoverished people and their environment.

The Capitalization of Nature

The ecological crisis of Central America is grounded in a particular model of capitalist development that has been promoted by the United States for the last four decades. At the end of World War II, the nations of Central America remained economically and socially "underdeveloped," highly dependent on the markets of the first world (particularly the United States) for their own prosperity. In 1954, just two commodity crops, coffee and bananas, dominated the region's exports, generating nearly 90 percent of Costa Rica's, El Salvador's and Guatemala's total foreign exchange earnings.[3] Although the prices for these exports improved immediately after World War II, they suffered relative price decreases by the mid-1950s, revealing the region's economic vulnerability.[4]

In the 1950s, the U.S. government assumed a more active role in expanding "dependent" capitalist development in Central America. This policy can be traced to the rise of political influence of corporate

47

interests linked to the Rockefeller family, particularly the National Security Council, the primary foreign policymaking body during the Eisenhower administration.

For instance, John Foster Dulles, secretary of state during most of the Eisenhower years, was proponent of the U.S.-orchestrated coup that overthrew the democratically elected government of Guatemalan President Jacobo Arbenz; he had been chairman of the board of trustees of the Rockefeller Foundation and was on the board of the Rockefeller-dominated Bank of New York. He was also a partner in Sullivan and Cromwell, a Wall Street law firm specializing in the representation of transnational corporations. Dulles, along with his brother Allen (then director of the Central Intelligence Agency), reportedly held direct financial interests in United Fruit, the direct beneficiary of the Guatemala coup.[5]

Washington's role was enlarged even further with the creation of the Alliance for Progress in 1961. Formed largely in response to the Cuban Revolution, the Alliance aimed to promote "social and economic stability" (or the creation of "middle classes") in Central America through the modernization, diversification, and expansion of capitalist export agriculture and industry. However, potentially progressive aspects of capitalist development under the Alliance were negated by U.S. military assistance, which gave the region's landed oligarchs, bankers, and military officers the power to appropriate the lion's share of the newly created wealth. The resulting impoverishment later stimulated the revolutionary struggles that erupted in the late 1970s.[6]

The social and ecological impact of the Alliance in the various Central American countries was similar. In El Salvador, Guatemala, and Nicaragua, the traditional oligarchies and surrogate security forces (along with the Somocista bourgeoisie) used U.S. economic and military assistance to promote the development of large-scale agricultural estates.

Pristine forest land, unique wildlife habitats, and peasant communities alike were "cleared" to make way for vast *latifundios* devoted to the production of traditional and nontraditional export crops, primarily coffee, cotton, sugar, bananas, and cattle. In Honduras and Costa Rica, on the other hand, foreign capital was used by small peasant farmers, the urban bourgeoisie, and landed oligarchs to modernize and expand smaller coffee farms and cattle holdings; large-scale banana plantations also grew rapidly. Since capitalist development took a more mixed *minifundio-latifundio* form in these two countries, state repression of the popular classes was much less significant.[7]

One of the first areas to be developed was the Pacific coastal plain (see Chapter 3). Guarded by a long chain of majestic volcanos, these fertile lowlands were ideal for the cultivation of two of the new export commodities, sugar and cotton. Prior to World War II, the Pacific littoral remained lightly settled in most areas, occupied by isolated haciendas that combined extensive cattle grazing with tenant sharecropping by resident families, or *colonos*. State initiatives, such as malaria and disease eradication projects, road and port construction, and land speculation, spurred by infusions of financial capital from the U.S. Agency for International Development (USAID), the World Bank, the Inter-American Development Bank (IADB), and other international development agencies, quickly created the appropriate conditions for the production of export agriculture.[8]

From the 1950s to the 1970s, virtually all of the coastal humid hardwood forests were destroyed, as well as coastal savannas, evergreen forests, and large areas of mangroves. With their habitats destroyed, many species of animals, including howler monkeys, anteaters, and white-lipped peccaries, were eliminated. Numerous other lowland deciduous forest mammals were either exterminated or reduced in numbers, including the nine-banded armadillo, agouti, coyote, gray fox, tepesciuntle, puma, and white-tailed deer, as well as large birds such as the ornate hawk-eagle, scarlet macaw, yellow-headed parrot, and great curassow.[9]

Peasants were evicted from their traditional landholdings, often through the use of brute force. For many dispossessed peasants, the only income-earning opportunities that remained were as wage-laborers during the short cotton-picking season.[10] By the late 1970s, the landed oligarchy and newly emerging agrarian bourgeoisie had carved out over 10,000 farms and over one million acres of cotton fields from the ancient tropical forests and employed one-half million workers. By then Central America was the third leading producer of cotton in the world.[11] Only 2 percent of the original coastal forests remained.[12]

Another export commodity that transformed the Central American landscape was beef cattle. Cattle ranching was less restricted geographically than cotton or coffee production. Beef could be raised wherever pasture grass would grow, although it was particularly suited to the lush lower montane and lowland Caribbean rainforests. Funded by grants and/or loans from U.S. government agencies, as well as by international financial institutions and the Central American Bank for Economic Integration, large-scale cattle ranches quickly expanded toward the rolling mountains and valleys of the interior, displacing peasant farmers from their traditional agricultural lands. The World Bank alone spent $154 million on the livestock industry in Central America and the Caribbean in its first two decades of development lending, amounting to 56 percent of its total direct commitments to agriculture.[13]

In Nicaragua and Guatemala, thousands of peasants who resisted eviction were killed in U.S.-supported counterinsurgency operations during the 1960s and 1970s. Military officers and government officials have historically promoted such counterinsurgency programs, as a means of capitalizing or privatizing nature for their own personal gain (see Chapter 4).

The expansion of cattle ranching quickly proved to be an ecological as well as social disaster. During the height of the cattle boom, from 1970 to 1980, 15 percent of the region's total forests, covering an area larger than Belgium, were destroyed.[14] As a result of this expansion, deboned frozen beef emerged as the region's most dynamic export, with a 400 percent increase in trade between 1961 and 1974 alone.[15]

Over two-thirds of Central America's lowland and lower montane rainforests, the largest expanse north of the Amazon Basin, have been destroyed since 1960.[16] Today, over 22 percent of the region's land mass—more land than used for all other agricultural commodities combined—is in permanent pasture (see Chapter 4).[17]

The Ecological Costs of Disarticulated Development

Under the Alliance for Progress, Central America was more fully integrated into the world economy as a supplier of cheap agricultural commodities and raw materials. By the mid-1970s, cotton, beef, sugar, coffee, and bananas constituted between 82 to 85 percent of all trade outside the region and over 60 percent of export earnings.[18] In addition, the creation of the Central America Common Market (CACM) led to 7 to 9 percent increases in industrial output in every Central American country except Honduras and Belize between 1960 and 1976.[19] Export diversification has continued with the introduction of new fruits, winter vegetables, and flowers.

But rather than bringing greater economic independence, this has intensified Central American dependency on U.S. and international capital. In short, capitalist development has left the region both *sectorally* and *socially disarticulated*.[20] An understanding of this pattern of capitalist development provides a basis for analyzing Central America's social and ecological crisis.

In Central America, neither backward linkages—industries that produce commodities (producer goods or inputs) necessary for the production of agricultural products and raw materials (such as farming equipment)—nor forward linkages—industries that process agricultural products and raw materials into another commodity form (e.g., hemp into rope)—have been developed in the processing of the primary commodities produced by the capitalist export sector. Thus, the region is sectorally disarticulated, despite the creation of the CACM and the development of some import-substitution industrialization (domestic manufacture goods that were previously imported), and despite more recent neoliberal trade policies under the Caribbean Basin Initiative (CBI).[21]

As a result, the capitalist export sector remains highly dependent on imported capital goods and highly vulnerable to trade and credit fluctuations in the international market. While nearly one-quarter of industry's raw material requirements were met by the CACM at the end of the 1960s, virtually 100 percent of the capital goods imports came from outside the region.[22]

The region is also *socially disarticulated*: it possesses little consumption capacity for commodities produced by the capitalist export sector, especially in those countries pursuing the more repressive *latifundio* path of development. The peasantry and poor working classes are not the primary sources of aggregate consumer demand. As a result, the region's economy is extremely vulnerable to world market conditions (falling prices for major exports, protectionism, overproduction, etc.), particularly now with the deepening economic recession in the United States and other advanced capitalist countries.

The United States supplied 36 percent of Central America's imports during the 1960s and 1970s, virtually the same percentage as its share of exports. Behind the U.S., the Federal Republic of Germany was the region's most important trading partner, receiving about a quarter of all exports (with coffee being the most important). Japan received the next highest percentage of exports, particularly hand-picked cotton.[23]

This condition is magnified by the extremely small size and openness of the region's economy. It is more like a corporation in a highly competitive global market than a group of truly independent national economies; contraction or expansion in the supply of Central America's leading agricultural exports has little impact on the world prices for these commodities. Hence the volume of these exports is "determined by production costs in Central American countries compared to costs elsewhere and the margin between world prices and production costs," as John Weeks notes.[24] With the primary market located abroad, both the production and consumption capacities of Central America's capitalist sector are increased by minimizing costs, including expenditures relating to environmental protection. Unburdened by effective environmental and community health and safety regulations that would impose greater production costs on capital, draining profits and damaging competitiveness, a host of Central American industries freely damaged the environment for decades.

Textile factories, tanneries, slaughterhouses, pesticide formulating plants, coffee processing units, and other industries that grew up under the Alliance are compelled to "externalize" the social and ecological costs of capitalist production in the form of harmful pollution, rather than "internalize" these added costs in the form of expensive pollution control equipment or other such measures. In partnership with multinational corporations, many of these plants are owned by the same oligarchs, government officials (including Somoza in prerevolutionary Nicaragua), and military officers who traditionally controlled the state and large sectors of the economy.[25]

Since the 1960s, Central America's workers and peasants and the larger environment have absorbed these costs (or negative externalities) in the form of increasingly polluted and disease-ridden water supplies, severe health problems, etc. Harm to the environment owned as private property by the capitalist firm figures into cost calculations; but harm to external nature not owned by the individual firm is ignored. Competition and the quest for higher profits pushes the individual firm to cut as many private costs as possible by not installing pollution control equipment or by rejecting less productive but less pollutive production processes, etc. Thus these private costs are externalized and become social costs to other appropriators of productive and/or consumptive nature—workers, peasants, and other capitalist producers.[26]

Enteritis and diarrheal disorders related to polluted water are major causes of death throughout the region (except in Costa Rica).[27] Water-borne disease accounts for 12 percent of all fatalities in Honduras, contributing to the third worst infant mortality rate in all of Latin America and the Caribbean.[28] Only one in ten Salvadorans has access to safe drinking water.[29]

Some of the worst offenders are *beneficios*—coffee processing plants which often discharge high levels of boron, chloride, and arsenic-laden wastewater into the environment. In El Salvador, more than 200 of the coffee oligarchy's *beneficios* dump contaminated wastewater directly into the country's rivers and streams. According to a USAID report, industrial and agricultural pollution is a "problem that now permeates almost every facet of Salvadoran life ... it includes toxic chemicals building up in soil, livestock, human and ecological food chain and urban waste disposal." El Salvador's principal dairy producing area is even using boron-laden wastewater from the *Laguna de Coatepeque* for irrigation.[30] During the dry season, pollution from thousands of Honduran *beneficios* causes serious environmental health problems in thirteen of the country's eighteen departments. In some places, cattle have died from drinking water downstream from the plants.[31]

In Costa Rica, *beneficios* produce 66 percent of the country's water contaminants. Tanneries are also a major source of pollution. The Costa Rican tanning industry processes some 200,000 hides daily and discharges some 100,000 cubic meters of toxic effluents like chromium directly into the nation's waterways. Taken together, effluents from both these industries are considered to be the country's most serious pollution problem. Much of the Central Valley's underground aquifers, which underlies the most highly populated area of Costa Rica, are already contaminated.[32]

In Nicaragua, thirty-seven industrial plants located on Lake Managua, the second-largest freshwater lake in Central America, were permitted by the Somoza dictatorship to dump toxic wastes. The worst polluter was the U.S. corporation Pennwalt, which escaped environmental regulations in the United States to dump an estimated forty tons of mercury in the lake between 1968 and 1981. In January 1980, environmental health officials found that 37 percent of the workers at the plant were suffering from chronic mercury poisoning.[33] Despite conservation efforts initiated under the Sandinista government during the 1980s, contaminated water from Lake Managua is seeping toward neighboring Asososca Lagoon, threatening the drinking supply for the capital city of Managua.[34]

The primary means by which Central American capital maintains its competitive position in the world economy is by minimizing the cost (while maximizing the productivity in both relative and absolute terms) of labor in the agricultural-export sector. To this end, capital resists costly procedures designed to protect worker health and safety as well as the environment. Dangerous working and living conditions are particularly evident for seasonal, unskilled laborers involved in the export harvests of cotton, coffee, bananas, and other commodity crops. These workers seldom have access to protective devices such as gloves, boots, and masks, resulting in massive exposure to lethal pesticides used on the crops.[35]

Only 10 to 15 percent of Costa Rican field workers, for instance, have the necessary protective clothing.[36] Approximately 1,000 Costa Rican banana workers have been rendered infertile through exposure to the nematicide DBCP, while another 4,000 to 5,000 exposed workers are considered at risk.[37] As a result of these and many other abuses, it is estimated that as many as 73,230 pesticide poisonings occurred in the region during the 1970s.[38]

Honduras and Nicaragua were world leaders in per capita illness and deaths from pesticide poisonings during the 1960s and 1970s. Even today, Nicaraguans and Guatemalans have more DDT (as well as other organochlorine pesticides) in their body fat than any population of human beings on earth. Since nineteen of the twenty-five most commonly used organochlorines prove carcinogenic in laboratory tests, the future may reveal higher cancer rates among Central American workers.[39]

Ecological Impoverishment of the Peasantry

The key factor in determining labor costs are wage rates. Labor costs are of particularly critical importance to the agricultural export sector in that the three-month seasonal harvest period for the region's primary commodity crops—cotton, sugar, coffee, and bananas—requires the availability of hundreds of thousands of migratory wage laborers. And because these seasonal workers are not the principal source of aggregate consumer demand for the agricultural-export sector, low wage rates have been essential for insuring and/or increasing the competitiveness and profitability of Central American capital.[40]

But how, given the region's predominant working conditions and wage rates, was this large, superexploitable labor force created? And how has the capitalist export sector maintained this labor supply during the six to nine months of unemployment between harvests without excessively raising production costs and damaging profitability?

The answer: Central America's capitalist export sector reduces labor costs by perpetuating the peasant subsistence sector. Since part of the subsistence costs of hired wage labor are provided by unpaid family members laboring on small subsistence plots or *minifundios*, the capitalist sector offers wages lower than the cost of maintaining the worker for the whole year.[41] The production of maize, beans, rice, sorghum, wheat, fruits, and other crops on peasant plots lowers the cost of labor-power, but is inadequate to insure the freedom of the peasant family from the bonds of wage slavery.

Maintenance of the peasant subsistence sector as a source of semi-proletarian wage labor on a seasonal basis has been the main "functional" prerequisite for continued accumulation in the capitalist export sector, a relation Alain de Janvry calls *functional dualism*.[42] Over the years, functional dualism has given competitive advantages in the world economy to Central American capital. For example, the wages for Guatemala's semiproletarian cotton workers in 1979 and 1980 represented only 10.3 percent of total production costs, compared to around one-third for Argentina, Mexico, and Paraguay.[43]

The proper "balance" between the two sectors is rather precarious, however. If the peasantry were to become completely proletarianized, the socially necessary labor time required for the production and reproduction of seasonal wage workers for the export sector (and therefore costs) would be increased, damaging the competitiveness of Central American capital in the world market.[44] Likewise, if the vast majority of peasant families were provided with sufficient natural resources (or ecological conditions of production in the form of fertile land, water, wildlife, and wood fuel supplies) and sufficient social resources (or means/relations of production in the form of technical and financial assistance, fertilizers and equipment, favorable marketing arrangements) to appropriate these natural resources to meet their subsistence needs, the capitalist export sector would be denied a sufficient supply of exploitable wage labor.[45]

In effect, functional dualism in Central America involves the "overdevelopment" of the export sector and "underdevelopment" of the subsistence sector that is manifest in the *social* and *ecological impoverishment* of the peasantry, whose need for survival forces them to work as migratory, semiproletarian laborers.

Since World War II, functional dualism has become institutionalized by a variety of state policies and development practices. The most important mechanism for the social and ecological impoverishment of the peasant involved land tenure. Initially, development of the Pacific coastal plains during the 1940s benefited the peasantry, since families were allowed to migrate into and establish new farms in the area. During this period, the expansion of the subsistence sector exceeded population growth in every Central American country except Nicaragua. Since alternative agrarian reform measures were unlikely, the development of the coastal lowlands offered a promising opportunity for resolving the peasantry's acute land shortages and reducing dependence on imported foodstuffs.[46] But by the early 1950s, the rate of subsistence agricultural expansion slowed dramatically, as the traditional oligarchy and newly emerging agrarian bourgeoisie monopolized the majority of new landholdings and financial resources for cotton, coffee, sugar, banana and cattle production.[47]

With the increased flow of U.S. military and economic aid under the Alliance for Progress, this process accelerated. Between 1950 to 1968, the export sector grew by about 1,729,000 acres, claiming 73 percent of all newly developed agricultural land. Although the number of farms worked by the peasantry also increased significantly, these farms occupied only 8 percent of the newly developed farm land.

Central America's rapidly growing population of peasants became increasingly land poor. In the major cotton-producing departments of El Salvador, for example, the number of farms twenty-five acres or smaller increased by 72 percent from 1950 to 1961, while the average farm size in this category declined by 54 percent. Likewise, average small-to-medium farm size in the major cotton departments of Nicaragua declined 20 to 38 percent from 1952 to 1964.[48]

By the early 1960s, 6 percent of Central America's largest farms controlled 72 percent of the farm land and employed 28 percent of the rural labor force. Conversely, 78 percent of Central America's farms occupied only 11 percent of the region's farm land. Too small to provide adequate income or full employment for the peasant families living on them, these *minifundios* provided 60 percent of the rural labor force for the export sector.[49]

Despite such widespread marginalization of the subsistence sector, labor shortages persisted in some areas of Central America, particularly along the Pacific plains. These shortages damaged the profitability of the export sector and impeded the expansion of cotton and coffee estates. Capitalist growers were forced to attract workers to their estates through more inefficient modes of labor exploitation, namely by granting peasants use rights to small agricultural plots in exchange for their labor.[50]

During the mid-1960s, however, large-scale cattle ranches expanded into ecological and geographical zones previously immune to capitalist development, including vast zones of campesino agriculture. By 1975, over ten million cattle were grazing on twenty million acres of pasture, an area exceeding all remaining agricultural land in the region.[51] Even though beef exports jumped from approximately $9 million in 1961 to $290 million in 1979, primarily to serve as fast-food hamburgers and pet food in the United States, marginalization of the peasantry resulted in declining beef consumption per capita over the same period, as well as falling income and food production. Between 1948 and 1978, food production declined substantially in every Central American country, particularly Guatemala and Honduras. In fact, domestic food production reached its lowest point *after* two and a half decades of capitalist agricultural development, a telling indicator of the peasantry's marginalization.[52]

In contrast to the rise in beef export, domestic beef consumption in Central America is extremely low (see Chapter 4).[53] This human impoverishment is a direct consequence of the cattle boom, which by continually displacing the subsistence sector, serving as an efficient instrument for land speculation and monopolization, and requiring little in the way of a labor force, has been the most important mechanism for maintaining the ecological impoverishment of the subsistence sector.

The vast majority of Central America's *minifundios* are today less than seventeen acres, the minimum farm size required to provide a family with adequate sustenance.[54] But quantitative figures on land tenure only partly convey the magnitude of the peasantry's impoverishment. The expansion of the capitalist export sector also displaces peasant farmers onto unfertile lands ecologically unsuitable for slash-and-burn (or swidden) agriculture, particularly the steep hillsides of the Pacific mountains and rugged interior highlands and nutrient-poor rainforest soils of the Caribbean lowlands. These lands are prone to severe erosion and fertility loss.

In El Salvador, for example, 40 percent of the land designated as ecologically unsuitable for agriculture became occupied by peasant cultivators during the 1970s.[55] In some areas of the country, peasants are clearing and cultivating land so steep that some farmers must tie themselves to a stake pounded into the ground to keep from falling down the hillside.

In Honduras, over 60 percent of the population lives in the fragile Choluteca Valley and western hills bordering El Salvador and Nicaragua, even though a mere 14 percent of the country's total land deemed suitable for intensive agriculture is located in these areas.[56] Likewise, as much as 6,950 square miles, or 23 percent, of the terrain considered unsuitable for agriculture or pasture in Panama has been deforested and put to this use.[57] As a result, peasant families displaced from twelve acres of fertile land to eighteen acres of degraded hillside improve their landholding position in quantitative terms, but in reality, they experience deteriorating living standards.[58]

Ecological impoverishment of the subsistence sector is aggravated by state policies and private practices of social impoverishment that deny favorable marketing, financial, and technological assistance and services. The capitalist export sector receives over half, and in some countries nearly three-fourths, of all the institutional credit allocated through national banking systems, often at usury rates.[59] As a result of these policies, even where the land is of high quality for agriculture, subsistence-based methods often result "in extremely inefficient yields, and a general deterioration of the soil and water quality," according to USAID.[60]

Thus, social and ecological impoverishment of the peasant subsistence sector creates the necessary *human conditions of production* for disarticulated capitalist development—a large army of semiproletarian wage labor. Since the late 1970s, the vast majority of Central America's rural peasantry have lived on subfamily subsistence plots incapable of satisfying the most minimum needs, forcing family members to engage in superexploitative wage work under a system of functional dualism for survival. Coffee, sugar, and cotton growers have seasonal fluctuations in their labor requirements, with the April-to-June planting and November-to-January harvest being the periods of greatest labor demand.

Therefore, the harvest of most export crops (except bananas) occurs during the dry season, while basic grains raised on peasant plots are cultivated during the rainy season. Peasant families can migrate for the export harvests and minimally impact the production of their own subsistence crops. If not for these climatic-crop specific variations, functional dualism would not have been a viable system of labor exploitation in Central America. The low availability of semiproletarian labor during the rainy season is a major reason why large-scale rice production has been highly mechanized.[61]

Hundreds of thousands of impoverished semiproletarian peasants, over 40 percent of Central America's total work force, migrate each year to the coastal and interior zones to pick export crops during the dry season harvest and then return to their small *minifundios* to plant subsistence crops in time for the rains. The health effects of functional dualism on migratory families include increased malnutrition, endemic parasite infestation, infectious disease and work injuries, as well as increased alcoholism and stress-related and sexually transmitted diseases, and the related detrimental impact on family and community relations.[62]

In the 1970s, roughly half a million wage laborers, over 17 percent of Central America's total work force (for a total of thirty-six million person days) were employed in the weeding and harvesting of one commodity crop alone—cotton—at an average wage of $1.25 to $1.50 *a day!*[63] As Jeffery M. Paige notes, wage levels were absolutely crucial because any substantial increase in labor costs would have destroyed the competitiveness of Central America's cotton bourgeoisie in the world market.[64]

Semiproletarianization and marginalization of the peasantry under a system of functional dualism is particularly advanced in El Salvador and Guatemala, as it was, to a lesser extent, in prerevolutionary Nicaragua. There, the rapid expansion of large-scale coffee, cotton, and sugar estates has created the greatest demand in the region for seasonal wage workers. Labor costs and productivity (i.e., the rate of exploitation in both relative and absolute terms) were central to determining the volume of agricultural exports.

Methods for the mechanization of coffee harvesting have not been effectively developed. In addition, Central America's cotton exports to Japan enjoyed competitive advantages over other world competitors due to its superior hand-picked quality. A large semiproletarian labor force, contracted an average of seventy days from mid-December through mid-March, was essential for hand-picking the cotton crop (and chopping by hand earlier in the season); a process that yielded a cleaner product and premium market prices and demand.

State repression, carried out to establish and maintain such conditions, has reached new heights of brutality in these three "latifundio road" countries, which, since the late 1970s, have seen the rise of powerful mass-based revolutionary movements.

In Guatemala, more than three-fourths of the seasonal agricultural workers came from the degraded Indian highlands of the northwest, particularly Huehuetanango and Quiche. Most were "recruited from the most destitute of the peasant households, from the families with the least land and livestock, and from the poorest and most remote of the mountaintop villages," writes Robert Williams. In the 1960s, temporary employment on large capitalist estates accounted for 66 percent of available labor time spent and 57 percent of annual incomes earned by semiproletarian peasants from the highlands. Each year, between 118,000 to 150,000 migrant pickers harvested the cotton crop, while coffee employed some 167,000 to 237,000, and sugar some 17,500 to 21,000.[65] By the late 1970s, about 60 percent of Guatemala's economically active population in the highlands, some 600,000 peasants, worked for the capitalist export sector and constituted one of the largest migratory wage labor forces (per capita) in the world.[66]

In El Salvador, capitalist export agriculture expanded into the volcanic highlands, interior valleys, and Pacific coastal plain, resulting in the near-complete dispossession of the peasantry. In the mid-1960s, 97 percent of the agricultural work force were employed during the export harvests. During the off-seasons, employment dropped to 32 percent of the available labor force.[67] Up to one-tenth of the pickers for Guatemala's cotton crop were impoverished Salvadoran peasants, while tens of thousands of others migrated to work the export harvests in Nicaragua and Honduras.[68]

In Nicaragua, the seasonal wage-labor force consisted of some 240,000 semiproletarian workers, 38 percent of the country's entire work force, by the late 1970s.[69] Urban-based landless workers, who played a major role in the insurrection that toppled the Somoza dictatorship, comprised another 32 percent of the work force.[70] The Nicaraguan peasantry represented 60 percent of the rural economically active population—some 260,000 people. Of these, approximately 22 percent were medium-sized peasant producers—the rest were semiproletarian. However, the pattern of capitalist development in Nicaragua, due in great part to the political weakness of the traditional coffee oligarchy, created a mostly impoverished subsistence sector in the Pacific zones and northern mountains and a relatively medium and rich peasantry in the interior.[71]

In contrast, capitalist development in Honduras and Costa Rica was less dependent on the creation of a large semiproletarian peasantry, and therefore the ruling bourgeoisie had less incentive (as well as less power) to impoverish the subsistence sector. (In Honduras, the underdevelopment of a nationally owned capitalist export sector resulted in a weaker state; when worker and peasant organizations gained strength, the military was not strong enough to suppress them.)[72]

The relative stability of the subsistence sector in Honduras and Costa Rica was rooted in the particularities of the two countries. These included: (1) the development of a relatively large, relatively prosperous class of family coffee farmers in both countries; (2) relatively higher incomes and better employment and living standards for banana workers in both countries; (3) the relatively small number of large-scale cotton estates, and therefore a lesser demand for labor; (4) the dominance of cattle ranching, particularly among small farmers compared to the "*latifundio* countries," and (5) more secure land titles and better services for Costa Rica's peasantry, as well as more extensive agrarian reform programs in Honduras. Honduras also exports a lower percentage of its agricultural production than any other country in the region.[73]

In summary, class struggles over the capitalization of nature reflected efforts to *create the appropriate conditions of production* for the capitalist export sector. Before production can take place, capital must gain favorable access to a sufficient quantity and quality of labor-power (human conditions), land and natural resources (ecological conditions), and infrastructure (communal conditions). Since these "conditions of capitalist production" are not produced as commodities in accordance with the law of value, the state must attempt to make these production conditions available to capital via social and environmental policy.

In short, the state regulates the exploitation of the conditions of production by capital; but capital and the state rarely have a free hand in their attempts to appropriate and restructure the production conditions according to the rules of the market, i.e., exchange value. As previously stated, these conditions are also means for the reproduction of human beings and their communities (and life itself) according to the rule of cultural norms and social values, i.e., use value. Hence, the massive resistance to capitalist exploitation and restructuring of production conditions in Central America.[74]

Ecological Collapse of the Minifundio

In the context of functional dualism, the peasantry depends for its survival upon access to adequate social and natural resources. Central America's peasantry are for the most part denied access to state extension programs that promote more sustainable models of agriculture (such as intercropping, organic and biological fertilization, technical training, etc.), as well as adequate financial credit and other social services. With the marginalization of the subsistence sector, conventional methods for both obtaining and maintaining these resources becomes increasingly disrupted.[75]

In addition to selling their labor-power to the capitalist export sector for the seasonal harvests, the peasantry responds to their growing impoverishment by overexploiting the limited natural resources to which it has access. The surrounding forests and other sources of wood fuel, land and agricultural soils, water supplies, fish and wildlife populations, and other critical resources are suffering from growing ecological deterioration, particularly in the highlands of Guatemala, El Salvador, Nicaragua, and Honduras.

However, disarticulated capitalist development in Central America not only *produces* severe ecological exploitation, but *depends* on it for the subsidized reproduction of semiproletarian labor and generation of a larger mass of surplus value. To appropriate (and therefore exploit) capitalized nature for the purpose of producing use-values (commodities) for sale in the world market, the export sector requires adequate supplies of exploitable wage labor.

Likewise, to exploit human nature (or labor) for the purpose of producing surplus value and profits in the world market, the export sector requires the overexploitation of noncapitalized nature in the peasant subsistence sector to generate and maintain these needed supplies of exploitable wage labor.[76] In effect, exploitation of labor and the environment are two different sides of the same coin, namely, functional dualism, and reflect the class privileges and power of Central America's ruling oligarchies and agrarian bourgeoisie.

An ecological crisis is a turning point, a moment when the reproduction of an established ecosystem (or systems) on which a given social formation or mode of production is dependent becomes threatened with collapse. Today, there is growing evidence that the environmental conditions of subsistence production in many areas are in a state of ecological collapse. Symptoms can be found in rampant deforestation; declining fallow cycles and land degradation; severe soil erosion and watershed destruction; critical fish, wildlife, and wood fuel shortages; declining food production and increased poverty; disease; widespread migration; growing problems of drought in the dry seasons and damaging floods in the rainy seasons, and other ecological problems.

Overexploitation of agricultural soils is perhaps the most ecologically destructive response to functional dualism. Traditionally, *milpa* or slash-and-burn (swidden) agriculture has worked relatively well for the peasantry, making use of an abundant resource (land), while economizing on scarce resources in the form of labor and capital. Peasant families cut and burn vegetation on a plot of land and plant a mixture of crops (typically maize, beans, sorghum, and other basic grains and/or semi-perennial plants) for two to four years. An idle or fallow period of a few years is critical for regenerating soil fertility after cutting and burning. With the end of the fallow period, the area is cleared once again for planting. If properly practiced, these methods are usually sustainable, minimizing deforestation, habitat destruction, soil erosion, and other problems of land degradation.[77]

But with increased social and ecological impoverishment of the peasantry, sustainable systems of rotating swidden agriculture are evolving into semi-permanent or permanent agriculture without the fallow periods necessary for nutrient recovery by successional vegetation.[78] This soil-destructive system and the abandonment of other soil conservation efforts, including contoured or terraced planting, reforestation, protection of vulnerable areas with forest cover, etc., results in accelerated erosion and fertility loss, watershed degradation, desertification, and climatic changes.[79] Land tenure and title arrangements are particularly important. Studies in the Choluteca basin have shown that campesinos who own their land are more inclined to practice conservation measures than those who must rent or sharecrop the land.[80]

Land degradation is now reaching crisis proportions in many areas of the region, contributing to large decreases in per capita food production.[81] Over 17 percent of Costa Rica is severely eroded, and another 24 percent moderately eroded. Some 3 percent suffers extreme erosion and is now useless economically. Other studies estimate that one-third of the country's land surface is severely eroded, with another third undergoing more subtle forms of erosion and increased flooding.[82] Virtually every major watershed in the country is seriously degraded, particularly in areas of subsistence agriculture and cattle ranching on the Pacific side. Both severe and extreme erosion effects 30 percent of the Pacific terrain, with an additional 30 percent of the land suffering moderate erosion. Soil losses, primarily from degraded pasture lands, are estimated at an astounding 680 million tons a year.[83] (*Moderate erosion* is defined as moderate sheet, rill, and occasional gully erosion or fluvial erosion in limited areas. *Severe erosion* is characterized by surface horizon truncation and frequent or scattered deep gullies and occasional small landslips; or severe fluvial erosion. *Extreme erosion* is characterized by exposure of subsoil or parent material over large areas; or stream terraces obliterated by fluvial erosion.)

Problems with soil erosion and compaction on overgrazed lands is magnifying the water crisis for much of the Costa Rican peasantry, particularly for those outside the coffee belt. In the Guanacaste area, soil compaction is increasing rapid water runoff and creating widespread gully erosion, decreasing the proportions of moisture penetrating the soil that is stored underground beneath the barren slopes. Researcher Susan Place has noted that "rivers formerly deep enough throughout the dry season for swimming and diving, and also of abundant fishing ... now carry a mere trickle of water during the summer."[84] Falling water tables and decreased river flows are necessitating the construction of deeper wells and other hardships. The burden is often borne particularly heavy on the backs of women and children, who must carry the heavy vases of water over increasingly long distances.

These ecological problems have contributed to a 5.1 percent decline in per capita food production during the 1980s.[85] An estimated 4,470,700 acres of degraded land currently under agricultural use are in need of immediate reforestation if the processes described above are to be halted.[86]

The ecological situation is somewhat worse in the highlands of Honduras, where the landscape is being reduced to a degraded patchwork of small farms occupying highly eroded, acidic soils laced with scattered trees and rocky surfaces. Severe land degradation and even desertification is also advancing in western Honduras, particularly in Choluteca.[87] In a country where more than 75 percent of the land possesses slopes greater than 25 percent, soil erosion averages a phenomenal 40 to 202 metric tons per acre over nearly 5.44 million acres of agricultural land.[88] Two-thirds of the peasant families in the Southern highlands cannot produce enough food to meet their own subsistence needs.[89] Aggravated by the elimination of nutrient-restoring fallow cycles, per capita production of beans and other basic grains common to the *minifundio* has declined 22.2 percent since the mid-1970s.[90] Sorghum, which grows much better on rocky and degraded soils but is much less valued by small farmers as a human food source over corn, now comprises up to one-half of food production in Honduras.[91]

Elsewhere, the ecological crisis is even worse. Despite its abundant water resources and fertile land, Guatemala is home to the third-lowest "physical quality of life" index in Latin America, trailing only Haiti and Bolivia. Over 65 percent of the country's original forests have been destroyed in the last 30 years.[92] Traditional Indian systems of the Central and Western Highlands—which had, according to a USAID report, "constructed terraces, planted and cultivated on the contour of the hills, reserved steeply sloped land for forests, and replaced soil nutrients by fallowing"—are rapidly being replaced with highly destructive practices. As a result, the moderately fertile andosanic surface soils and clayish subsoils (which together consists primarily of unconsolidated volcanic ash) are literally being washed down the mountainsides. Soil losses in some highland areas now average two to fourteen tons per acre a year.[93] In the northern rainforests of the Petén, annual soil losses in zones of cattle ranching and peasant colonization vary between an incredible 270 to 425 metric tons per square mile.[94]

Only 18 percent of the rural population has access to safe drinking water—one third of all deaths are due to preventable infectious and parasitic diseases. Life expectancy for Guatemala's Indian majority is now forty-four years, and for non-Indians, sixty years, one of the lowest rates in the Western Hemisphere.[95]

Nowhere is the situation more critical than in El Salvador, the most ecologically devastated country in Latin America. According to the United Nations Food and Agriculture Organization (FAO), the country is undergoing a process of desertification. More than 95 percent of the original tropical deciduous forests have been destroyed. Scientists estimate that only 3 percent to less than 7 percent of the country (compared to a regional average of just under 40 percent) is covered with tracts of woodland large enough to be considered forests.[96] Roughly 86.7 percent of all small farmer families live on ten acres of land or less, and of these *microfundios* over 50 percent are less than three acres in size.[97]

Aggravated by transitions from shifting to permanent or semi-permanent subsistence agriculture, overexploitation is causing extensive fertility loss, soil erosion, ravine and gully formation, and widespread collapse of the agricultural resource base. Much of the land base is already abandoned due to its destruction by abundant gullies, exposure of subsoil, landslips, and large landslides. More than 77 percent of the country suffers serious soil erosion, including the severely eroded peasant plots in the central volcanic highlands.[98]

Much of the fragile highlands of the *Cordillera Norte*, home to hundreds of thousands of desperately poor semi-proletarian peasants, are already irreversibly destroyed by erosion, gully formation, laterization, and "scorched-earth" counterinsurgency programs. Only an arid, rocky terrain remains, marked with ravines, landslides, and gullies.[99] With the evaporation of groundwater sources and severe degradation of virtually every watershed in the country (including the huge Rio Lempa), many campesinos are finding their wells dry and must spend more of their valuable labor-time and energy searching for increasingly scarce supplies of usable water. Lowered water tables are particularly noticeable around Volcán San Salvador, an area that supplies the capital city with its drinking water.

One result is that per capita basic grain production declined more than 29 percent between 1975 and 1985. While campesinos traditionally eat corn tortillas as a staple protein, many now make tortillas from the animal feed sorghum—which grows more easily in rocky and eroded land.[100] Sorghum acreage in tiny El Salvador equals that of Nicaragua, Honduras, and Guatemala combined, a telling indicator of the magnitude of the ecological crisis.[101]

Deforestation and land degradation is aggravated by the peasantry's dependence on wood as a source of energy. Some 14.5 million people, or nearly three-fourths of all Central Americans, consume more than 22 million cubic meters of wood annually—47 percent of the region's total energy use.[102] Denied access to alternative energy sources, more efficient stoves, and state-sponsored reforestation programs, peasants experience acute shortages of firewood in many localized areas, particularly the more arid highlands of El Salvador, Guatemala, and Honduras.[103] Urbanization and capitalist agricultural development in the Pacific littoral and interior valleys is also severely degrading fuelwood sources along the western slopes, as well as fragile watersheds surrounding major cities. For example, the hillsides surrounding the Honduran capital of Tegucigalpa are now virtually denuded of once-rich stands of pine and hardwood forests.[104] Many urban and rural households which once gathered wood free by walking to nearby lands, must now purchase fuels transported from far greater distances, diverting scarce economic resources from the family budget for increasingly expensive commodity fuels.[105] (Although wood fuel collection has exacerbated localized problems of soil erosion and other forms of land degradation, overall it is not a primary source of deforestation in Central America, despite its large consumption. In Panama, fuelwood would account for only 25 percent of the area deforested in one year, if all fuelwood was extracted from primary forests.)[106]

Another symptom of the peasantry's ecological crisis is protein malnutrition, a major health problem in Central America. Many peasants depend quite regularly on fish and game obtained from local forests, fields, and streams, and in the face of declining agricultural production and other resource problems, poor rural families are turning increasingly to wildlife for supplemental food and income.[107] But here, as with wood fuel, the capitalization of nature and marginalization of the peasantry has reduced the supply, while increasing the demand for wildlife.

Susan E. Place noted that in Guanacaste, Costa Rica,

> Every "old-timer" that I interviewed told the same story: each claimed that twenty or thirty years ago people used to live better, although they had little money. There was plenty of land available on which to grow crops, there was abundant game to hunt and more domestic animals products available. Diet was apparently more varied and food was more abundant. *Campesinos* were basically self-sufficient and could support a family with relatively little effort. Today, they have no access to land because affluent investors have moved in and taken over, and *tierras baldías* (public lands) have disappeared. They have to buy food now, but wages are insufficient to cover a family's needs.[108]

The destruction of localized fish and wildlife populations is especially severe in the highlands of Guatemala, El Salvador, and Honduras. In El Salvador, for instance, destruction of native flora and fauna is "so extensive that there appears to be no hope of meaningful recovery" (USAID)—almost all economically important wildlife species are now extinct.[109] Some 72 percent of the wild game sold in local markets is imported from Honduras, Nicaragua, and Guatemala.[110]

Coastal marine resources (shrimp, fish, sea turtles, etc.) also suffer heavy exploitation by commercial operators, contributing to the ecological impoverishment of the peasantry. Of these, the sea turtles (especially the green, hawksbill, and Pacific ridley) are the most vulnerable.[111]

Sedimentation, overfishing, and chemical pollution from nearby cotton fields is also devastating El Salvador's marine life habitats. More than 289,000 acres of mangroves have either choked to death from silt or been cut down, depleting the fish that breed there. El Salvador's shrimp industry, an important export earner, has been seriously affected.[112] At least 40 percent of Guatemala's original coastal mangroves have been seriously degraded since 1965.[113] The devastation of these unique habitats is posing a grave threat to the fishing and shrimp industries of both countries because 90 percent of the commercial marine species pass part of their life cycle in the mangroves.

In Honduras, some 5,000 families have formed The Committee for the Defense and Development of the Flora and Fauna in the Gulf of Fonseca (CODDEFFEGULF), to oppose the mass destruction of mangrove forests by USAID-sponsored shrimp export projects controlled by local military officers and wealthy leaders of the Honduran Congress. Nearby fishing communities have successfully harvested shrimp for local consumption for years from the mangroves, but with the advent of football field-sized artificial shrimping pools, local communities are losing access to their once-sustainable ways of life as "no trespassing" signs and fences seal off access to the coastal commons. On numerous instances, CODDEFFEGULF members have been threatened by the military and jailed.[114]

In Guatemala, the ecological and social crisis of the peasantry is magnified by the horror of the army's latest wave of repression. In direct response to widespread organizing by popular movements and the emergence of a persistent armed opposition by four guerilla groups joined under the banner of *Unión Revolucionaria Nacional Guatemalteca* (Guatemalan National Revolutionary Unity, UNRG), the Guatemalan military has systematically murdered civilians, eliminated entire villages, and destroyed vast areas of forests and fields.[115]

In September of 1982, the Dutch Catholic Congress reported on the violence, saying:

> The massacres were also destroying in a systematic manner all that sustains the life of the community; houses, woods, harvests; to the point that the water in the rivers is polluted to drive the people to desperation. The current wave of terror appears to have as a principal object to disarticulate the social life and the cultural inheritance of the Indian people and the peasant, to end the resistance of those that now won't support the weight of centuries of robbery, of maltreatment and of persecution.[116]

Since the early 1980s, military repression—"low-intensity conflict"—has claimed more than 45,000 lives, mostly Indians of Mayan descent, and caused the displacement of more than one million Guatemalans. Counterinsurgency operations have relocated some 60,000 people to some seventy so-called "model villages" (modeled on the "strategic hamlets" of Vietnam) over the last ten years, particularly in the northwestern highlands, as a means for providing maximum military surveillance over the civilian population.[117]

Another half-million Guatemalans live within the boundaries of existing "development poles," which the army defines as "organized population centers ... that guarantee the adherence of the population, and their support and participation with the Armed Institution against communist subversion."[118] Taken together, an interacting system of "model villages," "development poles," and "civil defense patrols" has ensured the army's control over many aspects of rural Guatemalan life and hastened the economic and ecological breakdown of peasant cultural practices. In El Salvador, the U.S. supported a bloody twelve-year war by the ruling oligarchy against the country's popular classes before reaching an uneasy peace agreement in January 1992. (Although a fragile truce remains in effect, death threats and killings by right-wing clandestine military groups have not ceased, and renewed conflicts seem likely. For more on the role of the U.S. in both military conflicts, see Chapter 6.)[119]

In 1988, community leaders in northern Morazán province, an area of intense government counterinsurgency activity, joined together to protest to the Salvadoran government, placing an ad in the Salvadoran daily *El Mundo* on February 24, which read:

We are very worried by the grave damages caused by the devastating forest fires caused by aerial bombing and indiscriminate mortar fire, as well as by soldiers carrying out patrols and operations. The armed forces commonly burn the forest during the dry season, accelerating the destruction of resources in the zone, including natural forests, logging areas, coffee crops and food crops. Because they have deforested large areas in our zone, the scorched earth and bombing campaigns have notably affected rainfall patterns. The length of the rainy season has shortened, and the levels of streams and rivers have dropped. The situation is becoming more critical, and we are worried now because it is affecting us directly. Our crops have diminished and this worsens our already agonizing economic situation.

Perhaps even more menacing than these direct blows are the indirect environmental effects of the war. War refugees are causing extensive ecological damage themselves, clearing forested areas or further taxing fragile natural resources in settlements that lack environmental planning or government social programs. According to a USAID report, 13 percent of San Salvador's mostly refugee population is located on "land regarded as unsuitable for ordinary development because of flooding, uneven terrain or proximity to pollution sources."[120] For example, the Salvadoran government allowed establishment of refugee settlements and neighborhoods at the base of Monte Bello even though it had been deforested by landless peasants and was known to suffer from massive erosion and flash flooding. When in 1982 torrential rains caused the mountain to give way, hundreds of homes were buried under forty feet of mud. While government estimates claim that 700 people died in the Monte Bello avalanche, it is widely believed that in fact more than a thousand died.[121]

Marginalization of Central America's peasantry is offset through migration, much of which merely displaces the ecological crisis of the subsistence sector and reproduces it in new forms.[122] Internal migration to urban barrios, the steep slopes of the western mountains, or the tropical rainforests of the agricultural frontier, has often proved highly useful for disarticulated capitalist development: providing a large army of reserve labor for the expansion of capitalist agriculture and industry along the Pacific coast; or efficiently clearing and colonizing lush rainforests for private land speculators, cattle ranchers, and military officers.

The lack of wilderness areas in El Salvador, particularly the vast Caribbean lowland rainforests held by its neighbors, has precluded many of the migration options available to other peasants in the region. As a result, many marginalized Salvadoran peasants migrated to neighboring countries to clear and cultivate new land, including some 300,000 peasants to Honduras during the 1960s. As William Durham points out, this factor contributed to the growing political friction over land between the Honduran peasantry (with the Salvadoran peasantry as their allies) and large cattle ranchers, which along with some disputes between the Salvadoran and Honduran governments over trade and the Central American Common Market, resulted in the so-called "Soccer War" between the two countries in 1969. Coupled with the severity of the current economic and ecological crisis of the peasantry, the lack of wilderness area is also an important factor in the development of the Salvadoran revolutionary movement.[123]

Today, as exemplified by the Monte Bello tragedy, migration as a survival strategy is becoming increasingly unviable. Peasant colonization of nutrient-poor rainforest soils and marginal agricultural land has proved to be a social and ecological disaster. More than 22,400 Honduran families have received over 97,000 hectares of national and ejidal (common public) land since 1978 under the national agrarian reform, but some 40 percent of the original farms have already been abandoned.[124] And with the failure of the Central American Common Market to generate a large, highly skilled industrial or agrarian working class, governments (Costa Rica and Panama excepted) have little incentive to invest social capital into the healthy reproduction of the large populations residing in the urban barrios.[125]

Some 423,000 man-years of new jobs were created (a growth rate of 2.3 percent) in the industrial sector from 1971 to 1975. Yet, the supply of labor grew at a faster rate—the equivalent of 5,000 to 6,000 man-years (or 2.7 percent) per year. Thus, not only did capital-intensive industrialization fail to reduce unemployment, but the unemployment gap actually increased 223,000 man-years between 1960 and 1975. The result was a rapidly expanding informal service sector which, in the words of DeWalt, represents a "euphemism for the thousands of shoeshine boys, street vendors, household servants and other underemployed and unemployed individuals who inhabit every Central American capital." By the end of the 1970s, declining incomes and worsening health and environmental conditions made the informal sector politically volatile.[126]

According to one USAID study of El Salvador's barrios, "these dense concentrations of underemployed urban dwellers, poorly supplied with potable water, sewerage and water treatment facilities, and garbage disposal services pose massive and growing environmental and natural resource problems." In San Salvador, 75 percent of the population lives in illegal settlements, "most of which lack public services such as waste disposal and treated water."[127]

Fewer than a dozen major sewage systems operate in the entire region. Most sewage is untreated and discharged directly into rivers, lakes, and local waterways, causing a flood of health problems for those poor workers and peasants who cannot afford bottled water or find their own private supplies. A USAID report on Guatemala suggests,

> It is the poor who suffer most from the effects of diseases resulting from contaminated water supply. Diseases such as typhoid, bacillary dysentery, Chagas' disease and onchocerciasis have been directly traced to water supplies contaminated by sewage.... Environmental degradation and poverty represent a classic example of circular causation with a downward spiral. The only effective way to break this spiral is to infuse a change into the system.[128]

The crisis of living conditions for some 40 percent of Central America's mostly unemployed population who live in urban areas is every bit as acute as those faced by their rural counterparts. In contrast with the developed world, the major causes of death in Central America are infectious diseases related to poor environmental quality and nutritional status.[129] As the economic crisis deepens and the ecological crisis widens, it is likely that emigration rates to Mexico and the United States will increase. Already, some 200,000 Guatemalans have fled to neighboring countries, especially Mexico and the United States.[130]

Population Dynamics and the Ecological Crisis

Growing impoverishment of the peasantry is transforming the household division of labor by gender. Women made up to 40 percent of Nicaragua's coffee pickers just prior to the revolution. In Guatemala, women make up 13.7 percent of the wage work force, and 10 percent of the total rural labor force in El Salvador.[131]

Typically, women produce petty commodities and means of subsistence on the *minifundio*, which cheapens the reproduction of semi-proletarian male labor. As Carmen Diana Deere states, this form of female labor "allows the payment by capital of a male wage rate insufficient for familial maintenance and reproduction ... less than the cost of production and reproduction of labor power."[132]

The increasingly difficult daily struggle to secure subsistence through the superexploitation of nature is often achieved through the superexploitation of familial labor. Deere notes: "If the wage is less than that required to maintain the wage worker so that familial labor power must be expended in the production of means of subsistence to reproduce the worker's daily expenditure of labor power, then, clearly, this would define the concept of the superexploitation of familial labor. Here, the moral-historical element of the wage is negative, for the wage is insufficient to provide the commodities for even the physiological subsistence of the wage worker."[133]

This burden falls particularly hard on women (along with children) in a double sense. They are charged not only with raising the animals, preparing food, gathering firewood and water, going to market, and in many cases cultivating the subsistence plot, but also with joining their male partners as seasonal wage laborers. Such tasks are exhausting and take a high toll on the health of poor women.

To offset these increased hardships, peasant households adopt a number of demographic strategies to insure family survival. One of the more important of these is the bearing of children as *production agents* for incorporation into the household labor process at an early age. In fact, for extremely poor peasant families, children are often one of the few productive resources available to assist with highly labor-intensive family tasks.[134] As social and ecological impoverishment worsens, it becomes necessary to have larger and larger families to generate income, guard against high child and infant mortality rates, and provide protection for parents in case of disability, unemployment, old age, and changing economic conditions.[135] By age seven, for instance, children in the subsistence sector are usually producing more on-and-off farm income for the family than what they cost.[136] Most peasant migrants into Central America's cities are older children in search of wage jobs and income, frequently bringing in a higher return for their labor than would be achieved on the family farm.[137] For example, almost two-thirds of all migrants to Honduran cities in 1974 were less than twenty-four years of age.[138]

Back on the *minifundio*, additional offspring are procreated to replace migrating children, and, as Alain de Janvry describes, "to maintain a constant stock of working children—a stock which itself needs to increase with poverty." Through migration, optimum family size in the peasant sector is brought yet closer to the biological maximum for women.[139]

Today, Central America's combined population is well over twenty-five million people, of which over 44 percent are under fifteen years of age. The demographic dynamics associated with functional dualism and disarticulated capitalist development have combined to produce the world's highest population growth rate (2.8 percent), a rate at which the region's population will double in less than twenty-four years.[140]

The most rapid growth rates occur among resource-poor and semi-proletarian peasants, with the poorest women in both households reproducing at the limits of their biological maximum. For instance, average family size in Costa Rica during the 1970s was 8.6 children.[141] This high rate of growth has largely benefited the oligarchy and agrarian bourgeoisie over the past four decades, providing a growing supply of workers for the expanding export sector.

The dynamics of human population are historically specific to the mode of production and social formation in which they occur. In Central America, the Malthusian current to the contrary, it is not rapid population growth but the monopolization of resources by the capitalist export sector and the systematic impoverishment of the subsistence sector, that is causing hunger and ecological devastation.[142]

In El Salvador, which is often cited by many environmentalists as an "overpopulated country," more than half of all agricultural land is devoted to export crops and cattle grazing—one of the highest percentages in Central America.[143] Over 60 percent of the rich farmland on large estates over 500 hectares remains uncultivated.[144] A small elite, referred to as the "fourteen families," comprises less than 2 percent of the population, yet enriches itself from ownership of more than 60 percent of the country's arable land.[145]

In other words, the country's best farmland, which could be used for growing domestic food crops to feed the people in place of ecologically unsuitable land, is guarded by the military power of the oligarchy. Were this land redistributed and production reoriented, concludes the University of Wisconsin-based Land Tenure Center, the poverty underlying rapid population growth could be addressed.[146]

This situation is repeated regionwide. Almost twenty million of Central America's twenty-five million people live on less than 25 percent of the region's land mass, usually the least environmentally suitable.[147] In fact, taken individually, the Central American countries have quite small populations relative to their land base.[148] But in the context of functional dualism, the economic conditions that fostered ecological impoverishment have also spawned rapid population growth as a survival strategy, which is contributing to the fragmentation of the *minifundio*, and therefore indirectly exacerbating degradation of the peasant's natural resource base (particularly in the region's highlands, where population density is greatest).[149] In El Salvador, population densities in areas of subsistence agriculture before the war ranged from about 100 persons per square kilometer in the ecologically devastated northern mountains, to well over 700 persons per square kilometer in the central volcanic highlands.[150] In the words of Alain de Janvry, "under functional dualism, sheer individual economic rationality in reacting to the pressures of poverty leads to quantitative and qualitative demographic contradictions that reinforce ecological contradictions and reproduce conditions of impoverishment and misery in rural areas."[151] These once essential demographic strategies may be increasingly unviable as a survival strategy in the face of a deepening ecological crisis.

With the inability of the export-agricultural and industrial sectors to absorb the growing numbers of unemployed, and thereby creating the conditions for militant protest, the region's oligarchs and the U.S. national security state have become increasingly alarmed. With good reason: when wage employment stagnated in prerevolutionary Cuba and Nicaragua, the growing informal urban sector (IUS) emerged as hotbeds of anti-government struggle. (This also proved true of Guatemala between 1981 and 1985.) Economists Xabier Gorostiaga and Peter Marchetti point out: "The informal urban sector was in fact the principal theme of a recent meeting of Central American business organizations held in San Pedro Sula, in Honduras, which affirmed that survival of the private sector depended on taking the IUS into account."[152]

But rather than developing strategies to address the systemic sources of poverty and rapid population growth, population control programs and policies have historically been for the most part coercive and reactionary and therefore highly ineffective. These population control programs were designed to (a) maintain control over the populations they allegedly serve in order to meet the labor requirements of international capital; and (b) to perpetuate the myth that poverty is created and reproduced by the oppressed themselves, by blaming them for unequal distribution of resources, wealth, and political power that characterizes underdevelopment.[153]

Sponsored by the U.S. government, tens of millions of dollars spent on "family planning" programs have been concerned less with "population control" and more with "controlling the population." As stated by Dr. R.T. Ravenholt, Director of the U.S. Office of Population in 1977, population control is needed to maintain "the normal operation of U.S. commercial interests around the world. Without our trying to help these countries with their economic and social development, the world would rebel against the strong U.S. commercial presence."[154]

One national fertility study in El Salvador found that 52.5 percent of all women seeking contraception were sterilized during the 1970s under pressure by government health workers, many without their consent.[155] In Guatemala, paraformaldehyde (a chemical poison) was used to involuntarily sterilize a much smaller number of women in the late 1960s.[156] And even in Costa Rica, a national scandal erupted in the 1970s over illegal sterilizations of women.[157]

These and other programs to reduce population growth in Central America have failed because they leave the origins of high birth rates—poverty and economic exploitation—untouched, treating a symptom instead of the cause.[158] In Central America and around much of the world, population growth has slowed only when living standards rise and health, education, and other services are provided to the majority of workers and peasants.[159]

Costa Rica's population growth rate declined in the 1960s and 1970s as social welfare programs and living standards for much of the population improved, particularly in urban areas. The largest drop occurred between 1965 and 1970, when there were no organized nor foreign assisted family planning programs in the country.[160] The problems underlying rapid population growth require the implementation of truly progressive and liberating political, economic, and social reforms.[161]

Ecological and Economic Damage to Capital

Ironically, the ecological crisis of the subsistence sector is affecting profit rates in the capitalist export sector in the form of negative environmental externalities. Negative externalities are simply defined as social or environmental costs (such as pollution or sedimentation) resulting from productive activity in one industry or economic sector that harms productivity (or quality of life) in another industry or economic sector. In capitalist economies, externalities assume the form of higher costs of one variety or another for the injured party.

Problems stemming from the ecological deterioration of the peasantry's resource base are damaging the ecological and communal conditions of capitalist production throughout the region. Thousands of lives have been lost, and damage amounting to billions of dollars has occurred to hydroelectric projects, state infrastructure, export crops, industry, etc.[162] The ecological and economic damage inflicted to these productive conditions is a significant factor in the advent of state fiscal crises and national debt/balance of payments crises throughout the region—an important "external" barrier to the continuation of disarticulated capitalist development.[163]

At the Cashi Dam site in Costa Rica, for example, an estimated $133 to $274 million has been lost to sedimentation damage.[164] Repair costs for the degraded watershed around the dam site are estimated at nearly $1 billion, as were those for the El Cajón and El Níspero hydroelectric projects in Honduras. El Salvador's Cinco de Noviembre Project and Guatemala's Pueblo Viejo Quixal Project are experiencing similar problems.[165] In Panama, improper land use and the ensuing soil erosion have tripled the siltation rate in Alajuela Lake, a leading supplier of water to the canal and Panama City. At current rates, one study estimated that the lake could lose up to 80 percent of its storage capacity by the year 2020.[166] Sedimentation has also reduced the capacity of the reservoir that provides water for the Honduran capital of Tegucigalpa, endangering an adequate supply of water for the city and adjacent export-sector irrigation projects.

Flooding, often the result of watershed destruction, is causing serious crop losses and infrastructural damage throughout the region. Flooding in the Sula Valley (a 370-square kilometer area), Aguan River and Atlantic littoral watersheds, Choluteca River valley, and other degraded watersheds in Honduras, causes some $40 to $50 million in damage *annually* to the capitalist export sector and state infrastructure.[167] In Nicaragua, heavy rains in May 1982 led to floods that destroyed almost all of the bridges in the León and Chinandega area, costing the Nicaraguan government some $20 million.[168]

Toward a Sustainable Future

U.S. policy in Central America has only deepened poverty, inequality, and natural resource destruction. Today the region's social and ecological crisis has reached a critical juncture. Is there an alternative future for the people and environment of Central America?

Throughout the region, environmentalists are pursuing a number of programs for ecological preservation and reconstruction. With some important exceptions, however, they are making little headway in the face of Central America's enormous ecological crisis. As one Salvadoran environmentalist explained to me, "Resolution of the environmental problems in our country cannot come from purely conservationist activity. There must be changes in the economy and in social relations to achieve effective conservation."

Central America's popular organizations—trade unions, farmer associations, women's and student groups, as well as revolutionary political parties—are seeking such changes. They include a respect for human rights; genuine democratization of the state in terms of broad-based participation, rather than "demonstration elections"; authentic economic reform and a just distribution of land and natural resources; a foreign policy of nonalignment, and an end to U.S. military and economic intervention. To overcome the root causes of environmental destruction in Central America, these reforms are essential. Only when the basic obstacles to achieving them are removed can Central American environmentalists hope to protect and restore the region's natural resources.

However, new governmental and structural economic reforms will not in themselves guarantee ecological sustainability and prosperity for Central America's popular classes. Restoring the balance between the region's resource base and human needs will also depend on specific long-term efforts. *Comprehensive agrarian reform* is needed: first, in the form of redistribution of export estate land to bring small farmers off marginal lands (such as eroded hillsides) and reduce soil erosion and deforestation. According to a 1982 USAID report, some 494,000 acres of degraded land currently in subsistence food production need alternative uses. Fertile land held idle or in pasture by large growers could go into sustainable production, for basic food crops, allowing marginal lands to be restored.

Agrarian reform must also apply to agricultural policy originating in the representation and empowerment of small farmers. Redirection of credit, and training and technical assistance to small farmers to improve yields and promote sustainability is necessary. Recognizing the need to address the dual crisis of rural poverty and environmental degradation, the U.S.-based solidarity organization New El Salvador Today (NEST) Foundation is working on a five-year program, *Tierra Viva* (Living Earth). Its goal is to help more than 10,000 peasant families in 155 communities in converting from chemical-intensive to appropriate agricultural methods, enabling them to improve their living conditions and help bring land back to life. Other projects with similar goals have been undertaken by solidarity groups, including Oxfam America.

Environmental and social restoration efforts must include an extensive campaign of reforestation, watershed production, toxic cleanup, and habitat recuperation, funded by international aid (especially from the United States) and progressive taxation. Other restoration needs include government promotion of appropriate technology, soil conservation, and new techniques of land use; extensive public investment in social programs to promote basic human services, including voluntary family planning based on the participation of women; and strict regulation of industry and agriculture to protect the environment and workers' health.

Finally, international support for radical ecology is urgently needed. Foreign governments and international environmental organizations are called on to assist reconstruction efforts and to bring about changes in the international economy. Regulation of transnational corporations and financial institutions, promotion of food self-reliance, price supports for primary commodities such as sugar, and accountability of private and multilateral lenders to environmental and social concerns are measures that speak realistically to the depth of the crisis. To ensure the continuation of the process, a lasting U.S. policy of peace and reconstruction for Central America is called for.

Overcoming the root causes of Central America's social and ecological crisis means transforming disarticulated capitalist development. Only then can the ecological conditions of production be reconstructed and protected in such a way as to benefit the vast majority of Central Americans. But as demonstrated in Nicaragua (see Chapter 5), it takes pressure from environmental activists to ensure that any development model is ecologically sound. The role of U.S. environmentalists is to challenge Washington's role in this tragedy and to begin working with their Central American counterparts for a new path of development with justice for the land and the people.

3
POISONING
FOR
PROFIT

Now we're close to León. Liberated territory.
A burning reddish-orange light, like the red-hot tip
of a cigar.
Corinto:
the powerful lights of the docks flickering on the sea.
And now at last the beach at Poneloya and the plane
coming in to land
the string of foam along the coast gleaming
in the moonlight.
The plane coming down. A smell of insecticide.
And Sergio tells me: "The smell of Nicaragua! ..."

Father Ernesto Cardenal[1]

The "first wave" of capitalist development in Central America during the late nineteenth and early twentieth centuries transformed both the rich oak-pine forests of the interior highlands into vast coffee estates and impoverished peasant plots and pockets of the Caribbean lowland rainforests into large banana plantations. Meanwhile, the Pacific littoral escaped relatively unscathed. Pristine coastal mangroves and vast tracts of virgin tropical forests (dry and moist), interspersed with open grassland, still flourished among isolated cattle haciendas and the plots of their resident tenant families, or *colonos*. Peasant families living on haciendas were advanced money or goods, or allowed to rent small plots on the estate, in exchange for their labor and/or payments in kind. In many cases, these arrangements between *colonos* and large landowners existed for generations.[2]

One traveler through the Pacific lowlands of El Salvador in the early twentieth century remarked how he rode, "mile upon mile through magnificent timber-tree lands," where stands of ebony, cedar, mahogany and granadilla stood "so close together that daylight seldom enters, and sunlight never."[3] These forests and fields teemed with an abundance of animal life.

As the early twentieth century progressed, the expropriation of small farms by commercial coffee producers in the central highlands forced peasants to migrate and clear forests for subsistence cultivation in the Pacific lowlands. Nevertheless, huge areas of the coastal plain remained forested until World War II.

Today the protective canopy of dense forests is gone. In the now dusty and eroded agricultural fields of Central America's Pacific coastal plain, hundreds of thousands of poor seasonal workers come from distant highland farms and nearby urban *barrios* to toil in the hot tropical sun harvesting cotton, the bourgeoisie's "white gold." Added to the burden of long hours, backbreaking work, and some of the lowest wages in Latin America, is the familiar roar of crop-duster planes flying overhead, symbol of the worst toxic threat to the environment and people of Central America: pesticides.

The Capitalization of the Pacific Coastal Plains

In the years following World War II, international capital and local oligarchs increasingly recognized the profit potential for capitalist agriculture that lay in the lush Pacific coastal plain of Central America. Guarded by a long chain of majestic volcanos and the steep slopes of the western highlands, the plain extends from Mexico down through Panama almost to the tip of South America. The hot dry climate and rich volcanic soils of the Pacific lowlands were particularly ideal for growing cotton and sugar and for raising cattle, all for export. However, the prevalence of tropical diseases such as malaria, especially closer to the sea, and the lack of adequate roads and public infrastructure, posed significant barriers to the immigration of labor and capital.[4]

To overcome these ecological and infrastructural barriers, a radical reconstruction of the Pacific landscape was required. Spurred by international agencies—including USAID, the World Bank, the Inter-American Development Bank (IADB), the Pan American Health Organization, and the World Health Organization—this process of ecological reconstruction was initiated during the 1950s and later accelerated under the Alliance for Progress. In brief, the aim of these agencies was to create the appropriate ecological, communal, and human conditions for capitalist export agriculture in the Pacific lowlands (as discussed in Chapter 2).

Eradication programs aimed at the disease-carrying Anopheles mosquito were launched, using chemical pesticides, particularly environmentally persistent and carcinogenic organochlorines such as DDT and dieldrin. Backed by international health agencies, eradication programs utilizing pesticides left untouched the existing forms of land tenure or political institutions dominated by the oligarchies.[5] In addition, an elaborate network of all-weather roads was constructed, designed for the rapid, high-volume, and low-cost transportation of agricultural commodities. By 1970, a highway stretched along the Pacific coast from the Mexican border into Costa Rica.[6]

These programs raised the value of land and facilitated large-scale deforestation and conversion to pasture and cropland, particularly for cotton. During the 1950s and 1960s, the high differential rent potential of the Pacific littoral created a frenzy of land speculation, leading to deforestation and fencing as a means of claiming title in order to realize this rent through capitalist agriculture. In Marxist economic terms, land values took the form of differential rent rooted in the favorable natural properties of the soil, geographical location, and climatic conditions of the coastal lowlands. The fertile volcanic soils, nine-month dry season, hot temperatures, and other environmental characteristics were extremely advantageous for agricultural production, particularly of cotton.

However, these favorable ecological conditions were not accessible to capital due to inadequate infrastructure and roads (or communal conditions of production). The all-weather highway system, ports and warehouses, etc., not only unlocked this potential but also raised land values in the second form of differential rent, stemming from investments of labor into the land. Highway systems promoted the efficient circulation of capital and labor, raising the financial value of the land. In 1971, 88 percent of El Salvador's cotton was grown in the twenty-five *municipios*, through which the recently constructed Pacific highway ran. Four-fifths of Nicaragua's cotton acreage was in the fifteen *municipios* of that country through which the Pacific highway traveled. The road was partly constructed with $16.1 million in loans from the World Bank.[7]

These economic processes resulted in the destruction of the established lowland ecosystems for agriculture. In the 1940s, tropical semi-deciduous forests almost totally blanketed Guatemala's Pacific coastal plain, adjacent foothills, and lower slopes of the highlands; in just thirteen years, between 1950 and 1963, roughly 380,000 acres of these forests were destroyed in what would become Guatemala's eight most important cotton and cattle producing *municipios*.[8]

Pristine forests, wildlife habitats, and peasant communities alike were "cleared" to make way for the roads and fields. Virtually all of the remaining humid hardwood forests were destroyed, including stands of old-growth ebony, cedar, mahogany, and passion flower (granadilla), quebracho, cedro, laurel, balsamo, aceituna, and jiote. Coastal savannas, evergreen forests, and large areas of mangroves were also cleared in the onslaught. Even gallery forests of ceiba (kapok), donacaste, fig, and volador found along the edges of rivers were eliminated. With their habitats destroyed, many species of animals were eliminated (see Chapter 2). Other unique species, such as the spider monkey, tayro, tree squirrel, tamandua, tapirs, crocodile, and caiman, were severely depleted.[9]

Capitalization of the Pacific lowlands also transformed existing land tenure arrangements and land use practices by the peasants of the old haciendas. Before the development of cotton export-agriculture, cattle ranchers and migrating subsistence farmers cleared many areas of the Pacific coastal plain but maintained a "balance" with the regional ecosystem. Although some zones of primary forest cover were cleared, the land was exposed only temporarily to the sun and elements before the cultivator moved on, and secondary vegetation cover of small trees and scrub reestablished itself.[10]

While this system of farming was inefficient, it did not degrade or transform the natural environment on such a gross scale as did capitalist cotton production. David Browning noted, "The practice of allowing a *colono* to use a piece of land on the estate in part exchange for his labour was discontinued, and the tenant-farming of subsistence crops decreased as the value of the land increased and the area of unused land diminished." In most cases, the switch to money-rents escalated very quickly beyond the affordability range of former peasant tenants.[11]

As a result, most of the former *colonos* were expropriated by landlords; a new class of cotton entrepreneurs and cattle ranchers, often urban-based professionals, were willing and able to pay higher money-rent. In both Nicaragua and El Salvador, 52 percent of the cotton land was rented.[12] Those tenant-farmers who remained found their only income-earning opportunity came during the short cotton-picking season.[13]

The capitalization of the Pacific lowlands transformed the old social relations—sharecropping on extensive *haciendas*—to the exploitation of permanent and seasonal wage labor on capital-intensive export estates. With the internal subsistence sector—peasants barely surviving on the old *haciendas*—eliminated, *colonos* all along the coast were evicted and transformed into impoverished small farmers, semi-proletarian wage laborers living *external* to the capitalist estates, but still dependent upon them for survival.

Independent peasant families were evicted from their traditional landholdings as well, often through the use of brute military force. The expansion of cotton was responsible for most of the damage, with beef cattle, sugar, and other export commodities assuming periodic importance.[14] Along Nicaragua's entire Pacific plain, cotton land expanded 400 percent between 1952 and 1967, while peasant lands devoted to corn, beans, sorghum, and other food grains dropped by over 50 percent. During this time, the country had shifted from a net exporter to a net importer of basic grains.[15]

In fact, cotton was grown on 80 percent of the Pacific plain's total arable land—40 percent of all the cultivated land in Nicaragua. Cotton lands expanded from 25,900 acres in 1960 to 535,990 acres by 1977, leaving virtually no undisturbed stands of Pacific forest. During the mid-1960s, the magnitude of deforestation for new cropland in Nicaragua began approaching that of El Salvador a decade earlier, but remained inadequate to absorb those peasant corn producers displaced by cotton. By 1963, the cotton fields of León and Chinandega spread over 196,000 acres, claiming three-fifths of the land in annual crops and reducing corn to less than one-fifth of the available cropland. Overall, only one-fourth of the new cotton growers were peasant families, cultivating an average of five acres of cotton on farms smaller than 17 acres. Conversely, estates larger than 364 acres accounted for 60 percent of the cotton area harvested.[16]

In Guatemala, some 221,312 acres of the Pacific lowlands were used for cotton by 1972, almost completely displacing the area's poor *campesinos*. Corn land declined by about 25,000 acres between 1950 and 1963, while cotton expanded by 192,000 acres to occupy 70 percent of the area's cropland. Estates larger than 1,100 acres cultivated 62 percent of the country's cotton.[17] The largest 3.7 percent of farms along Guatemala's Pacific coast monopolized 80.3 percent of the land, according to some estimates—reportedly the highest degree of land concentration in all Latin America.[18] By 1980, a mere fifteen families controlled nearly 50 percent of Guatemala's cotton production. The 1979 census also showed that 309 large *fincas* (landholders) controlled 99.95 percent of Guatemala's cotton crop.[19]

The monopolization of the Pacific lowlands by the oligarchy and urban bourgeoisie had a devastating impact on El Salvador's peasantry as well, indirectly escalating environmental problems in other parts of the country. As in Guatemala and Nicaragua, many of those displaced by the expansion of coffee during the late nineteenth and early twentieth centuries occupied ecologically fragile lands subject to rapid deterioration.

In 1954, a Salvadoran government study of soil conservation recommended that 50 percent of the national area under subsistence cultivation be returned to forest in order to avoid excessive use and erosion. Since land reform was politically impossible, the report suggested that the only alternative that would not create "intolerable hardship" for the farmers would be to make the fertile coastal lowlands accessible to them.[20] Development of the coastal lowlands offered a promising opportunity for resolving the peasantry's acute land shortages and reducing dependence on imported foodstuffs throughout Central America.[21]

The report was ignored by the government. From 1948 to 1972, large cotton growers expanded their acreage by more than 20.5 percent each year, denying small farmers the best farmland in the country.[22] One-fourth of the entire cotton crop came to be controlled by only eighteen families. Even these figures do not reveal the concentration of economic power by the cotton bourgeoisie, because many of the larger families rented additional property on top of what they already owned.[23]

The result was the virtually complete dispossession of the country's peasantry from lands ecologically suitable for agriculture. Between 1942 and 1965, cotton acreage in El Salvador increased from 24,200 acres to 302,100 acres, leaving only scattered and isolated stands of trees and uncleared mangroves along the swampy coastal lagoons. Only a very small segment of the peasantry benefited. By the early 1960s, 58 percent of the country's cotton growers were small farmers planting an average of five acres of cotton on farms smaller than twenty-five acres.[24]

As cotton expanded along Central America's Pacific coast, the excluded peasant farmers increasingly moved into crowded urban *barrios* or onto unfertile land ecologically unsuitable for their slash-and-burn (or swidden) agriculture, particularly the steep hillsides of the Pacific mountains and rugged interior highlands, and the nutrient-poor rainforest soils of the Caribbean lowlands.

In El Salvador—which lacks rainforests—peasant cultivators in the 1970s occupied the 40 percent of the land designated as ecologically unsuitable for agriculture, with disastrous results. Rampant defores-

tation, declining fallow cycles, severe soil erosion and land degradation, watershed destruction, critical fish, wildlife, and wood fuel shortages, declining food production and increased poverty—all proved
that the resource base for much of Central America's peasantry was
reaching a point of ecological collapse, as discussed in Chapter 2.[25]

Only 2 percent of the original woodland canopy along the Pacific
coast remained by the early 1980s.[26] By the early 1980s, some 10,000
farms occupied an estimated 1,004,796 acres of cotton fields in the
ancient tropical forests and employed half a million workers. Central
America was producing over one million bales of cotton a year (a bale
is equal to 480 pounds), ranking the region third in sales, behind the
United States and Egypt.[27]

Following the blocking of Cuban sugar from the U.S. market, sugar
production had also risen substantially and along with cattle contributed to further deforestation and peasant displacement along the coast
and interior valleys. From 1950 to 1980, the area planted in sugar cane
increased 30 percent in Costa Rica, 154 percent in El Salvador, 392
percent in Guatemala, 279 percent in Honduras, and 131 percent in
Nicaragua.[28]

Due to a variety of factors, including government lending policies,
shortages of wage laborers, and the narrowness of the Pacific lowlands, cotton production assumed much smaller proportions in Costa
Rica and Honduras. By 1977, cotton fields in Costa Rica occupied only
34,086 acres, earning about $5.5 million in export earnings. In Hondu-
ras, only 31,000 acres of the coastal plain were planted in cotton.
Instead, large landholders focused more on cattle ranching to expand
their holdings onto richly forested municipal and national lands.[29]

The capitalization of the Pacific lowlands was seldom accompanied
by land conservation investments in soil cover, drainage systems,
wind barriers, etc. Many growers were tenant speculators who were
renting tracts from large landlords and operating on short-term credit.
In a highly competitive market, these farmers had little economic
interest in laying out money to protect the long-term viability of the
land.[30]

In fact, just the opposite was the case. As David Browning's study
points out, there were "seldom regulatory clauses in the contract
against maltreatment of the land, or payments to the tenant for improvements made by him." Thus, the tenant was "encouraged in his

inclination to maximize his profits regardless of the costs in terms of soil deterioration." On the larger privately owned and operated cotton estates, landholders also degraded the soil to minimize costs and maximize yields in the short run. As the lowlands became exhausted, these owners often extended their holdings onto steeper lands along the northeast margins of the Pacific plans. The better lands were sometimes left to recover in pasture but often continued to be over-exploited. Overgrazing and lack of soil conservation investments often led to further leaching and erosion.[31]

The cultivation methods utilized also worked against soil conser-vation. Trees necessary to protect the fields from wind erosion were removed to facilitate cheaper forms of pesticide application by aircraft. Rather than practicing crop rotation, weeds and protective ground cover that prevent erosion were eliminated as well, since they could host potential cotton pests between plantings. The soil was prepared at the beginning of the rainy season, plowed to a fine tilth, and left unprotected until the middle of the rainy season before being planted. The exposed soil readily eroded under the heavy rains and high winds.[32]

An estimated sixteen to twenty tons of topsoil were being washed and blown from the cotton fields each year, leading to the severe clogging and sedimentation of nearby waterways, causing dangerous flooding in the rainy season and damaging drought in the dry season.[33] In Nicaragua, erosion and sedimentation combined with heavy rains to cause heavy flooding in May 1982 that destroyed almost all of the bridges in the León and Chinandega areas, costing the Nicaraguan government some $20 million.[34] In many areas of the Pacific lowlands, there was ample evidence of sheet erosion, often in severe form.[35]

As the Guatemalan author Mario Payeras describes, "By the second half of the twentieth century, with the expansion of the cotton indus-try, the Costa Grande ceased to exist as rainforest ... the Pacific rains ran unchecked through the verdant waterways, filling the rivers with volcanic sands; and the extinction of the broad-leaved forest trans-formed the area into a desert environment which is intermittently flooded."[36]

The Pesticide Treadmill

Deforestation was devastating, but perhaps the most ecologically destructive practice involved the abuse of pesticides. At the beginning of the cotton boom in the early 1950s, organosynthetic insecticides were considered the "miracle drugs" for combating the insect pest problems inherent in many large-scale capitalist monocultures.

Nicaragua quickly became a laboratory for pesticide experimentation in the early 1950s. In 1951, the German multinational corporation Bayer tested methyl parathion, a derivative of a nerve gas developed by the Nazis during World War II, in the area around León. By 1952, over 1.2 million pounds of this deadly chemical were applied to over 74,347 acres of cotton, causing dozens of deaths and hundreds of illnesses among Nicaraguan field workers and their families. The following year, the Ministry of Agriculture banned methyl parathion, only to have Somoza reverse its decision in 1954 under pressure from cotton growers, who praised its effectiveness as an "atomic bomb" against the boll weevil and other costly cotton pests.[37]

From that time on, pesticide use expanded exponentially. By the mid-1950s, methyl parathion and other organosynthetic pesticides were being used extensively throughout Central America. By boosting yields and profits, pesticides (along with fertilizers) helped to create the appropriate ecological conditions of production for capitalist cotton monoculture. As a result, a sustained increase in productivity and acres planted occurred during the decade.[38] By 1960, average yields for the region had increased to 2,026 pounds of cotton (with seed) per acre, compared to 1,385 pounds per acre in 1950.[39]

In the 1960s, a great variety of new organosynthetic insecticides appeared on the Central American market, mainly organophosphates and carbamates. But the miraculously profitable advantages of these pesticides were short-lived. Throughout the region, several traditional cotton pests, once easily exterminated by insecticides, developed resistance to them. A 1971 study found populations of the bollworm, a cotton fruit-eating pest, to be forty-five times more resistant to methyl parathion than any field population previously recorded.[40] But the chemicals decimated the populations of economically beneficial insect predators and parasites that attacked potential cotton pests. Relatively benign cotton pests, once controlled by natural predators during the

1950s, quickly emerged in the 1960s as newly malignant secondary cotton pests.[41]

By the mid-1960s, these two processes created an explosion of old and new cotton pests, particularly the cotton bollworm, armyworm, virosis vector tobacco whitefly, cabbage looper, and aphid. In El Salvador, eight new economically important cotton pests emerged during the decade. In Nicaragua, the number of economically important pests jumped from five (prior to 1955) to nine in 1965 to 1966. In Guatemala, where the cotton boom started somewhat later, the number of harmful species increased from two in the 1950s to eight in the 1960s.[42]

The economic boom of the "exploitation phase" during the 1950s had given way to an "ecological-economic crisis phase" in the 1960s.[43] In response, growers steadily boosted their use of fertilizers and pesticides to kill the explosion of cotton pests and restore crop yields and profits. The average number of pesticide applications jumped from about five to ten a year during the mid-1950s, to about twenty-five to twenty-eight applications in the mid-1960s, an incredible two to three sprayings a week during the growing season.[44] But these measures only worsened the problem.

The cotton bourgeoisie had become trapped on the "pesticide treadmill" of declining yields, increasing costs, and falling profits. For example, Nicaragua's cotton yields plummeted 30 percent between 1965 and 1969.[45] The situation was further compounded by poor soil conservation practices, resulting in the leaching of soil nutrients, sheet erosion, and declining fertility. Pesticide abuse combined with these practices to further destroy beneficial microorganisms, insects and earthworms (annelids) necessary for naturally maintaining soil vitality.[46] By the latter half of the 1960s, pest control expenditures commonly reached roughly 50 percent of total production costs and had combined with poor soil management measures to force many growers out of business.[47] Some 300,000 acres of cotton land went out of production during this period. In El Salvador, half of the country's cotton growers went out of production between 1963 and 1968, while the area under cultivation plummeted 43.8 percent, from a high of 302,100 acres to less than 128,000 acres.[48]

In response to the pesticide treadmill and crisis of cotton agroexport in the mid-to-late 1960s, growers adopted a number of alternative strategies. For many, one of the most effective alternatives involved agricultural diversification away from cotton into other export crops such as mechanized rice and sugar production.

About 160,000 acres of land went into sugar production alone from 1965 to 1971, particularly in Nicaragua and Honduras. During this period, the price of sugar increased an average of 5 percent a year. Growers supplying two of Nicaragua's largest sugar mills in the cotton belt expanded sugar production over 17,000 acres during the cotton slump. In Honduras, the completion of the Los Mangos sugar complex in 1967 converted the country's most important cotton *municipio* into a leading sugar producer of more than 22,000 acres of cane. Countrywide, cotton acreage in Honduras declined from 31,000 acres in 1967 to only 19,768 acres in 1972.[49]

In Guatemala and El Salvador, with the sugar mills located in the upper piedmont away from the cotton belt, growers converted primarily to cattle ranching and corn. This resulted in the contamination of these products with pesticide residues left over from cotton. In El Salvador, 47.6 percent of the 29,482 hectares of cotton land taken out of production in 1966 was immediately put into corn production, while another 30.5 percent were turned into pasture. Large-scale corn production had the effect of contributing significantly to the stagnation of corn production by competitively disadvantaged peasant farmers.[50]

Regardless of the commodity, however, agricultural diversification resulted in the concentration of landholdings, while greatly reducing income for Central America's desperately poor peasantry. The number of jobs in the cotton harvest, which grew from 15,000 in the early 1950s to over 350,000 in the mid-1960s, had been reduced by more than 100,000 by 1971, due to pesticide treadmill and crisis of cotton.[51]

Not all of Central America's cotton bourgeoisie opted for agricultural diversification. A more common response was to reinforce existing structures of economic dependency on ecologically unhealthy productive forces, such as pesticides imported from the advanced capitalist countries (which were responsible for the crisis in the first place), thus reinventing and deepening the pesticide treadmill. Working with the state and multinational chemical producers, large growers began looking for more "effective" pesticides as part of a technical solution to the economic-ecological crisis of cotton.

In Nicaragua, dictator Anastasio Somoza established the Cotton Experimental Center in Posoltega in 1967, which quickly became the vehicle for the proliferation of pesticide products in Nicaragua's cotton-growing region.[52] For $1,000, pesticide corporations could test products for commercial use and avoid more expensive industry testing procedures in their country of origin. Many of the chemicals tested were environmentally damaging compounds later restricted or banned for agricultural use in the United States during the 1970s, such as DDT, endrin, dieldrin, kepone, leptophos, and lindane. By 1968, multinational corporations were marketing over seventy-five commercial formulations in Nicaragua.[53]

For example, leptophos (or phosvel), an organophosphate nerve toxin, causes serious disorders of the central nervous system in contaminated workers. In 1976, workers at the Veliscol Chemical Corporation, which manufactured the chemical, named themselves the "phosvel zombies" as they lost their coordination and their ability to work, talk, and think clearly. Although banned for use in the United States, phosvel was exported to Central America and other third world regions during the 1970s as part of a U.S. foreign aid program.[54]

The development of new insecticide varieties encouraged Central America's cotton bourgeoisie to further intensify the pesticide treadmill as a short-term solution to the crisis of cotton. Transnational chemical corporations such as Bayer, Ciba-Geigy, Chevron, DuPont, Shell, Stauffer, and Hooker flooded the Central American market with extremely toxic organophosphates and environmentally persistent organochlorines. By the mid-1960s and through the 1970s, a whopping 40 percent of all U.S. pesticide exports went to Central America, making the region the world's highest per capita consumer of pesticides.[55] The Pacific plain became washed with immense quantities of poison. Newer types of more dangerous, more lasting, or more toxic chemicals were introduced to replace those to which insects had developed a resistance.

Growers also dramatically increased applications of older insecticide varieties (often in combination with new varieties) at much higher doses and in much shorter intervals. Instances of over fifty sprayings per growing season were common in the cotton belt of Guatemala, El Salvador, and Nicaragua.[56] By the late 1960s, some of El Salvador's cotton growers were making up to fifty-six applications a growing season with DDT and other environmentally persistent chlorinated hydrocarbons, while others used some fifty different pesticide combinations, or "chemical cocktails," representing nearly half of the growers' total production costs. In Nicaragua, by comparison, a number of cotton growers were spraying their fields up to thirty-five times a year, claiming one-third of total production costs.[57]

As the pesticide treadmill accelerated during the first half of the 1970s, particularly as chlorinated hydrocarbons became increasingly ineffective, even greater quantities of poison were required. In El Salvador, growers sprayed 58.4 kilograms on each hectare (kg/ha) of cotton in 1972. Three years later the figure was 70.0 kg/ha. In neighboring Guatemala, these figures rose from 45.6 to 79.9 kg/ha. DDT consumption in El Salvador skyrocketed threefold from 555,200 kg in 1970 to 1.6 million kg in 1977. Despite the implementation of Integration Pest Management (IPM) programs in Nicaragua, designed to rationalize the country's use of pesticides, imports of DDT leaped from 29,000 kg in 1974 to 521,600 kg in 1976. Overall, some 27,300 metric tons of pesticides were consumed in Guatemala, El Salvador, Nicaragua, and Honduras in 1974 alone, an amount equal to over seventy-five kilograms per square kilometer of surface area and two kilograms (or 4.5 pounds) of poison for every person in those countries. El Salvador and Guatemala were the biggest consumers, followed by Nicaragua, with Honduras a distant fourth, where the small size of the cotton export sector restricted pesticide use.[58]

Many cotton growers, particularly in El Salvador and Guatemala, intensified their use of extremely dangerous phosphate-based poisons such as malathion and parathion. Some 400 Guatemalan workers died each year as a result.[59] By 1975, tiny El Salvador, a nation the size of Massachusetts, alone consumed 20 percent of the world's entire parathion supply to supplement its already massive use of DDT, an average of 4.5 pounds of this deadly chemical for each acre of cropland in the country. It is estimated that some 2,400 pounds of insecticides were annually dumped on every square mile of cotton land in El Salvador during the mid-1970s.[60]

Regionwide, the cotton bourgeoisie annually applied an average of 3,380 pounds of pesticide to every square mile of cotton land—an incredible 4.4 pounds for every man, woman, and child in Central

America. The Pacific coastal plain of Central America was drowned in a sea of poison.

During this period of increased pesticide use, Central America's cotton yields temporarily ranked among the highest in the world. Guatemala's yields stood second only to Israel, while El Salvador and Nicaragua were in the top five. Nicaragua's yields were almost twice the average production per hectare of the United States (947 kg/ha).[61] However, growers found an increasing share of their profits going for chemical inputs. In the mid-1970s the cotton bourgeoisie was spending $70 million a year for pesticides, but contributed only $82 to $117 million to the gross international production (GIP).[62] By 1978, total pesticide imports in the region totaled $165 million, of which over $110 million were used on cotton.[63] In Nicaragua, which was importing roughly 2.36 million pounds of technical grade (100 percent) DDT— almost a pound for every Nicaraguan—by the end of the decade, the national cotton harvest produced net deficits as production costs exceeded export revenues.[64]

While damaging to Central America's cotton growers, this situation proved highly profitable for international chemical companies. Not unlike a street dealer pushing heroin to strung-out addicts in need of "more and better" drugs to get the same high, multinational corporations pushed dependency-creating pesticides to growers in need of "more and better" chemicals to get the same crop yields—creating a growing demand for their own supply of chemicals.

In fact, many of the leading exporters of pesticides to Central America and the third world are the very same companies that sell agricultural seeds. Between 1968 and 1978, petrochemical giants such as Monsanto, Ciba-Geigy, and Union Carbide bought thirty major seed companies. As Jack Kloppenburg, Jr. and Daniel Lee Kleinman note, "by cornering the global seed market, the companies apparently plan to insure that farmers the world over are dependent on their seeds, as well as their fertilizers and pesticides."[65]

Chemical corporations developed and marketed broad-spectrum pesticides in order to maximize their market share in Central America (the world's highest per capita consumer in the 1970s), and the rest of the world. The broader the spectrum, the less predictable and controllable the chemical became in the long term, thereby contributing to the pesticide treadmill for Central American growers.[66]

Multinational chemical companies favor broad-spectrum chemicals because development of highly specialized chemicals is not as economically feasible nor as profitable. This preference is indicated by the great efforts put into research and development. Often 10,000 to 20,000 compounds are screened before a marketable one is identified. It often takes eight to ten years to develop a compound from synthesis to market introduction. Add high economic risk and costs: each new pesticide product costs approximately $25 to $50 million to develop. Lack of research and development innovation in recent years had led to pesticide dumping and increased experimentation in the third world, where worker health and safety and environmental regulations are less strict.[67]

As the treadmill expanded, the region became a giant experimental laboratory for multinational pesticide companies to profitably test and market new products and dump old ones as well. By 1980 there were approximately 463 generic types and 3,061 different formulations in Costa Rica's pesticide market, including at least nineteen chemicals prohibited or restricted for use by the Environmental Protection Agency in the United States[68]

However, the pesticide dependency would eventually prove highly precarious for international capital in the 1980s and 1990s. When enough agricultural "users" eventually "die" of a pesticide "overdose" and go bankrupt, the overall market demand for the "pushers'" chemical commodities may be significantly reduced.

The Health Costs to Workers

As the landed oligarchy, cotton growers, and multinationals reaped short-term financial benefits from pesticides, the majority of Central Americans have suffered. One Pan-American Health Organization study reported some 19,000 poisonings between 1971 and 1976. The great majority (17,283) of these cases were recorded for El Salvador and Guatemala, suggesting a much higher level of nonreported cases elsewhere in the region.[69]

In Nicaragua, another study reported an average of more than 3,000 acute insecticide poisonings of workers each year between 1962 and 1972, nearly eight times greater than the United States per capita rate.

During the 1978–1979 harvest alone, over 280 cases of pesticide poisoning were reported in the San Vicente Hospital in León.[70] Honduras and Nicaragua were world leaders in per capita illness and deaths from pesticide poisonings during the 1960s and 1970s.[71] Therefore, it is more reasonable (although still somewhat conservative) to assume that at least 73,230 cases of acute pesticide poisoning actually occurred in Central America during the 1970s.[72]

Poisonings continue to plague Central America as the predominant occupational illness. Surveys conducted in 1988 and 1989 by the Ministry of Health in Nicaragua show that 12 percent of small farmers in the country's principal agricultural region reported being poisoned at work; an estimated 5,000 of the region's 650,000 workers required medical treatment.[73] In Guatemala, an average of eighty-eight pesticide poisonings are recorded each month, although unreported poisonings are estimated to be much higher.[74] In Costa Rica, some fifty-four agricultural workers die each year from overexposure. From a regionwide study, researchers found some 6,500 poisonings—twenty-five for every 100,000 people—are registered each year.[75]

But as stated by Dr. Douglas Murray, an expert on pesticide-related worker health and safety problems in Central America, "for every recorded poisoning, my experience is that there are generally two to three other cases which go unreported." Given this reality, it is reasonable to conclude that over the last twelve years (from 1980 to 1992), some 200,000 cases of pesticide intoxication have occurred in Central America, one of the highest per capita rates in the world.

Many growers maintain their own clinics, preventing the region's public health officials from documenting the seriousness of the situation on their farms. These clinics and public hospitals often fail to report poisonings to the state or instead report them as nonpesticide related illnesses. A 1972 Ministry of Labor survey in El Salvador found six times as many deaths as indicated by the data collected from the hospitals.[76]

Central American governments also disguise the problem. In Costa Rica, there were 1,500 official government cases of pesticide poisoning recorded over a five-year period. But in only three months during one of those years, doctors reported 700 cases in just two hospitals, suggesting a much higher rate than those reported in state documents.[77]

Victims often do not go to hospitals because they lack money, fail to recognize the symptoms, or fear they will lose their jobs and income, while others do not trust the clinics run by the growers.[78] Many of the poisoning victims are children, but they are not recorded or covered by social security medical programs.[79] Children under age sixteen currently account for 15 to 20 percent of the reported poisonings in Nicaragua.[80] Usually only the most severe or life-threatening cases appear in hospital emergency rooms. More than fifty children died of pesticide poisoning in just one San Salvador hospital alone in 1987.[81]

The high volume of pesticides used in Central America only partly explains the region's high rate of poisonings. Just as the cotton bourgeoisie seeks to maximize crop yields at the lowest possible cost through the use of fertilizers and dangerous pesticides, they also seek to maximize the productivity of agricultural workers per unit of labor time at the lowest possible cost by offering slave wages, cutting expenses on worker health programs, eliminating rest periods, and timely safety procedures, etc. In other words, it is capital's drive to exploit labor and produce surplus value (or profits) that systematically exposes workers to unhealthy working and living conditions.

This systematic marginalization of the peasantry under a system of functional dualism provides the cotton growers with hundreds of thousands of desperately poor seasonal workers—expendable labor-power (see Chapter 2). Since cotton picking is a skill easily acquired (despite the grueling nature of the work), laborers who are injured, grow sick, or die from pesticide exposure and other abusive working conditions are quickly replaced with other hungry peasants desperate for income.

The oligarchy, cotton bourgeoisie, and state officials see little economic incentive to invest social capital in protection or improvement of the lives of agricultural workers and their families, particularly in highly competitive periods of economic crisis. Outlays of money by cotton growers for worker/community health and safety do not typically increase labor productivity or profits sufficiently to balance such expenditures and therefore serve as a drain on their earnings.

As one Salvadoran leader from the National Association of Farm Workers (ANTA) explained in a personal interview, "the owners think of their own interests and not the interests of the workers. So even if a different kind of pesticide application would be safer, the owner won't adopt it if there are cheaper ways for them to spray." The unionist adds, "in El Salvador there isn't any protective law for workers with regard to pesticides and other work conditions."[82]

Workers seldom have access to protective devices such as gloves, boots, and masks. USAID estimates that only 10 to 15 percent of Costa Rican field workers wear protective clothing. Some workers have even been known to stir chemicals with their hands because "it's faster," and spray herbicides from backpacks while walking shirtless and shoeless through the fields.[83]

It is simply more profitable to poison. Cotton growers and governments actively suppress environmental regulations and trade unions that could otherwise protect agricultural workers and their families. Compounding the neglect of the growers is the fact that more than 75 percent of Central America's cotton workers cannot read. For those who can, understandable instructions and warning labels on pesticide products are often absent, permitting growers to save extra costs and exert greater control over a labor force that might otherwise resist dangerous and unhealthy work practices. According to Catharina Wesseling of the Pesticide Program of the National University in Costa Rica, "not one pesticide label in Costa Rica has *any* reference to its ingredients' ability to cause cancer, birth defects, neurological damage or any other chronic effects."[84]

When workers and union leaders do complain about wages and working or living conditions, they are often threatened or fired. Some are arrested, tortured, and/or murdered. Jesús Hernández, Secretary General of the National Association of Farm Workers (ANTA) in El Salvador, was one such case. In 1987 he was kidnapped by the Third Infantry Brigade and tortured. His body was found several weeks later.[85] One death squad in Guatemala even kidnapped a doctor for reporting pesticide poisonings to the state.[86]

In the cotton belt, 80 percent of the workers live in mud-floored wooden shacks or *champas* within 100 meters of the fields. To maximize total acreage, many growers plant their cotton crop right up to the edges of waterways, worker residences and adjacent towns, suggesting significant contamination for farmworkers and their families beyond that encountered directly in working with pesticides and in pesticide-treated fields.[87] Much of the growers' housing for temporary workers have no walls to offer protection against pesticide drift; and most often lack running water, leaving workers and their families little option but to bathe in pesticide-laden irrigation ditches or streams surrounding the fields.

Many of these facilities can best be described as cages. About 60 percent of the so-called "houses" have no toilet. Only 25 percent have running water, while less than 25 percent have bathrooms with shower facilities. Over 80 percent of the houses were found to have insect and rodent pests inside the structure. The deplorable conditions of worker housing is a major contributor to worker pesticide contamination, especially when one considers that ten percent of the total volume of poison applied to cotton falls within a 100-meter area just outside the boundaries of targeted fields.[88]

Mothers in the cotton regions have been found to have as much as 42 to 185 times more DDT in their breast milk than levels deemed "safe" (0.05 parts per million) by the WHO. Separate studies have shown average residues of 2.29 parts per million (ppm) and matabolites (maximum over 5ppm) in human milk fat samples from women in the León Department. Other chlorinated insecticides, including lindane and aldrin, were also found in trace amounts.[89]

Most of the insecticide on Central America's cotton is applied by aircraft. The vast majority of the planes utilize ultralow volume (ULV) spray equipment, which offers the advantage of a larger payload of chemicals. The growers enjoy significant savings in labor and fuel costs, since the aircraft and its pilot spend more of their valuable time in the air applying pesticide and less time on the ground reloading during critical periods in the pest cycle. In other words, this equipment supposedly saves growers money because it allows a smaller fleet of planes to cover a larger area in a shorter period of time.

Although more profitable for the export sector, ULV-spray equipment poses a grave danger to workers. In contrast to higher volume sprays, ULV equipment produces smaller and more concentrated spray droplets, offers poor coverage of plant surface, and is far less effective against smaller pests such as aphids, mites, and white flies.[90] To minimize weed and pest damage to the crops and cut costs associated with employing and housing an idle labor force, growers often order workers back to the fields after a pesticide application before it is safe. This results in high incidences of poisoning, as workers rub against and absorb the concentrated droplets into their systems.

Organophosphate pesticides pose the greatest danger, since these chemicals have the highest acute toxicity for mammals of all those used in cotton production. It takes sixty times more DDT to kill 50 percent of an insect population than would be required if methyl parathion were used.[91] El Salvador reports a higher number of worker pesticide poisonings per hectare in many studies because the country uses a higher proportion (48 percent) of organophosphates than other Central America countries. Guatemala showed a big jump in reported poisonings since that country's cotton bourgeoisie adopted more lethal organophosphates in response to the pesticide treadmill of the 1970s: 1,039 official cases were reported in 1976, although many claim that the actual figures are much higher.[92]

When one considers that cotton workers typically pull a twelve-hour shift (for which the pay is usually $1.25) each day, some six or seven days a week for one to three months a year, it becomes clear that they are being exposed to tremendous quantities of poison. In some instances, crop dusters spraying fields even disregard those working below or use human spotters as targets for dumping their loads. Villagers in Guatemala report that sometimes there is no warning that spraying is about to take place. A nurse at a clinic near La Noria noted that these drenchings contribute to some thirty to forty poisonings a day.[93]

Although highly toxic organophosphates and carbamates cause the vast majority of Central America's acute pesticide poisonings, this family of pesticides does break down rather quickly once released into the environment. However, chlorinated hydrocarbons (or organochlorines) such as DDT (dichlorodiphenyltrichloroethane), chlordane, and heptachlor are highly stable and environmentally persistent; the half-life of DDT, or the time it takes a given mass to degrade by half, is twenty years. Furthermore, they are easily absorbed by the fatty tissues of humans and other animals.

Throughout the 1970s, organochlorides were being dumped on the world market by multinational chemical companies in response to heavy restrictions and/or bans of their use in the United States and other advanced capitalist countries. During this period, Guatemala, Nicaragua, and El Salvador were among the world's leading users of DDT and other organochlorines. In Nicaragua, of the total 19.5 million pounds of pesticides applied in the 1974–1975 cotton season, nearly fifteen million pounds were organochlorines.[94]

Although the use of organochlorines is declining in the 1990s, these compounds may, in the long term, continue to create even more serious chronic health problems in the region. Today, the 700,000 people living in Central America's cotton region have more DDT in their body fat than any other population of human beings in the world. During the 1970s, Nicaraguans and Guatemalans showed an average of 520.6 parts per billion of DDT in their body fat—more than any general population in the world. In 1980, Nicaraguans still showed the world's highest levels (ninety-seven parts per million), sixteen times the global average. The only exception is a population of DDT manufacturing workers in California, who measured at 590.5 ppb. Costa Ricans have recently been found to have average DDT levels of 33.16 parts per million, more than three times the world average.[95]

Since nineteen of the twenty-five most commonly used organochlorines prove carcinogenic in laboratory tests, the future may reveal high cancer rates and other chronic health effects among Central Americans. In 1979 and 1980, a program to monitor the poison Galecron in Central America's cotton workers found that 40 percent of the samples yielded contamination levels 50 to 200 times beyond acceptable WHO standards. Galecron's chief toxic agent, chlorodimeform (CDF), is a carcinogen.[96] No one knows how many people will eventually die.

The Health Costs to Communities

Another social-ecological cost of cotton agroexport and the pesticide treadmill concerns the new outbreak of malaria, a deadly disease that has struck millions of Central Americans. Malaria is a human disease caused by sporozoan parasites (genus Plasmodium) in the red blood cells. Transmitted by the bite of anopheline mosquitoes, malaria is characterized by periodic attacks of chills and fever, which in severe cases can result in death (particularly among malnourished and poverty-stricken people).

Chemical eradication programs begun in the 1950s by the Pan American Health Organization and the World Health Organization proved highly successful in containing the malaria mosquito (*Anoph-*

eles albimanus), reaching a "consolidation phase" by the mid-1960s. However, as cotton agriculture increasingly inundated the Pacific lowlands with pesticides, mosquitoes gradually developed resistance to standard chemicals, particularly organochlorines. Conventional health programs lost their effectiveness, creating an alarming resurgence of malaria.

By 1970, malaria infection rates had grown to previously unknown levels. Between 1965 and 1975, the incidence of malaria jumped three times higher in El Salvador, Nicaragua, and Honduras, exceeding the number of cases before eradication programs even began.[97] By 1976, some 83,000 malaria cases were reported in El Salvador alone, with an additional 48,000 cases in Honduras, and another 26,200 cases in Nicaragua.

One of the prime reasons for the malaria resurgence was the acquired mosquito resistance to the eradication insecticide carbamate, resulting from exposure to another agricultural organophosphate pesticide, parathion. Other products, such as OMS-33 (bygon), which supplemented DDT, showed effectiveness for about four years before mosquitoes once again developed resistance.[98]

To combat the health crisis, government eradication programs reverted back from their "consolidation phase" of the 1960s to an "attack phase" in the 1970s. As planned, intensive time-limited sprayings were to be launched to eliminate mosquito populations. If these tactics prove successful, and active cases of malaria drop to near zero, then the attack phase gives way to "consolidation," where specific maintenance sprayings are sparingly used to maintain the consolidation phase.[99] In practice, a newly defined stage of "permanent attack" increased government health expenditures, but also spewed more poisons into the bodies of workers, their homes and communities, wildlife and the environment—all under the advice of the WHO, which continued to promote a chemical fix to the malaria crisis.

This strategy proved to be an utter failure. Effective chemical "consolidation" of increasingly resistant mosquito populations was prevented by the deepening pesticide treadmill in cotton production. DDT-susceptible mosquito populations declined from nearly 100 percent in 1959 to 5 percent in 1980.[100] Between 1972 and 1975, mosquito resistance in Central America (directly related to the pesticide treadmill) increased from 58 to 86 percent.[101]

According to a report by the Central American Institute of Technology (ICAITI) in 1977, for every two pounds of insecticide added to the Central American environment, roughly 100 new cases of malaria would result: "a change of 1 percent in the area of the country planted with cotton in relation to total planted area may result in an increase of 0.136 cases of malaria per 1,000 population."[102] By 1980, malaria incidence had reached 65.7 cases per 1,000, compared to an average of 39.2 cases per 1,000 in 1972. In Nicaragua, reported cases of malaria increased over 400 percent between 1972 and 1983.[103]

Today, the malaria epidemic continues to escalate, requiring more expensive chemicals and diverting resources needed for combating a growing health crisis. In Costa Rica, the number of malaria cases has increased fourfold since 1981. In response, the Costa Rican government has replaced DDT, toxaphene, and other conventional mosquito controls with malathion and propoxur, which are four to fourteen times more expensive.[104] The 1984 Kissinger Commission report on Central America also expressed alarm at the serious resurgence of malaria and dengue fever in Belize, Guatemala, Honduras, and El Salvador, but neglected to point out any connection between the malaria epidemic and the use of pesticides.[105] Today, some 17 million people inhabit the malaria zones of Central America, and roughly 200,000 of them fall victim to the disease each year.[106]

The Ecological Costs of Cotton

Drowning the Pacific coastal plains in a sea of poison has led to the long-term contamination of the land surface, water table, and food chain. A major cause is the use of ULV spray equipment, which produces smaller and more concentrated droplets. Adding to the dangers discussed previously, HVL sprays create severe problems with pesticide drift. Some 50 to 75 percent of the insecticide applied by aircraft under normal conditions never reaches the target crop. Instead, the droplets drift widely, commonly up to fifty miles or more, contaminating local ecosystems, including groundwater sources, river and estuaries, fish and wildlife, nearby villages and towns, their food crops, and adjacent cattle herds. In the words of one ICAITI report, "organosynthetic pesticides have become a part of the natural and human environment."[107]

Some planes empty their tanks at the end of the day by dumping the "excess" pesticides in lakes and bays.[108] Airborne pesticide residues from the cotton fields of Central America and Mexico have even been found by scientists as far away as the upper Great Lakes of the United States and Canada.[109]

Wildlife is suffering the brunt of this ecological assault, as deforestation and chemical drenchings disrupt animal reproduction and kill off smaller prey for birds and larger animals. Broad-winged hawks, crested forest eagles, pelicans and all insect-eating birds have diminished dramatically in recent years.[110] Ironically, many of the organochlorine chemicals (like DDT) banned in the United States because of their devastating impact on wildlife continue to harm North American bird species that make Central America their winter home.

Although less toxic than organophosphate pesticides, which break down relatively quickly once introduced into the environment, organochlorines such as DDT, heptachlor, and chlordane pose a particular threat to the reproductive systems of birds. These pesticides accumulate over the years in agricultural soils, pond and river bottoms, insects and animal tissue, and the larger environment, to be taken up later by plants and birds or released by soil organisms to further poison the environment.

The half-life of the organochlorine pesticide toxaphene is fifteen years in soil, meaning that fifteen years after application, one-half of the pesticide remains in the soil as poison. About one-third of the fifty-three North American bird species that spend their winters in western Central America have now suffered significant population declines.[111]

Other species of wildlife, such as raccoons and iguana, have been found to be highly contaminated with chlorinated poisons.[112] In Costa Rica, pesticides have all but exterminated armadillos, fish, and crocodiles along many of Guanacaste's rivers.[113] In Guatemala, pesticides have blown from lowland areas up mountainsides, killing the bark beetle's natural predators and causing the worst beetle attack recorded in that country's history. Other beneficial and productive insects, like honeybees, have almost completely disappeared. This process has spurred secondary pest resurgence in nearby corn and bean crops, excluding their successful cultivation in many cotton-growing areas.[114]

The biologically impoverished Pacific coastal plain has become an increasingly real example of Rachel Carson's *Silent Spring*, an ecological nightmare in which the songs and sounds characteristic of a "living environment" are absent. Lethal chemicals such as DDT, dieldrin, toxaphene, and parathion also permeate food and water sources. Many supplies of drinking water, such as those in the Choluteca and Olancho regions of Honduras, are heavily contaminated with these chemicals.[115]

Scientists are worried that pesticide contamination in the 3,475 square miles of mangrove forests on Central America's Pacific coast is causing a decline in fish catches. In the Gulf of Fonseca, shared by El Salvador, Honduras, and Nicaragua, high levels of DDT and organophosphates are believed to be a major factor in the declining catches of fish and shrimp, a leading export. As El Salvador's fourth leading export commodity, the destruction of the coastal shrimp breeding grounds by pesticides represents a potentially serious blow to the Salvadoran economy. The country's most important source of edible clams in Jiquilisco lagoon has also been decimated. (In Corinto Bay off the coast of Nicaragua in 1980, a time when cotton production was severely disrupted by the revolution, pesticide levels were found to be much lower than in neighboring El Salvador.)[116]

In the region's coastal bays and estuaries along the cotton belt, massive fish kills occur twice a year. In the coastal mangroves surrounding Jiquilisco lagoon, the country's most important fishing zone, thousands of fish are killed during the months of September through January. Virtually no fish are caught during this period. Samples taken from seven of the lagoon's fifty-six different species of fish in 1975 and 1976 showed four different pesticides: three chlorinated (DDT, endrin, and dieldrin) and one organophosphate (methyl parathion).[117]

The first casualties come with the rainy season when downpours wash chemicals from the soil into nearby waterways, such as the once-rich Guayape River in Honduras.[118] The second kill comes at the beginning of the dry season in August when aerial spraying of cotton begins, and peaks in December and January. According to one report, the "sight of dead birds along the mangrove channels is common during the cotton spraying season ... when migratory as well as resident birds are numerous."[119]

The Circle of Poison: The Costs to Consumers

The people of Central America are not the only ones being poisoned by pesticides used in the region. Central American agricultural exports contaminated with pesticides come back to the United States and other countries in a vicious "circle of poison."

Although the U.S. environmental movement was successful in legally restricting or prohibiting the use of many hazardous chemicals during the 1970s, multinational corporations continued to manufacture and export these same pesticides to the third world. Up to 150 million pounds of these blacklisted products, worth more than $800 million—about one fourth of U.S. pesticide production—are marketed overseas each year. An estimated 75 percent of the pesticides applied in Central America are either banned, restricted, or unregistered in the United States[120] The circle of poison closes when people in the United States and other countries consume Central American exports contaminated with these pesticides.[121]

Along the entire Pacific cotton belt, cattle are contaminated with dangerous chemicals by eating pasture and drinking water laced with pesticide drift and runoff. While contaminated beef is also sold within Central America, the domestic market is unable to absorb the supply of beef, particularly in periods of declining U.S. imports or embargoes.[122] Residues of DDT and other chlorinated insecticides average about twenty parts per million (ppm), and range as high as 100 ppm in cow's milk along the cotton belt.[123] Some ranchers even turn their cattle into the cotton fields to feed on the infected stubble after the harvest.

Average DDT levels in cow's milk in Guatemala are ninety times higher than that allowed by U.S. standards; the level found within Central America's cotton belt in 1977 was a dangerous 9.46 ppm. The level of contamination was much higher in Nicaragua. Just prior to the revolution, cow's milk was found to contain an average of 35.5 ppm of DDT, a level far exceeding the WHO's safety limit of 1.25.[124]

In fact, the U.S. Environmental Protection Agency (EPA) has found DDT levels of up to 106 parts per million in the fat of imported Central American beef destined for the hamburger and fast food industries. U.S. Food and Drug Administration (FDA) inspectors have repeatedly denied entry to Central American products, owing to excessive levels of DDT and other chemicals found in port-of-entry tests. In one year alone, the FDA rejected Honduran beef shipments on five separate occasions, while in Costa Rica the discovery of organochlorine residues led to a U.S. embargo on all four of the country's meat companies for three months, costing the country's beef exporters an estimated $10 million. Similar embargoes costing tens of millions of dollars have also been placed on El Salvador, Nicaragua, and Guatemala.

It is unknown how many other contaminated shipments have passed inspection undetected, but the U.S. Government Accounting Office (GAO) estimates that 14 percent of the meat entering the country is contaminated.[127] In some FDA inspection procedures, a small sample is removed for analysis while the rest of the shipment proceeds to the market and consumer. By the time tests are completed—showing poisons such as dieldrin, parathion, or DDT—the product has already been consumed.[128]

One typical example occurred in April 1988 when chlordane (a suspected carcinogen) in beef imported from Honduras to the United States was detected at levels eight times the allowable U.S. standards. By the time test samples were analyzed and the U.S. Department of Agriculture notified, 40,200 pounds of the 42,000 pounds of imported beef had been absorbed in the U.S. market. In a similar incident two months earlier, 45,000 pounds of boneless Honduran beef was distributed in Florida and Kentucky before test results came back showing levels of chlordane more than three times the standard. All the beef had been processed and sold by that time. During 1986, the Food Safety and Inspection Service did not test at all for either chlordane or heptachlor in meats or poultry.[129] This circle of poison adds yet another ecologically devastating dimension to the Central American hamburger connection (see Chapter 4).

Conclusion

The disastrous impact of cotton and the pesticide treadmill on Central America reveals how the self-expanding, profit-based character of dependent capitalism contradicts basic principles of human decency and ecological sensibility. Protected by the military power of repressive states, the oligarchs and cotton growers are unloading the social and ecological costs of agricultural production through severe worker and community health hazards, livestock and crop contamination, wildlife depletion, and ecological pollution.

To maintain profitability in a highly competitive world market, the cotton elite are slowly killing the laborers and natural environment that are the foundation of their wealth and class privileges. A 1977 United Nations report on pre-revolutionary Nicaragua, for instance, estimated that insecticide-caused environmental and social damage had a total yearly economic cost of $200 million, while foreign exchange earned for cotton amounted to a maximum of $141 million.[130] Clearly, the costs of cotton are obscene.

The degradation of capitalized nature along the Pacific coastal plan has created yet another set of ecological contradictions. The dynamics of the pesticide treadmill and soil degradation, combined with declining world market prices, appear to have once again damaged the profitability of cotton. In the early 1980s, the world price of cotton plummeted 25 percent, and the price of sugar 75 percent. Together, these two commodities represented 15 percent of Central American exports.[131]

Some 90 percent of Costa Rica's cotton growers have gone bankrupt since the mid-1980s.[132] In Guatemala, where cotton has traditionally constituted the country's second most important export, cotton acreage has plunged roughly 247,000 acres since the late 1970s.[133] Region-wide, cotton production has steadily fallen from 1.15 million bales in 1980 and 1981 to only 276,000 bales in 1991 and 1992, while total area planted has dropped from a high of 1,172,015 acres in 1978 to less than 188,500 acres in 1990 (and is even less today).

In the words of economist John Weeks, "the decline in cotton production could merely be a consequence of world prices dropping below the break-even point for capitalist producers, in which case the problem is transitory. More likely is that the heavy use of chemical fertilizers and related methods of raising yields have affected the soil. Indeed, this ghost of over-exploitation of the soil haunts agribusiness throughout Guatemala."[134] This view has been confirmed in a major study conducted in 1990 by the World Bank and the United Nations Food and Agriculture Organization (FAO), which concludes that the ecological crisis of cotton is so severe that it is no longer economically viable to produce the crop in that part of the world.[135]

These repeated ecological and economic crises of cotton agroexport represent a classic example of the manner in which dependent capitalist development is destroying its own material foundations of existence (or ecological conditions of production). As seen with other traditional crops, the case of cotton is also symptomatic of the larger social, economic, and ecological disaster that chemical-intensive capitalist export agriculture has created in Central America since World War II.

Bananas are a special case in point. Central America currently produces the majority of the world's bananas, with Costa Rica alone being the world's second leading exporter (behind Ecuador). The banana industry alone imports 25 to 30 percent of all the pesticides used in Costa Rica, which is equivalent to seven times the world's per capita average. In 1991, Costa Rica produced 76 million forty-pound boxes of bananas. Just two companies, Dole and Chiquita, own or lease nearly 190,000 acres of land, principally in Costa Rica and Honduras (the original "banana republic"), as well as Panama and Guatemala.[136]

As with the cotton industry in neighboring countries, Costa Rican levels of pesticide contamination in the banana industry are among the highest in the world. According to government records, some 250 to 300 agricultural workers suffer pesticide intoxications a year, although researchers who examined the country's hospital records estimate the actual number to be around 5,000 cases of acute poisonings annually. In addition, upward of 1,500 to 2,000 male workers from the Atlantic banana-growing region of Costa Rica have been rendered infertile through overexposure to the nematicide DBCP, while another 5,000 exposed workers are considered at risk.

The problem originated when an American company, Standard Fruit, continued to use the U.S.-manufactured pesticide DBCP on its plantations even after the EPA outlawed this dangerous chemical for domestic use. When the Costa Rican government banned DBCP in late 1978, Standard Fruit shipped more than twenty-two tons of stockpiled DBCP to Honduras, where hundreds of that country's banana-plantation workers are now also complaining of sterility. A multimillion-dollar lawsuit brought about by the law firm Barron and Budd on behalf of the affected Costa Rican workers against Shell, Dow, and Occidental chemical companies—makers of DBCP—and Castle & Cooke, Inc., which owns Standard Fruit, was settled out of court in

1991 for an undisclosed sum. It is likely that a similar suit will soon be filed on behalf of the Honduran workers.[137]

The ecological impacts of banana plantations are also disastrous. From 1989 to mid-1992, there were over seventy-five documented incidents of pesticide pollution killing massive wildlife populations. In 1990, for instance, contamination by American Cyanamid's insecticide terbufos killed one million fish and ruined drinking water in the Barra de Matina on the Atlantic Coast. Discharges from one pesticide facility in Chomes, in the western Puntarenas province, which has formulated Velsicol's heptachlor, American Cyanamid's terbufos, and Rhone Poulenc's ethoprophos, has reportedly resulted in repeated fish and shrimp kills and water contamination of the Lagarto River. The river empties into the Nicoya Gulf, an important, once-productive fishing area.[138] The coral reef off the country's Caribbean shore is now about 90 percent dead as a result of pesticide run-off and sedimentation, principally from the banana plantations.[139] In addition to massive fish, lobster, and shrimp kills, thousands of acres of former banana lands have been rendered irreversibly damaged by excessive chemical contamination.[140]

The pesticide treadmill is also reappearing in the wave of nontraditional fruit and vegetable crops, such as broccoli, snow peas, strawberries, pineapples, melons and mangoes, currently being promoted in the region by USAID as a substitute for the economically declining cotton, beef, and sugar export base.[141] In Honduras, currently the leading melon exporter in Central America, pesticide-related illnesses have increased dramatically in recent years, even though cotton production has declined dramatically.[142] The FDA reports that in 1989, forty-five shipments of cantaloupe and snow peas from Guatemala were rejected for entry into the United States due to illegal pesticide residues. At least seventeen shipments of contaminated Costa Rican fruits and vegetables, including coconuts, pineapples, strawberries, and chayotes, were also rejected that same year.[143] Traditional agricultural exports from Central America such as bananas, coffee, and mangoes are also contaminated with pesticides. Between 30 to 50 percent of all coffee imports into the United States show contamination with DDT, lindane, and BHC, and other totally banned chemicals. BHC, commonly used on Guatemalan and Costa Rican coffee plantations, has been found to cause tumors, premature births, and other reproductive damage, and to kill fetuses, even when used in tiny concentrations.[144]

However, the GAO estimates that FDA testing fails to detect 60 percent of the chemicals used on imported foods. In addition, the FDA test less than 1 percent of all imported foods, including some 33.5 billion pounds of imported fruits and vegetables (equal to 135 pounds for every man, woman and child in the country), placing U.S. citizens at a growing risk.[145] Of that imported food that is tested by the FDA, some 5 percent is found contaminated with illegal pesticides—twice the rate for domestic foods.

Despite the problem, in 1984, the Reagan administration cast the lone "no" vote in a United Nations resolution called "Protection Against Products Harmful to Health and Environment." This measure (which passed 146 to 1) called for countries importing pesticides to be provided with information necessary to safeguard health and the environment.[146] In response, the environmental, labor, and consumer movements convinced some twenty-five U.S. Senators to cosponsor "The Circle of Poison Prevention Act of 1991," a legislative act that might lead to some significant progress in the battle against this form of "ecological imperialism."[147]

There is little actual government control of pesticide use in Central America today. Over the past twelve years, only Nicaragua and Costa Rica have launched a comprehensive effort to use pesticides in a safer, more efficient manner (see Chapter 5).[148] In Honduras, the Pan American Agricultural School in Zamorano has developed a training course for technical personnel and agricultural workers in pesticide application which is being recognized by the EPA. However, it is fair to say that without greater democracy and popular mobilization against the abuses wrought by multinational corporations and the agrarian bourgeoisie, the poisoning of Central Americans and consumers internationally, and of the global environment, will continue.

4
REVOLUTION
IN THE
RAINFOREST

The creation of the first guerrilla detachment in the Guatemalan jungle was one of the richest and most rewarding revolutionary experiences for our organization.

Mario Payeras[1]

Ten-year-old Tomás León lives at the edge of the rainforest on the eastern slopes of a Central American country. Six months after he was born, his family was forced by their own government from the fertile interior highlands they had farmed for generations. Government officials insisted that prosperity lay just down the new road built to the agricultural frontier. The León family joined a government-sponsored rainforest colonization project and received more land than they'd ever had before. However, three years after clearing trees to plant crops, the Leóns were forced to move deeper into the forest, this time by a cattle rancher who mysteriously produced titles to the land they worked. The Leóns were evicted a third time three years later.

Today Tomás and his mother farm the new family plot while his father earns a dollar a day on the nearby cattle *hacienda*. Despite their hard work, the family often goes hungry. The forest animals Tomás and his father hunt grow scarcer each year. Although young and illiterate, Tomás understands that his family has lived with injustice for far too long.[2]

The story of Tomás León is a microcosm of Central America's social and ecological crisis. There are hundreds of thousands of families like the Leóns throughout the region. Their continued political domination and economic exploitation by local oligarchs and allied foreign powers, namely the United States, has brought about widespread poverty and environmental destruction—problems that have produced revolutionary movements and civil war in much of the isthmus in recent decades.

The magnitude of this crisis is reflected most dramatically in the destruction of Central America's tropical forests. In 1960, woodlands blanketed nearly 60 percent of the region. Today less than one-third of the original forests remain standing; the rest have vanished. Even more devastating is the felling of Central America's (broad-leafed) lowland and lower montane rainforests, one of the richest reserves of biological diversity found anywhere in the world, which has proceeded at a rate between 1,351 and 1,545 square miles a year over the last decade. Although slowing, if current deforestation rates continue, most of the remaining rainforests could be completely destroyed within the next twenty years, except for small remnants in parks and preserves.[3]

The loss of genetic material is astounding. For instance, in Costa Rica, a country the size of West Virginia but home to 5 to 7 percent of the world's known species, there are over 8,000 plant species and 758 bird species—620 of which are residents—a greater variety than that found in all of North America above the Tropic of Cancer. Although only 1,803 acres in size, the La Selva Forest Reserve alone contains 320 tree species, 42 fish, 394 birds, 104 mammals (including 62 bats), 76 reptiles, 46 amphibians and 143 butterflies—a diversity of species equal to about half that of the entire state of California.[4] For the last ten years, an area of jungle the size of the La Selva Reserve has been destroyed every six hours in Costa Rica. In fact, more than two thirds of the country's tropical forests have disappeared since 1950; less than 4,418 square miles remain, largely on the Cordillera de Talamanca and Cordillera Central mountain ranges, and in the northeast. Prior to colonization, over 99 percent of Costa Rica was originally forested.[5] Since about 15 percent of some 1,500 trees inventoried in Costa Rica's forests were evaluated as having potential for cancer treatment, their destruction represents an incalculable loss for both present and future generations of humanity.

Occupying only 6 percent of the earth's surface (it used to be 12 percent), rainforests are home to 80 percent of the world's vegetation and half of the earth's living species, up to four million life form varieties. Half of the world's medicines originate from tropical forests, including aspirin, quinine, digitalis, cyclosporin, and vincristine, which has been highly successful in the treatment of leukemia in children.[6]

In the fall of 1991 an agreement was reached between the National Biodiversity Institute of Costa Rica, a private, nonprofit organization promoting the preservation of the country's richest biological resources, and Merck & Company, Inc., the world's largest pharmaceutical company. This agreement was the first time a major drug manufacturer collaborated directly with a tropical country to hunt the rainforests for new medicines ("chemical prospecting"), providing economic incentives to preserve biodiversity.[7]

The roots of deforestation can be traced to decades of development policies that have favored the expanded production of traditional and nontraditional capitalist agricultural exports over the sustainable use of natural resources for meeting the needs of the Central American people. Along with chemical-intensive cotton production, the production of beef cattle has proved to be the most important, as well as the most socially and ecologically destructive, commodity for promoting the diversification, modernization, and expansion of capitalist export agriculture in the region since World War II.

This approach to development continues to enjoy the active support of local oligarchs and military officers with the assistance of the United States government and international lending agencies, increasingly rolling back huge areas of *selva* for cattle and concentrating the richest lands and resources under control of the capitalist export sector. It has also condemned the majority of small farmers to a life of brutal poverty and hardship. Therefore, to understand the current social and ecological crisis it is necessary to look at the expansion of the capitalist export sector, in particular the cattle stampede into the rich tropical forests of Central America.

Deforestation and the Cattle Stampede

Export beef production first began along the western territories of Central America in the late 1950s and early 1960s. The financial capital and technical assistance necessary to develop the cattle industry came from United States government agencies and international financial institutions, principally the World Bank, Inter-American Development Bank (IADB), U.S. Agency for International Development (USAID), and the Central American Bank for Economic Integration (CABEI).

Most of the funding for cattle and export agriculture was provided by the Inter-American Development Bank. The IADB invested some $3.037 billion in Latin American agriculture between 1961 and 1978, 22 percent of their total distribution of loans.[8] The World Bank provided massive financial support, spending $154 million on the livestock industry in Central America and the Caribbean in its first two decades of development lending, some 56 percent of its total direct commitments to agriculture. During the 1960s, more than one-fourth of the private loans made to agriculture also went to cattle production, converting it from a system of hoarding to an instrument of capitalist production for money profit.[9]

In fact, all of the agricultural credit provided by the International Development Association (IDA, a division of the World Bank) in the western hemisphere between 1961 and 1970 went for livestock improvement. In addition to the credit provided by the IDA, loans to the cattle industry by the International Bank for Reconstruction and Development (IBRD) between 1961 and 1965 comprised 28 percent of its total agricultural allocations made to Latin America and 51 percent from 1966 to 1970.[10]

As was the case with cotton and other export crops, the flood of development assistance gave Central American governments the financial tools for creating the appropriate ecological and communal (or infrastructural) conditions for export beef production. This was first accomplished through improving the quality of existing pasture in the Pacific coastal lowlands, ensuring suitable feedstock for the dry season, and reconstructing the "biological character" of the cattle herds.

One of the primary barriers to the export of Central America cattle was the poor quality of the criollo stock, a breed inherited from the Spanish colonists. Slow maturation rates and relatively modest weight gains were serious obstacles. To be competitive in the world market, ranchers required breeds that would maximize the rate of quality beef formation in the shortest amount of time. Santa Gertrudis, purebred Brahman, Zebu, and other new breeds of beefier, faster-maturing cattle, more resistant to disease and the environmental conditions of the tropics, were imported to replace and upgrade the inferior quality of the existing stock.[11]

Commodities and techniques for improving the health of the herds were also purchased and adopted, including vaccines, medicines, and vitamin supplements for combating diseases, such as leptospirosis, and parasites like screwworms, vampire bats, and ticks (which transmit protozoal diseases like anaplasmosis and paraplasmosis). In Costa Rica, animal medicines were the third-largest imported agricultural input during the mid-1970s, behind only pesticides and fertilizers.[12]

The "biological character" of the existing landscape was also reconstructed. A number of high-yielding African grasses were imported to replace the unproductive varieties native to Central America.[13] Combined with the increased use of chemical fertilizers, pesticides, wells and irrigation, the productivity of pasture grasses jumped significantly, particularly on those ranches that fattened cattle for slaughter. Pasture improvements also raised land values and required fencing the once-open fields and forests as a means for securing title as capitalist private property.

Before these improvements, cattle expended great amounts of energy roaming vast areas of unfenced and unimproved pastures. This traditional pasturing technique produced malnutrition, insect infestation, disease, and infertility in the cattle, thereby lowering the rate of beef formation and increasing gristle content.[14]

Finally, the influx of foreign capital financed construction of an elaborate system of highways, feeder roads, and bridges leading to the Pacific ports, as well as the truck fleets, packing plants, warehouses, and facilities necessary to efficiently transport and process this beef for the world market. By 1960, ships laden with frozen beef for the U.S. fast-food hamburger and pet food industries sailed from Guatemala every five days.[15]

With these investments, the modernization and expansion of export cattle production caused massive deforestation in the Pacific coastal lowlands and coincided with the development of large-scale cotton and sugar estates. Cattle proved to be a very effective and highly flexible instrument for wealthy land speculators since herds could be moved from titled to untitled areas and sold (along with the "newly developed" land) when market conditions were most favorable (unlike agricultural crops, which were fixed investments that had to be harvested and sold in a specific period of time). This process also accelerated deforestation and habitat destruction, since stripping the land of its tree cover, or "land improvements," demonstrated not only de facto ownership but also expanded the pasture area for growing herds.

In some areas, cattle ranching was the dominant force behind the destruction of dry and moist tropical forests along the Pacific coast. A tropical dry forest formation is characterized by a low, semideciduous canopy of trees, usually twenty to thirty meters tall with short, stout trunks and large spreading crowns. Tropical moist forests are usually taller, multistratal, semi-deciduous or evergreen forests.[16]

In Escuintla, Guatemala, a mere 12 percent of the land was in pasture while 48 percent stood forested in the early 1950s. By 1964, Escuintla had emerged as the country's largest cattle-raising department, holding one-fifth of the nation's herd. Some 42 percent of the land was in pastures of imported pangola and other African grasses. Only a paltry 16 percent of the area remained forested.[17]

Cattle ranching was particularly expanded in the Pacific lowlands of Honduras and Costa Rica because cotton production assumed much less importance there in comparison to the rest of the region. The western department of Choluteca developed into Honduras' largest cattle raising department by the early 1970s, for instance, with one-tenth of the national herd.[18]

In the northern Pacific province of Guanacaste in Costa Rica, wealthy ranchers utilized discriminatory state banking policies, land laws, and tax credits to double their pasture acreage from 765,621 acres in 1963 to 1,468,027 acres in 1973, forcing 22.12 percent of all small peasant farmers to leave the province. Of the more than 701,000 acres of new pastures of jaragua grass developed in the province, 587,860 acres (or 82 percent) went to farms 247 acres or more in size.

The displacement of peasants by increased land values (and rents) and discriminatory state policies resulted in the decline of every food crop except rice.[19] By 1974, 65 percent of Guanacaste was in pasture, its rich forests slashed from 34 percent to a mere 13 percent in a decade.[20] Similar processes also occurred in the neighboring provinces of Puntarenas and Alajuela.

Today, only a few patches of Costa Rica's original woodlands of guayacan, amarillo, granadilla, madrone, and other trees remain, typically in the most inaccessible areas of the Pacific lowlands and surrounding mountains. These remaining forests have lost some of their regenerative capacity, not only because of the small size of the remnants, but also because of the decline, and even local extinction, of animal populations that have co-evolved mutualistic relationships with the wild plant species.[21]

Once home to an abundance of North American birds, such as the broad-winged hawk, stripe-headed sparrow, the American wideon, great blue heron, and the solitary sandpiper, these provinces now support hordes of cattle. As noted in chapter 2, peccaries, agoutis, pacas, coatimundis, jaguars, pumas, ocelots, foxes, tapirs, caimans, crocodiles, scarlet macaws, parrots, great curassows and other animals found in the forest have been either eliminated or greatly reduced. White-tailed deer and howler monkeys are still present in areas with some remnant forest and secondary growth, but in reduced numbers. Coatimundis, collared peccaries, agoutis, pacas, and tapirs are still found in some forested areas, generally near streams, although the last two have become very scarce. The big cats are become exceedingly rare and are probably extinct in most of lowland Guanacaste, except in parks and reserves. The harpy eagle and hookbilled kite, the latter almost exclusively restricted to dry forest habitats, are both almost completely gone. Only a few generalists such as rabbits, coyotes, squirrels, armadillos, and iguanas have adapted to the open grassland monoculture.[22]

Revolution and Repression, Life and Death in the Rainforests

As "development" of the narrow Pacific coastal plains was completed during the course of the 1960s, Central America's landed oligarchs and bankers turned their attention to the vast wilderness areas and peasant communities in the rugged eastern territories. They soon realized that large profits could be garnered from the conversion of these less-accessible zones (previously immune to capitalist export agriculture) into extensive cattle ranches.

Beef cattle take four to six years before they reach the most profitable slaughtering weight of 400 to 450 kilograms (880 to 1,000 pounds). This maturation rate for cattle grazing on more marginal lands, particularly in nutrient-poor rainforest areas, requires the creation of extensive cattle ranches for moving herds to new pastures as older pastures degrade over time, and therefore contributes to deforestation. Unlike more geographically specific commodities such as cotton and coffee, cattle were less restricted and could be raised wherever pasture grasses would grow. In fact, the longer rainy season in the region's interior, particularly in the lower montane and lowland rainforests of the Caribbean slope, offered the possible year-round growth of pasture grasses. Mature cattle from the enlarged herds in the wetter interior zones could then be culled and sold to the more modern ranches on the Pacific coast to be fattened for slaughter and exported.[23]

Fueled by increased financing from bilateral and multilateral lending agencies, Central America's large cattle ranchers moved quickly to realize the profit potential, expanding toward the rolling mountains and valleys of the interior. Through the economic processes of land speculation, higher rents, legal trickery, and land titling from "sympathetic" government officials, these cattle ranchers displaced tens of thousands of peasant families from lands they had traditionally farmed for generations. In areas where peasant communities organized against eviction, government repression, including U.S.-sponsored military counterinsurgency operations, was used to expropriate their farmland.

In the interior department of Olancho, Honduras, a series of peasant massacres by the army and private security forces in coordination with the National Federation of Farmers and Cattlemen (FENAGH) and sectors of the business establishment were carried out in the 1960s and 1970s. The aim of the repression was to attack leading organizers in Olancho's peasant movement, who were resisting the expansion of cattle ranches onto their farmland and adjacent forests. By the 1970s, Olancho had the fastest growing cattle herd in the country. Nearly half of Olancho's farmland was untitled national land occupied by peasants. Ironically, many of these peasants were displaced migrants from the Pacific coastal region of Choluteca. Thus, peasant and export sector conflicts along the Pacific coast in the 1960s were displaced into the interior during the 1970s.[24]

The use of repression to "capitalize nature" was even more widespread in Nicaragua. In the mountainous northern department of Matagalpa, the country's leading producer of corn and beans in the early 1960s, most of the farmland was worked by peasants without title. By the mid-1960s, the area emerged as the country's most important cattle-producing department, as President Somoza's feared National Guard evicted families from their traditional plots of land. In 1963, 30 percent of Matagalpa was in forest, compared to only 5 percent in 1976. Pastures, on the other hand, increased from 39 percent to 94 percent of the farm area over the same period.[25]

Conflicts between small family farmers and large cattle ranchers intensified. By 1967, the rural guerrilla movement, the Sandinista National Liberation Front (FSLN), emerged with the support of the peasantry to combat the capitalization of Matagalpa.[26] The Somoza dictatorship quickly declared the area a counterinsurgency zone, and with U.S. assistance, launched a brutal campaign of repression that devastated the guerrilla movement (including the killing of 13 senior members of the FSLN leadership). Those families resisting eviction from then on were routinely arrested, tortured, killed, or imprisoned in the nearby Zelaya concentration camp.[27]

Spurred by the militarization of the countryside, as well as government colonization projects and road-building programs, ranches quickly spread eastward into the country's lower montane and southeastern Caribbean lowland rainforests, particularly along the boundaries of the Rama road.[28] Cattle ranching destroyed more than 386 square miles of Nicaragua's broad-leaved and coniferous forests annually during the 1970s, the highest level of any country in Central America. Pasture lands expanded to blanket 10,888 square miles by 1978, compared to 6,602 square miles in 1961.[29]

By this time, Nicaragua possessed the largest cattle herd in all of Central America and had become the United States' number one Latin American beef supplier. Beef export from Nicaragua jumped from $6.7 million in 1965 to $26.6 million in 1970.[30] Officers of Somoza's *Guardia* and local magistrates took advantage of the repression to establish their own ranches. The Somoza family itself utilized its control of the country's military apparatus to appropriate a lion's share of the profits from the cattle export boom.

By 1979, land holdings belonging to Somoza and associates expanded to more than two million acres, more than half of which was extensive ranchland.[31] Six Miami meatpacking plants and the largest slaughterhouse in Central America, all owned by Somoza, were key ingredients in this recipe for rainforest destruction.[32]

Perhaps the most brutal repression occurred in Guatemala. Between 1950 and 1964, the departments of Zacapa, Izabal and Chiquimula experienced heavy deforestation and peasant displacement by large cattle ranchers. During this period, pasture acreage tripled in Izabal and nearly doubled for Zacapa. Deforestation was particularly severe along a road running eastward from Guatemala City through the richly forested Motagua River Valley to Puerto Barrios and Matías de Gálvez, major beef ports on the Caribbean.[33]

Discontent quickly ripened into rebellion at the edge of the rainforests. By the mid-1960s, as in Matagalpa, Nicaragua, a guerrilla organization emerged. Rebel Armed Forces (FAR) formed widespread alliances with desperately poor peasant villages in Zacapa and Izabal to resist the appropriation of their land. (In March 1965, these two rebel fronts split into two separate revolutionary organizations.)[34]

In 1966, at the urging of the U.S. State Department, the Guatemalan government declared these eastern districts a counterinsurgency zone, launching a series of merciless attacks on peasant communities to break the resistance. U.S.-supplied-and-piloted helicopter gunships, T-33 fighter jets, and B-26 "invader" bombers armed with napalm and heavy bombs assisted the Guatemalan army in the carnage, killing some 6,000 to 10,000 people between 1966 and 1968.[35]

The "success" of these military campaigns quickly opened up the farms and rainforests found on the "agricultural frontier" to huge cattle ranches owned by landed oligarchs, local and national government officials, military officers, and paramilitary personnel. The U.S.-trained commander of the counterinsurgency, Colonel Carlos Arana, known as "The Butcher of Zacapa," became one of the largest ranchers in northeast Guatemala and later president of the military government.[36] The political career of Colonel Arana is indicative of the manner in which Guatemala's military officers and government officials have promoted rainforest destruction as a means for acquiring large cattle ranches and assuming their own personal fortunes.[37]

By the mid-1970s, the cattle stampede had spread to the pristine rainforests in the Mayan Indian departments of Alta Verapáz, El Quiché, Huehuetenango, and northwest Izabal (also known as the Northern Transversal Strip). The Guatemalan government was particularly anxious to "develop" the tropical evergreen seasonal forests in the immense northern department of El Petén, an area comprising about one-third of the country. The Petén included upland forest of mahogany, Spanish cedar, ceiba, and zapote.[38]

An extension of Mexico's oil-bearing Chiápas rainforest, the discovery of nickel, oil, and the enormous hydroelectric potential in the Petén wilderness and other northern departments further increased the pressure to open up the region to foreign capital. This sparked an intensified wave of violence and state terror against church-backed peasant cooperatives and traditional Indian communities. By 1973, the $250 million Mineral Explorations and Exploitations (Exmibal) nickel mining and processing operation was conceded in the department of

Alta Verapáz. By 1978, seven international oil companies had received concessions in northern Guatemala.[39]

As the decade progressed, the receding edge of the tropical rainforest became the setting for growing peasant resistance to encroachment by large cattle ranchers and multinational resource companies. Another revolutionary organization, the Guerrilla Army of the Poor (Ejército Guerrillero de los Pobres, EGP), was born in this period. After a series of spectacular attacks by the EGP in northern El Quiché, the army launched massive counterinsurgency operations designed to "clear" the Transversal Strip of its small farmer inhabitants, including the massacre of more than 100 Kekchí Indians in the town of Panzós in 1978.[40] This massacre is considered a turning point that resulted in a upsurge of grassroots resistance by the Mayan Indians who make up more than half of the country's 8.7 million people. Entire Indian villages joined the popular movement or the armed resistance waging revolution in the rainforest.[41]

Despite the armed resistance, military officers, government officials, and landed elites continued to destroy rainforests. General Romeo Lucas García, who was in charge of the counterinsurgency operations in the Northern Transversal Strip before he became president of the country in 1987, acquired a number of ranches and timber properties on the strip ranging from 81,000 acres to 135,000 acres. This stretch became known as "The Zone of the Generals."[42] Other members of this cattle-military-industrial complex acquired properties, including the defense minister General Otto Spiegler Noriega, General Carlos Arana Osorio, and President Kjell Laugerud.[43]

Today, the army contributes directly to the deforestation of the Petén by building roads, clearing areas up to 300 yards on either side to prevent guerrilla ambushes, and opening up the jungle to further logging, cattle ranching, and colonization by landless peasants. The National Agency for the Economic Promotion and Development of the Petén and its temporary successor, the *Comisión Liquidador*, are operated by the Guatemalan Armed Forces and as such have been largely immune to government oversight as they continue to grant huge logging concessions in the Petén.[44] In fact, a 1983 USAID-financed study claimed that 60 percent of the Department of Alta Verapaz is owned by the army, and army land holdings are rapidly growing in the Petén as well.

It is widely suspected that government officials at the highest levels receive substantial bribes for granting illegal logging concessions, even in designated "protected areas." Archaeologists report that loggers enter the parks surrounding the archaeological sites to cut trees. According to one scholar working in the area, it is not unusual for loggers with a license for cutting a maximum of 2,000 board feet to cut two to four times that amount as the authorities look the other way.[45]

Park boundaries are also ignored by multinational corporations, such as Basic Resources International, Ltd. (BRI), a Canadian-backed company based in the Bahamas, which owns a concession in the northwestern part of the Petén, formerly belonging to Texaco. One active oil well, called *Xan I*, which suffered a major spill in 1989, operates on the boundary of the 174-square-mile *Laguna del Tigre* reserve, an area of pristine wetlands, grasslands, and subtropical semi-humid forest, and numerous endangered species. Additional wells are planned for the reserve's interior and will likely further increase land values and speculative deforestation. In 1989, Exxon planned exploratory oil drilling in the rainforests surrounding Ceibal, one of the country's most prestigious archaeological sites. Fortunately, Guatemala's environmental movement has successfully blocked Exxon's plans, at least for now.[46]

Mining and logging operations also take a toll. In 1977, Exmibal constructed a $220-million-dollar plant capable of producing 28 million pounds of nickel annually on the shores of the huge Lake Izabal. Partly owned by the Hanna Mining Company of Cleveland, along with Guatemala's military government, the plant employed fewer than 500 Guatemalans at between $2.50 and $7.50 *a day*, while its strip-mining operation and tailings waste irreversibly damaged the fragile environment around Lake Izabal. It finally shut down in 1981 under the weight of low world prices for nickel and high energy costs.[47]

To pay off a growing $490 million foreign debt, the Guatemala government has considered reopening a pulp processing mill in the small town of El Rancho. Called "Celgusa," the pulp plant was built in the 1970s with obsolete and environmentally contaminating technology and caused extensive damage before closing in 1986. Its reopening threatens to deforest an estimated 17,290 acres of coniferous highland forests per year and would release dioxins and other toxic chemicals into one of Guatemala's most important sources of water, the Rio Motagua. According to some environmentalists, the ecological damage caused by the original mill has exceeded the amount of the debt, and a reopening would further decimate the country's woodlands.[48]

Another environmental threat facing the Petén rainforests and peasant communities is a drug eradication program, using U.S. pilots and planes to spray lethal herbicides on allegedly burgeoning fields of opium and marijuana. The U.S. Drug Enforcement Agency has carried out the program, working with Guatemala's military intelligence division, the G-2, which is notoriously connected with the death squads operating in the country.

Human deaths, deformed children, ulcerations of the mouth and throat from drinking sprayed water sources, increased infant mortality, deaths of entire cattle herds and vegetable crops, as well as scores of endangered quetzals and other species, and the widespread defoliation of the Petén have all been reported as a result of the campaign over the last five years. Although the DEA claims to be using only the herbicide Roundup (glyphosate), most of these effects cannot be attributed to this chemical but are instead reportedly consistent with much more lethal chemicals such as paraquat, 2,3,5-T, and 2,4-D.[49] Many environmentalists argue that the sprayings are also concentrated in areas of guerilla activity in the Petén, San Marcos, and Huehuetenango, and are part of a military counterinsurgency program to decimate the growing revolution in the rainforest.

Poverty, Deforestation, and the Hamburger Connection

Central American peasants displaced by the stampede of cattle ranchers, loggers, land speculators, and multinational corporations face a number of options in addition to armed resistance. Tens of thousands of families are moving into the region's rapidly growing cities in search of wage jobs in factories or on nearby agricultural export estates harvesting cotton, sugar, or coffee.

Others settle on the steep slopes of the volcanoes and hillsides along the Pacific slope, clearing them of trees and other protective vegetation to plant food crops. Most of the deforested hillsides are inappropriate for agriculture and soon develop severe problems with erosion and fertility loss, flash flooding, and decreased productivity. Tens of thousands more are joining the urban informal service sector to look for incomes as street vendors, household servants, and any other tasks that offer the hope of survival.

The end results of cattle expansion therefore include the overcoming of potentially severe seasonal wage-labor shortages through the marginalization the rural peasantry. It also creates a large army of desperately poor workers residing in the city *barrios*. In this sense, the cattle boom has been (and continues to be) a safeguard for the economic viability of capitalist export-agriculture and industry along the Pacific coast.[50]

Many displaced peasants escape their landless condition by moving east in advance of the cattle stampede into the tropical rainforests of the interior. Often utilizing agricultural methods ill suited to the rainforest ecosystem, migrating peasants clear and burn the forest vegetation to plant subsistence crops such as corn, beans, rice, and manioc, as well as small-scale cash crops such as coffee, chiles, bananas, and cacao.[51] However, rainforest soils planted in crops are typically thin and poor; the nutrients normally stored and protected by the jungle canopy quickly leach out when exposed to the hard rains and burning tropical sun, and eventually the soil turns to brick. Denied access to critical financial and social services and technological inputs necessary to protect the land and improve their lives, crops soon begin to fail after a few short years. Yet, as biologist James J. Parsons points out, "enduring countless hardships and difficult living conditions on an isolated and malaria-infested fringe" is often the only available means to insure survival for the family which clears the forest and plants in its ashes.[52]

As invasive weeds and noxious insects take over the degraded soils, these families become forced to abandon or sell their plots to a second wave of land speculators and cattle ranchers. Many others simply have their farms appropriated by the military or paramilitary personnel acting on behalf of wealthy ranchers and government officials. In areas where government repression is less overt, cattle ranchers employ wage workers to slash and burn the trees and brush and plant pasture grasses. Many landowners rent forested parcels of land or *rozas* to subsistence farmers, who in exchange will clear the trees and grow food crops for a year or two, just long enough for the stumps to rot. After this time, they will be evicted and the land seeded for pasture. New forest parcels are rented, and the process will be renewed once more.[53]

In numerous instances, peasant families follow roads into the forests created by extensive logging operations, particularly in Honduras, Guatemala, and Costa Rica. The Honduran government's Forestry Development Corporation (COHDEFOR) has cleared large areas of tropical forest in the northern provinces, contributing to the destruction of over 4.94 million acres of Honduran forests since 1960. In addition, commercial loggers clear an estimated 123,500 to 148,200 acres of pine forests annually.[54]

Despite its potentially high economic value, however, most processes of small farmer displacement and land speculation usually waste the felled timber. Up to three-fourths of it is burned on the ground. For instance, an estimated $320 million worth of cut hardwood is burned or left to rot each year by land speculators and migrating campesinos.[55] The burnings create heavy influxes of ash and organic matter in local waterways, depressing oxygen levels and causing recurring fish kills, such as on the western shore of majestic Lake Izabal in Guatemala.[56] These patterns are repeated time and again. Peasants move ever deeper into the rainforests, only to eventually lose their farms to the cattle stampede. In effect, Central America's impoverished peasantry are mere pawns in a general's game, serving as an effective vehicle for clearing the rainforests, free of charge, for wealthy ranchers.[57]

As part of this larger process, destruction of Central America's tropical rainforest is further exacerbated by government-sponsored peasant colonization projects. More often than not, these projects only reinforce structures that benefit the capitalist export sector (particularly ranchers) and foreign capital at the expense of the region's majorities and environment.[58] Often called "land reforms," these resettlement projects are designed to serve as an outlet for potentially explosive social tensions caused by land-tenure conflicts and urban overcrowding elsewhere in the region. In many cases, however, these conflicts often reappear between colonizing peasants and ranchers on the agricultural frontier. Peasant colonists often refuse to move on when cattle ranchers are ready to take over their land, precipitating violent confrontations.

Such was the case in Honduras in 1975, when a cattle rancher was implicated in a grisly multiple murder of priests and peasant activists organizing against eviction. Recently, in Costa Rica, campesinos have reclaimed abandoned cattle lands, causing conflict between large ranchers and peasant families.[59]

Peasant colonization and destruction of rainforest as an alternative to comprehensive agrarian and economic reforms are often promoted by the United States. For instance, in response to the growing insurgency during the 1960s in Matagalpa, Nicaragua, the U.S. Agency for International Development and the Inter-American Development Bank provided an $80 million loan to the Somoza dictatorship for small-farmer colonization and road projects into the jungles of Zelaya, causing massive deforestation of the area.[60] Under the Nicaraguan Agrarian Institute (Instituto Agrario de Nicaragua, IAN) and, later, the Campesino Welfare Institute (Instituto de Bienestar Campesino, INVIERNO), a total of sixty-three colonies involving 2,651 families relocated from the Pacific coastal plain were established on the Atlantic coast and agricultural frontier by the mid-1970s.[61]

Pushed from behind by the cattle stampede, many displaced peasants deforested and settled land traditionally belonging to the Miskito, Sumu, and Rama Indians of Nicaragua's Costa de Miskitos, resulting in clashes between the two cultures.[62] In fact, throughout Central America the common woodlands and ways of life of other indigenous Indian communities—including the Kekchí and Chorti of Guatemala, the Paya and Miskito of Honduras, the Talamangquenos of Costa Rica, and the Kuna and Choco of Panama—continue to be threatened by expanding cattle ranchers and displaced farmer colonists.[63]

Under Somoza, peasant rainforest colonization and other "surface" reforms in the Pacific highlands of Carazo and central highlands of Matagalpa and Jinotega failed to stem the deepening poverty of the Nicaraguan people and therefore halt the growing social unrest and FSLN guerrilla activity in the countryside. In response, Somoza imposed a news blackout and state of siege in 1975, ordering the National Guard to carry out extensive "search and destroy" missions, which, with U.S. support, included the use of napalm, defoliants, and indiscriminate bombing of rural communities. As part of this state of siege, estimated to have killed some 3,000 people in thirty-three months of generalized terror, thousands of families saw their huts burned out and crops destroyed, their women raped and brutalized, their fathers and sons tortured—actions that invigorated the Sandinista-led revolutionary movement which overthrew the Somoza dictatorship on July 19, 1979.[64]

These actions were repeated in Guatemala's tropical rainforests of the Petén and other northern departments during the same period. Already spontaneously colonized in some areas by isolated peasant families engaging in primitive forms of shifting agriculture, the government sought to further develop these pristine rainforests by employing displaced small farmers through road-building programs and "official" colonization projects as a means for relieving land conflicts occurring in other parts of the country, particularly the eastern ranching districts.[65]

For instance, in 1976 the National Institute for Agrarian Transformation (INTA) utilized $5.6 million in USAID money to have some 5,000 families join a cooperative colonization project of former highland peasants from Huehuetenango in the Ixcán region of the Transversal de Norte development zone. However, as characteristic of the prevailing land tenure system in the rest of the country, these settlers were placed on the more marginal lands and provided little capital assistance. The better lands were distributed to large cattle ranchers. As the nutrient-poor soils of the Petén lost their fertility during the course of the 1970s, ever larger numbers of small corn farmers lost the land they had worked so hard to clear and cultivate to the expanding cattle latifundia. As a consequence, the 1976 harvest of 1.5 million quintales of maize fell to slightly over 500,000 in 1978.[66]

These injustices sparked a guerrilla operation by the EGP, which in June, 1976, killed landowner Luis Reina—"the Tiger of Ixcán"—virtual lord of the large, newly acquired tracts of land in the area. In retaliation, the army systematically murdered cooperative leaders in the Ixcán area operations the following month. As social unrest in the rainforest grew with the discovery of oil and conversion of land to large cattle, the army eventually launched a wave of terror in the late 1970s against peasant communities and cooperatives, further fueling the growing revolution in the rainforest.[67]

Spurred by the "first wave" of peasant colonization, deforestation and the expansion of Central America's cattle industry was further accelerated by the large market in the United States for imported beef. In what is often referred to as "the hamburger connection," exports of deboned, frozen beef from Central America feed the burgeoning fast-food hamburger joints, pet food industries, and processed and frozen food sections in U.S. supermarkets.

During the 1970s, as the U.S. fast-food industry grew 20 percent a year (2.5 times faster than the restaurant industry overall), the United States was the world's biggest importer of beef. It imported about 132 pounds per average citizen, accounting for about one-third of all international trade, compared to less than eighty-eight pounds of beef per citizen in 1960.[68] Deboned frozen beef quickly emerged as Central America's most dynamic export commodity, with a 400 percent increase in trade between 1961 and 1974 alone.[69] As a result, during the height of the cattle boom between 1970 and 1980, an area of tropical forests larger than Belgium was annihilated.[70]

By 1980, Central American beef exports to the United States skyrocketed to over $290 million annually, constituting 15 percent of the total U.S. beef imports (compared to only $9 million in beef exports, or 5 percent of U.S. total imports in the early 1960s). U.S. per capita beef consumption had risen to 117 pounds a year, a figure twice the yearly average for Western Europe. Exports rose from 20,000 tons a year in 1955 to almost 150,000 tons 20 years later, as 90 percent of total Central American exports went to the U.S. market.[71] According to the U.S. Department of Agriculture, from 1981 to 1992 Central America exported over 612,760 tons of beef to the United States.

Ironically, the cattle stampede and destruction of Central America's rainforests has resulted in declining beef consumption and growing hunger among the majority of Central Americans. Since the capitalist export sector monopolizes the best land, the rural poor cannot grow enough food to survive or afford to buy beef. In Costa Rica, where only 2,000 ranchers control more than half of all agricultural land in the country, beef production doubled between 1959 and 1973, while per capita beef consumption dropped from thirty to nineteen pounds over the same period.[72] Even in prerevolutionary Nicaragua, which became the only country in Central America with more head of cattle than people, per capita beef consumption declined during the 1970s.[73] As part of this general "protein flight," a typical housecat in the United

States now consumes more beef than the average Central American peasant.[74]

Central American beef exporters enjoy a number of competitive advantages in comparison to domestic producers in the U.S. market. In particular, North American ranchers suffer higher costs because of the need to supply feed grain to cattle during the winter, as well as higher land prices (rents) and labor costs. Central America's most important cost advantages over the United States lie primarily in the cheaper cost of equivalent areas of ranchland and freedom from the costs of corn and hay feed during the winter months. About 60 percent of U.S.-produced beef is fed grain, hay, corn, straw, and other roughage. These competitive advantages are rooted in the massive conversion of tropical rainforests into extensive pastures. In fact, Central American beef costs one-fourth of the amount needed to produce grass-fed beef in the United States.[75]

The rapid expansion of hamburger joints and pet and frozen food industries has created a market niche for the cheaper, leaner, grass-fed beef from Central America over the more expensive, redder cuts of U.S. grain-fattened beef. (The red, well-marbled meat of grain-fed cattle is graded by the U.S. Department of Agriculture as prime or choice cuts used for steaks, roasts, and other more expensive meats.) It is estimated that imports of cheaper Central American beef reduce the price of hamburger by about five cents a pound in the United States. For instance, the average price of imported Central American beef was $0.67 per pound in 1978, compared to $1.50 for U.S.-produced beef. Some U.S. officials have claimed that beef imports have done more to hold down food price inflation than any other single government initiative.[76]

Central American beef exporters also enjoy competitive advantages in the U.S. import market in comparison to South American countries, which are restricted by the presence of hoof-and-mouth disease. All beef produced south of the Panama Canal is banned for export into the United States, unless it is pre-cooked, which imposes a prohibitive cost.

In recent years, beef exports have declined because of regional military conflicts, growing protectionism, and falling prices, as well as declining per capita beef consumption by the increasingly health-conscious U.S. market. Between 1960 and 1980, beef production dou-

Table 1
Deforestation in Central America

	1961		1991		Average Annual Deforestation, 1980–1990	
	Total forested area(sq.mi)	% of total area	Total forested area(sq.mi)	% of total area	Square miles deforested per year	% of total area
Central America	116,300	58%	61,844	31%	4,208	1.6%
Belize*	3,907	44%	3,771	42%	34	0.7%
Costa Rica	10,996	55%	4,417	22%	479	6.9%
El Salvador	888	11%	325	4%	19	3.2%
Guatemala	32,432	77%	14,017	33%	347	2.0%
Honduras	27,413	63%	12,125	28%	347	2.3%
Nicaragua	24,834	49%	12,456	25%	467	2.7%
Panama	15,830	54%	14,733	49%	139	0.9%

*1972 figure.
Note: total area of Central America equals 201,992 square miles.
Sources: Myers (1981:5); Food and Agriculture Organization of the United Nations, *Production 42*, Statistics Series no. 88 (1988); WRI, *World Resources 1990–91: A Report by the World Resources Institute* (New York: Oxford University Press, 1990).

bled and exports tripled in Costa Rica, Guatemala, Honduras, and Nicaragua. Since then, however, beef exports to the United States have steadily declined, forcing the region's producers to scramble for new markets. Total beef exports declined from 162,000 metric tons (40 percent of total production) in 1979 to 61,000 tons (19 percent of total production) in 1985; total beef production dropped from 400,000 tons to 318,000 tons. In 1991, the United States imported only 46,231 tons of Central American beef, a substantial decline from the 1970s.[77]

Despite this decline in beef exports, deforestation has continued apace. Regionwide, an estimated 4,208 square miles of Central America's tropical forests and woodlands are destroyed each year. In 1961, 116,301 square miles of tropical forests and woodlands blanketed 57 percent of the region's total area. Today, only 52,340 square miles remain to cover 26 percent of total area, representing the destruction of over 63,960 square miles of forest in a mere 30 years (see Table I).

The impact on the landscape has been enormous. The isthmus of Central America is being ecologically transformed into one great stock ranch. Once traveling through hundreds of miles of dense woodlands in the 1950s, the entire paved length of the Pan American Highway (including its 3,700-meter summit in Costa Rica) is now surrounded by croplands and *repasto*, planted pastures of aggressive African grasses such as guinea, pará, molasses, jaragua, pangola, and African star.

In 1955, some 4.7 million head of cattle grazed on 8.5 million acres of pasture. Twenty years later, over 10 million cattle occupied 20 million acres, an area exceeding that of all other agricultural land combined. Without the importation of the more palatable, productive, and aggressive colonizing varieties of African grasses, the enormous expansion of export-beef production would not have been possible.[78]

The massive "Africanization" of Central America's forests and fields—the conversion of over 25 percent of its entire land mass into permanent pasture, more land than that used for all other agricultural commodities combined—is considered to be the most dramatic socially created ecological transformation in the region's history (see Tables 2 and 3).[79]

Countless numbers of unique animal, plant, and insect species found nowhere else in the world will soon be lost forever, along with the habitat for many migratory bird species that make Central Amer-

Table 2
Central America's Changing Landscape
(square miles)

	1972	1987	Average Annual Land-use Increases 1972–1987 (sq.mi)
Total Area	**201,992**	**201,992**	
Land Area	**196,822**	**196,772**	
Permanent Crop Land	23,579	26,282	+ 180
Arable Land	18,591	20,788	+ 146
Permanent Crops	4,988	5,494	+ 34
Permanent Pasture	30,347	51,845	+ 1433
Forest & Woodland	90,648	69,174	- 1432
Other Land	45,398	45,471	+ 5

Sources: same as Table 1

Table 3
Expansion of Cattle Pasture in Central America

	Total Area (sq.mi)	1961		1987		Annual Rate of Pasture Expansion
		Pasture (sq.mi)	% of area	Pasture (sq.mi)	% of area	
Central America	201,992	28,055	14%	51,845	25%	915
Belize*	8,885	143	1%	185	2%	1.6
Costa Rica	19,730	3,741	19%	8,880	45%	198
El Salvador	8,124	2,340	29%	2,355	29%	0.6
Guatemala	42,042	4,011	9%	5,290	12%	49
Honduras	43,278	7,747	18%	9,768	22%	78
Nicaragua	50,193	6,602	13%	20,270	40%	526
Panama	29,760	3,471	12%	5,097	17%	62.5

* 1972 figures
Sources: same as Table I

ica their winter home. For instance, the rapidly dwindling forests of Panama lie in the path of three of the four major bird migration routes between North and South America and support 800 bird species, more than the number found in the United States and Canada combined.

At least twenty-four major species of wildlife are now threatened with extinction in Honduras and Guatemala, including jaguars, pumas, river otters, manatees, tapirs, ocelots, giant anteaters, crested eagles, and other large animals (particularly mammals), which require expansive areas of primary tropical forest to survive.[80] These genetic storehouses are for all practical purposes nonrenewable, since certain lowland rainforest ecosystems require a successional process of 1,000 years after large-scale clearing before a full primary status can be achieved once again—if ever. The destruction of these unique and wonderful ecosystems represents, in Norman Myers' words, "one of the greatest biological debacles to occur on the face of the earth."[81]

Costa Rica is symptomatic of the crisis. Although it possesses the most extensive park system in Central America, covering some 22 percent (or 4,417 square miles) of the country, Costa Rica also has the highest national deforestation rate (6.6 percent) of any country in Latin America, including Brazil and Ecuador.[82] Often touted as a model of conservation for the third world, the Costa Rican government is finding itself increasingly unable and unwilling to reconcile the intensifying conflict that pits environmental protection and growing inequality against a debt-ridden economy dependent upon the export of cheap renewable and nonrenewable resources.

Numerous species of flora and fauna, particularly larger mammals, are dependent on these relatively small islands of preservation in a sea of ecological devastation. But their survival requires much larger territories than the rapidly dwindling forests remaining in the country's parks and protected areas in immediate danger of extinction. All species of cat and monkey are endangered, a condition aggravated by illegal commercial hunting. Also among the country's sixteen officially endangered animal species are the tapir, manatee, two highland squirrels, and the giant anteater. Eleven species of birds are also endangered, including seven birds of prey.[83]

Most of Costa Rica's parks are not even adequately maintained, but menaced by encroaching cattle ranchers and growing numbers of displaced peasants who move into protected areas to begin farming and/or mining. Over the last decade, United Brands and other producers switched from banana production on some of their plantations to the more profitable but less labor-intensive palm oil. Thousands of unemployed banana workers have since traveled into the tropical forests of Corcovado National Park to mine gold and poach wildlife, resulting in deforestation, habitat destruction, siltation, and soil erosion.[84]

The Failure of Deforestation for Development

Development on the agricultural frontier through the destruction of tropical rainforests has proved to be an economic and ecological disaster in Central America.

Unlike the rich volcanic soils found in the highland and Pacific coastal regions, which can support intensive cattle ranching indefinitely given the proper care, the soils underlying the Caribbean rainforests are mostly poor, their nutrients leached by millions of years of torrential rains. Rather than residing in the shallow and poorly drained soils underneath the ground, about 90 percent of the ecosystem's nutrients exist in the biomass which makes up the living canopy of plants and the thin layer of humus above the ground.

In the words of Douglas Shane, "some sixty million years of evolution have enabled the flora of the tropical forest to perfect methods of capturing and storing essential nutrients such as nitrogen, calcium, potassium and phosphorus before they are flushed into ubiquitous river systems."[85] Once this protective canopy is cut and burned, rainforest soils lose the ability to replenish nutrients, which quickly leach beyond the shallow root zones of newly planted pasture grasses and food crops. The natural biomass that sustains the maintenance of nutrients in the ecosystem is quickly reduced to a low biomass with little storage capacity.

Nearly 9,000 of the more than 22,400 families to have received land under the Honduran agrarian reform over the last thirteen years have been forced to abandon their plots.[86] Soils with high clay contents common to Central America's rainforest zones are particularly vulnerable, as noted above, literally turning into brick once exposed to compaction by grazing cattle, torrential rains, and the blazing sun.

Other soils high in acid eventually kill pasture grasses in a few short years, giving birth to noxious weeds and insect pests. The neurotoxins emitted by these poisonous weeds accumulate in the grazing cattle, often resulting in their death. James J. Parsons notes: "Unless carefully managed, and usually fertilized, both planted and natural grasses become sparse or woody with overgrowth, trampling, compaction, and declining soil fertility."[87]

What was once an oasis of jungle life is quickly reduced into a weed-infested wasteland. As the soil degrades, large ranchers clear new areas for pasture, exacerbating destruction of the jungle and displacement of small farmers. Ranchers then typically raise one head of cattle per 2.5 acres during the first seven years of production, but as the soil again deteriorates over the following five to ten years some twelve to seventeen acres of land are needed for each head of cattle. New areas are deforested once again. Grazing still occurs on older pastures until it is no longer productive, at which point it is abandoned. (In some areas, the poor condition of pastures and animal health, high operating costs, and low prices have combined to wipe out any potential profits for the cattle ranchers. Many would not survive economically without alternative sources of income.)[88]

By then the damage to the land is usually permanent. Unlike peasant-based agriculture, which allows for the regeneration of secondary forest growth after the land is abandoned, the use of African pasture grasses and overgrazing deters the secondary rejuvenation of the jungle, obstructing the processes by which nature "heals itself."[89]

One of the most serious long-term environmental impacts of overgrazing in both the Pacific and Caribbean lowlands is soil compaction (or hardening of the ground). In turn, this problem impedes drainage and reduces soil permeability, resulting in more rapid water runoff, accelerated wind and water erosion of the soil, and eventual gully formation, particularly in hillier terrains. Already over 17 percent of Costa Rica is severely eroded and 24 percent moderately eroded. Soil losses, 80 percent of which are caused by overgrazing on degraded pasture lands, reaches an astounding 680 million tons a year, choking waterways with sediment and causing millions of dollars in damage to hydroelectric facilities, which provide over 80 percent of the nation's electricity. Erosion rates are particularly severe on pasture lands in wetter forest zones, averaging an incredible 162 to 324 metric tons per acre annually. Virtually every major watershed in the country is seriously degraded.[90]

In the once-vast rainforests of the Petén in Guatemala, which have lost over five million cubic meters of wood since 1969, annual soil losses on degraded pasture lands is between 1,813 and 2,849 metric tons per square mile.[91] Such massive erosion leads to great fluctuations in the water table (including drought stress in the dry season and flooding in the rainy season), as rapid runoff from the compacted lands allows smaller amounts of moisture to be absorbed into the ground, disrupting the nutrient recycling systems of the soil.[92] Considerable soil erosion and sedimentation has already damaged the Motagua, Sarstún, and Polochic rivers and watersheds surrounding Lake Izabal, Guatemala's largest lake.[93]

The widespread destruction of forests for cattle ranching is also resulting in regional climatic changes. A pristine rainforest canopy acts as a protective umbrella, breaking the force of torrential downpours and recycling the moisture throughout the ecosystem. But with the clearing of the forest, water-recycling systems are destroyed. Daytime temperatures rise on the converted savannas, decreasing relative humidity and precipitation levels while increasing the rate of transpiration.[94] As a result, the grasslands and surrounding forests suffer from increased drought stress.[95]

In fact, regional rainfall is declining as much as one-third of an inch annually, reflecting marked alterations in the climate.[96] In central Panama, deforestation has reduced the average annual rainfall some 17 inches over the last fifty years.[97] When it does rain, the water rushes off the barren slopes to cause downstream flooding, soil erosion, and siltation of waterways.[98]

Localized climatic changes also occur with the cooler nighttime and warmer daytime temperatures radiated by deforested lands. According to a USAID report, almost 40 percent of Nicaragua's landscape is affected by significant changes in climate, hydrology, soil conditions, and biological complexity.[99] How the so-called "greenhouse effect" and global climate are affected by the destruction of Central America's forest and in particular by the release of carbon dioxide from burning forests and methane gases from cattle wastes, remains unknown.[100]

Conclusion

Despite the growing ecological and social crisis posed by the destruction of Central America's tropical rainforests, the region's ruling classes are showing little interest in exploring more sustainable and socially just modes of production.

Tropical rainforests are indeed a rich environment for efficiently and sustainably growing food—as various indigenous populations have demonstrated in practice. The Lacandon Maya's traditional system of rainforest agriculture produces almost 5,200 pounds of shelled corn and 4,000 pounds of root and vegetable crops per acre annually (compared to only 9 pounds of beef per acre under current capitalist forms of land use). The Lacandones produce these yields for five to seven consecutive years before the forest plot is allowed to recover for five to ten years under a system of agroforestry that conserves and regenerates the rainforest biome.[101]

The wasteful exploitation of rainforests, and the misery of small farmers who live at their edge, could be ended through the implementation of "sustainable agrarian reform measures," based on the replacement of cereals, roots, and grasses with alternative diversified tree-crops or multistoried forms of agriculture.[102] Another option would be to redistribute prime farmland in the capitalist export sector to the rural poor majorities of Central America, as was done in revolutionary Nicaragua during the 1980s. This not only reduced hunger and poverty in that country, but also greatly diminished peasant migration to the tropical rainforest.[103]

In either case, meaningful agrarian and economic reform offers the best hope of ending deforestation and bringing a more equitable, ecologically sustainable mode of life to the people of Central America. But due to the threat that these alternative measures pose to the economic wealth and political power of landed oligarchs and the agrarian bourgeoisie, the governments they control are unwilling to promote these more sustainable production systems. Their solution to growing ecological degradation is to keep destroying more tropical rainforests through the forces of repression, and in the process reproducing the social and ecological crisis endemic to the rest of the region.

Time is running out. The remaining jungle will be lost forever, unless major political and economic changes which present viable alternatives to the destruction of tropical rainforests soon take place. This must include the implementation of genuine and comprehensive agrarian reform designed to eliminate the impoverishment of the peasantry. With peaceful avenues to democratic change currently blocked by militarization and U.S. foreign policy, it may be that the only hope for an end to the destruction is the revolutionary struggle being waged in the rainforests of Central America.

KEY TO MAP

BELIZE, with little agricultural development and a small but growing cattle industry, has a relatively low deforestation rate of roughly 34 to 42 square miles annually. Forests cover 70 percent (some 3,475 square miles) of the country, with some 40 percent of the original primary forest remaining. Most deforestation results form small timber and commercial cattle industries, expanding citrus plantations, and an influx (45,000 and rising) of Guatemalan and Salvadoran refugees fleeing the region's repressive governments.

In HONDURAS, peasant farming, logging, and export-agriculture cut down roughly 250 to 300 square miles of rainforest each year. At current rates, the country's 8,880 square miles of rainforest will disappear within the next thirty years. Soil erosion eats away at 6.8 percent of the national territory.

In GUATEMALA, cattle ranching, oil and gas exploration, logging, peasant colonization, and government counterinsurgency operations contribute to the deforestation of 350 square miles annually. The Petén rainforest has lost 5 million cubic meters of wood annually since 1969. Less than 35 percent of the country's original forest cover remains.

Logging, peasant migration, and clearing for cattle grazing are destroying the remaining 10,810 square miles of rainforests in **PANAMA** at the rate of 310 square miles (or 197,600 acres) annually. Two-thirds of the nation's farmers squat on indigenous and national forest land; the Bayano Kuna Indians have lost at least 80 percent of their land to loggers and colonists in the last few years.

In COSTA RICA, Central America's leading beef, banana, and hardwood exporter to the United States, 4,054 square miles of lowland and lower montane tropical rainforests are disappearing at a rate of 230 square miles annually. By the year 2000 there may be no primary rainforests left outside of national parks, which are becoming increasingly degraded (the parks system covers some 25 percent of the country). Soil loss, caused mostly by overgrazing, reaches 680 million tons a year, with the result that approximately 10 percent of Costa Rica's land, some 1.24 million acres, has been abandoned (including one-fourth of all pasture land).

Prior to the revolution in NICARAGUA, the country's 16,000 square mile rainforest receded 386 square miles annually, the highest rate in Central America. Under the Sandinistas, government-sponsored agrarian reform helped to lower deforestation rates to 193 square miles a year, greatly reducing the destruction of Central America's largest rainforest. Privatization of state farms and many cooperatives by the Chamorro government has brought new pressures on the forests.

The Receding Rainforest

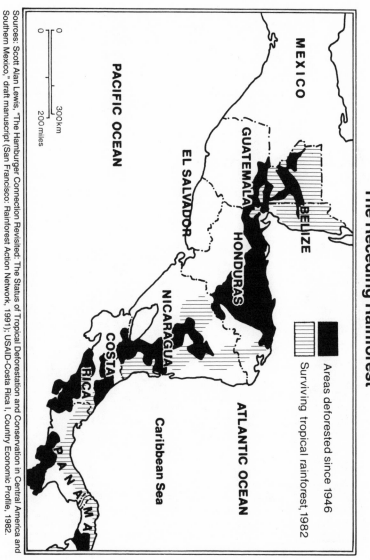

Areas deforested since 1946

Surviving tropical rainforest, 1982

MEXICO

GUATEMALA

BELIZE

EL SALVADOR

HONDURAS

NICARAGUA

COSTA RICA

PANAMA

PACIFIC OCEAN

ATLANTIC OCEAN

Caribbean Sea

0   300km

0   200miles

Sources: Scott Alan Lewis, "The Hamburger Connection Revisited: The Status of Tropical Deforestation and Conservation in Central America and Southern Mexico," draft manuscript (San Francisco: Rainforest Action Network, 1991); USAID-Costa Rica I, Country Economic Profile, 1982.

5
THE NICARAGUAN REVOLUTION
AND THE
LIBERATION OF NATURE

Not only humans desired liberation.
The entire ecology cried for it. The
revolution
Is also for lakes, rivers, trees and animals

Father Ernesto Cardenal[1]

On July 19, 1979, the Sandinista National Liberation Front (FSLN) assumed formal political power over the Nicaraguan government after a bloody popular insurrection toppled the brutal dictatorship of Anastasio Somoza Debayle.[2] The roots of the revolution lay in the legacy of widespread poverty and repression experienced by Nicaragua's popular classes, the products of a United States-promoted model of disarticulated capitalist development.[3]

By the time of the insurrection, large landholders representing a mere 1 percent of the population controlled half of the land in Nicaragua. Somoza himself owned 20 percent of the nation's prime farmland. Export commodity crops—cotton, coffee, sugar, tobacco, and cattle—dominated the agricultural landscape. Over 60 percent of rural people were deprived of the land they needed to feed themselves.[4] Over half of Nicaragua's children were undernourished under Somoza.[5] Impoverished Nicaraguan peasants working on the large export estates during the short harvest season received wages as low as a dollar a day. Malnutrition, disease, and illiteracy were rampant.

Somoza had used the coercive powers of the state to monopolize control of the economy, including the economic resources of Nicaragua's national and dependent bourgeoisie. This led to a profound split between the anti-Somocista bourgeoisie and the Somoza family. With Somoza's rip-off of international aid following the 1972 Managua earthquake and the assassination of respected businessman-lawyer Joaquín Chamorro on January 10, 1978, the split turned into open opposition. Many reluctant capitalists and private-sector leaders moved to form the Broad Opposition Front (Frente Amplio Opositor, FAO). In the ten months preceding the revolution, the FAO organized a series of general strikes that seriously weakened the regime.[6]

Some 50,000 Nicaraguans lost their lives in the revolution, with material damage estimated at an additional $480 million by the United Nations, a huge sum for such a small economy. To make matters worse, Somoza had sacked the national treasury before fleeing to Miami, leaving the country with a $1.6 billion foreign debt, the highest in Central America.[7]

The new Government of National Reconstruction (GNR) immediately faced the monumental task of not only rebuilding and transforming a society crippled by the 1972 earthquake, which had killed up to 20,000 people and caused a minimum of $772 million in damage, including the destruction of 75 percent of Managua's housing and 90 percent of its commercial capacity; but also with revitalizing a society devastated by civil war.

In addition to an economically devastated society, Somoza left behind something else. The Sandinistas discovered a national environmental crisis of massive proportions. Most of Nicaragua's Pacific coastal plain suffered serious pesticide contamination, including subterranean water resources. In 1977 alone, according to a United Nations report, insecticide-caused environmental and social damage amounted to $200 million a year. (The most foreign exchange cotton had ever earned amounted to maximum of $141 million in 1973.)[8] The country held the dubious distinction of being a world leader in pesticide poisonings; nearly 400 pesticide-related deaths were reported annually.[9] Pesticide runoff from cotton agriculture, toxic chemical pollution from lakeside industries, and untreated sewage dumped from the capital city had virtually killed Lake Managua, a body of water equivalent in size to California's Lake Tahoe.

The World Health Organization found that polluted water led to 17 percent of all Nicaraguan deaths.[10] Deforestation had caused widespread soil erosion, dust storms, and flash floods. In the eastern half of the country, cattle ranching was eating into Nicaragua's extensive tropical rainforests, 30 percent of which disappeared in the 1970s.[11] Many species of wildlife teetered on the brink of extinction, the result of habitat destruction and unregulated sale in local and world markets. These environmental problems merged with poverty and the lack of social services to give the Nicaraguan people the lowest life expectancy in all of Central America.[12]

For forty-five years, the Somoza family utilized its control of the National Guard and U.S. financial and military support to pillage the country's natural resources, often for direct personal gain. Profits derived from the exploitation of nature were seldom used to serve the majority of the population by building broad-based educational or health systems, but rather flowed into the bank accounts of the "Somocistas" and growing agrarian bourgeoisie. Foreign and domestic companies had access to the country's resources, as long as they paid the necessary "concessions" to the government and to Somoza himself. For example, Somoza received a "gift" of $1 million in exchange for granting the Japanese transnational Kawasaki rights to explore for geothermal energy. In another instance, the U.S.-owned Nicaraguan Long Leaf Pine Company (NIPCO) directly paid the Somoza family a percentage of the company's multimillion dollar timber business from 1945 to 1960, in exchange for favorable terms of trade, such as not having to reforest clear-cut areas. Thus, by 1961, NIPCO had cut all of the commercially valuable coastal pines (*Pinus caribea*) in northeast Nicaragua, leaving over 1,160 square miles denuded.

Between 1968 and 1972, Somoza granted eight forest concessions to foreign corporations covering 10,425 square miles. By the mid-1970s, these companies were processing eighty million board feet annually. In addition to the over-exploitation of the Atlantic Coast and Central Mountain Zone pine forests, virtually all of the valuable commercial forest species were cleared along the Pacific coast during the 1970s.[13]

Although there were a few United Nations-sponsored environmental projects in Nicaragua, most attempts by environmentalists, trade unions, and other popular organizations seeking a more equitable distribution and rational management of the country's social and natural resources were seen as a "Communist-inspired" threat to the "stability" of the system. In 1976, a group of Nicaraguan environmentalists proposed that the government create a Ministry of Natural Resources. Somoza quickly rejected their proposal and threatened the group with harsh reprisals if they met again. (Jaime Incer, considered the founder of Nicaragua's environmental movement, did manage to persuade the Somoza government to establish Masaya Volcano National Park, which protects fifteen square miles of extremely rare, dry tropical forest surrounding the volcano. Incer was also one of the small group of environmentalists who unsuccessfully petitioned Somoza to create a ministry of natural resources.)

The social and environmental crisis had reached the point where more and more Nicaraguans recognized the need for political change. Environmentalists saw that only a fundamental transformation in the country's power structure could open the door to ecologically sound and socially beneficial development policies. Many even took to the hills and streets to join the Sandinista guerrillas who were waging war against the Somoza regime. Some environmentalists, such as Ivan Montenegro Baez and Edguard Munguia Alvarez, perished in the struggle for liberation. As limnologist Salvador Montenegro, one of the proponents of the Ministry of Natural Resources, told me, "revolutionary struggle and environmentalism became one."

The Birth of Revolutionary Ecology

With the triumph of the revolution, Nicaragua's environmental movement was presented an opportunity for reorienting the country on a path toward sustainable development. On July 22, 1979, just three days after the FSLN came to power, the same group of environmentalists that proposed a ministry of natural resources to Somoza brought a similar proposal to the new government. The Sandinistas had already prohibited natural resource extraction by foreign companies by nationalizing Nicaragua's forest, mineral, and aquatic resources. Former Vice President Sergio Ramírez commented that nationalization gave Nicaraguans the ability to protect their natural resources and "to develop them and exploit them in accordance with our own needs and our own vision of the future."[14]

On August 24, 1979, the new government responded to the environmentalists' proposal by creating the Nicaraguan Institute of Natural Resources and the Environment (Instituto Nicaragüense de Recursos Naturales y del Ambiente, IRENA)—the country's first environmental agency—with the statement:

> The environment and natural resources are considered to have a great impact on society; they deserve the attention of the State, which aspires to socioeconomic change based on national sovereignty, self-determination, and the participation of the population. . . . The preservation of natural resources is not a goal for its own sake, but must be directed toward elevating the quality of life![15]

With the creation of IRENA, there developed within a limited sector of the Nicaraguan government an "ecological socialist" or "revolutionary ecologist" tendency. These Sandinistas recognized that comprehensive environmental programs and policies were absolutely essential for addressing the country's social and economic crisis, just as comprehensive social and economic reform of the existing model of disarticulated capitalist development was essential for addressing the country's ecological crisis.

IRENA immediately assumed a powerful and central role in the process of social transformation, taking responsibility for all of the country's renewable and nonrenewable resources, including the nationalized mining, fishery, forestry, and wildlife sectors. Within a few months, some 400 persons, including administrators and scientists, worked at the central IRENA office in Managua.[16]

The tendency toward "revolutionary ecology" came to be reflected in IRENA's environmental policies and policy battles, which included programs in reforestation, watershed management, pollution control, wildlife conservation, national parks, environmental education and the conservation of genetic diversity. Other government and nongovernmental agencies worked with IRENA, as well as mass-based organizations, on pesticide control and regulation, energy conservation, agrarian reform, appropriate technology, and worker health and safety.[17]

The basic aims of these programs were substantial. They set out, first of all, to reverse the social and ecological impoverishment of the subsistence sector. Secondly, the programs sought to reconstruct and protect the ecological and communal conditions of agricultural export production, including the development of more ecologically and economically appropriate productive forces, which would lessen Nicaragua's dependency on expensive oil imports and other inputs. They acted to eliminate or reduce work hazards and pollution, etc. Finally, the programs sought to preserve and protect unique natural wonders for scientific research and as a condition of consumption (e.g., national parks) for the majority of Nicaraguans—of present and future generations.

Supported by foreign aid, especially from the Scandinavian countries, as well as by multilateral aid agencies like the United Nations Food and Agriculture Organization (FAO) and the Organization of American States (OAS), these environmental programs were unique in that they contributed to a larger process of social transformation and national liberation. This process sought a new model of economic development devoted to the needs of the "popular classes."[18]

The Sandinista revolution also created the political environment where nongovernmental groups like the Nicaraguan Association of Biologists and Ecologists (ABEN), and later the Nicaraguan Environmental Movement (MAN), had access to the highest levels of government and were free to work without fear of repression (in contrast to environmental work in Honduras, El Salvador, and Guatemala, where repression is common). ABEN was assisted by HABITAT, the student environmental movement at the School of Ecology and Natural Resources, University of Central America.

The Somoza dictatorship's legacy of underdevelopment was devastating. It left Nicaragua with a lack of trained personnel and insufficient knowledge and information about tropical ecosystems and ecological processes. The responsibility for environmental legislation had been assigned to one governmental person, who had no specific experience in the field.

The new government also lacked the economic resources necessary to manage many of the proposed programs for ecological recovery. IRENA and other governmental agencies would, in fact, come to rely on the support and participation of both national and international environmental organizations for the implementation of governmental policy—a new form of grassroots environmentalism.[19]

In Defense of Nature, 1979–1986

Central to the process of revolutionary social transformation in Nicaragua was the pursuit of a nonaligned foreign policy, economic diversification, democratization of the state and social planning, and agrarian reform. Key industries and agricultural estates controlled by the Somocista agrarian bourgeoisie, including the one-fifth of the nation's farmland owned by the Somoza family, were confiscated and placed under the direct control of the government. Workers on the new state farms and peasant farmers were encouraged to join unions, grassroots organizations, and other participatory structures.

The aim of the state was to continue agricultural export production for the world market, but in the future the foreign exchange earnings (or social surplus) would be utilized to attack poverty, provide education, housing, and health care for the popular classes, and fund the process of social transformation.[20]

Many Nicaraguans saw the establishment of state farms as inadequate and soon landless and land-poor peasants began organizing land confiscations and demanding more comprehensive agrarian reform measures. By the beginning of 1980, increased political pressure by the Association of Rural Workers (Associación de Trabajadores del Campo, ATC) and National Union of Farmers and Cattle Ranchers (Unión Nacional de Agricultores y Ganaderos, UNAG)—along with the stagnation of domestic grain production—finally led the government to begin providing campesinos with better credit services, guaranteed prices, technical assistance, and agricultural inputs.[21]

But campesino impatience continued to grow, and on July 19, 1981, President Daniel Ortega Saavedra announced the proposed Agrarian Reform Law to the applause of one-half million Nicaraguans gathered to celebrate the second anniversary of the revolution's triumph. At the time the law was announced, the government estimated that roughly 30 percent of the country's agricultural land was abandoned, idle, or inadequately used.[22] With the enactment of the law and land redistribution in August, the government initiated the first comprehensive program in the country's history for reversing the social impoverishment of the Nicaraguan peasantry and promoting domestic food production.[23] By July 1984, the government had given to some 45,000 beneficiaries, as family farm owners or members of farm cooperatives, free titles to 2.4 million acres—more than one-fifth of the nation's farmland, and more than ten times all the land owned by poor peasants before the revolution.[24]

Despite its early political success, the agrarian reform program began encountering a number of organizational and technical difficulties.[25] In addition, ecological degradation of the Nicaraguan countryside contributed to severe flooding and drought in the 1982–1983 and 1983–1984 growing seasons, seriously impairing peasant-based corn and bean production. Spurred by heavy rains (twenty-one inches in one day alone!), the 1982 flood was particularly devastating, killing 35 people while affecting over 35,000 others, by destroying 4,500 homes and 39 bridges and 60 percent of the corn crop. Damage estimates totaled $357 million dollars. These problems were magnified by the poor ecological conditions and inadequacy of land distributed to some of the peasantry, including the formerly poor and landless campesinos organized communally into the Sandinista Agricultural Cooperatives (CAS).[26]

In response to the corn crisis, the government shifted its focus back to the state farms of the Pacific region in 1984, this time initiating a massive program of irrigated corn production heavily dependent on expensive inputs and equipment. Michael Zalkin notes that while significant social resources were invested in campesino farms and cooperatives, "a popular mobilization to guarantee timely grain marketing was never attempted, nor was a systematic program of improvements in grain production and storage methods implemented."[27]

As the agrarian reform failed to provide fully adequate social resources, tensions increased among the peasantry. This led some small sectors to collaborate with the U.S.-supported counterrevolutionary forces, or contras. Fighting under the leadership of former National Guard officers, the contras sought to destabilize and overthrow the revolutionary government.

Gradually, the FSLN realized that their continued emphasis on state farm production, their "over-respect" for reactionary and patriotic sectors of the agrarian bourgeoisie, and their lack of commitment to the full revitalization of the subsistence sector, was creating political unrest. A series of peasant demonstrations in 1985 was coupled with low support for the FSLN in some rural areas during the 1984 national elections, as the U.S. contra war and trade embargo expanded. (The FSLN received 63 percent of the total vote.) The Sandinistas shifted their development focus once more in 1985, redistributing large quantities of land to individual small farmers for the first time.[28]

Under the reformulated Law of Agrarian Reform in January 1986, land redistribution of "underutilized" farms (including smaller holdings) to both cooperatives and individual families continued. Meanwhile, state marketing schemes attempted to improve terms of trade and consumer goods distribution for peasant producers. Eventually, the government would give private and cooperative land titles covering nearly 5.2 million acres (over one-third of Nicaragua's farmland) to about 120,000 peasant families—more than half of the country's peasant population. In addition, the revolutionary government prevented the new land titles from being held as collateral on bank loans, removing the primary "legal" means by which land had been appropriated from small farmers in the past.

This stability meant that peasants took a greater interest in the long-term potential and productivity of their own lands and laid the groundwork for the implementation of soil conservation and other small-scale projects with clear environmental benefits.[29]

As part of this larger process of agrarian and economic reform, the Sandinista government also launched a series of projects designed to reverse the ecological impoverishment of the peasantry. As in much of Central America, the ecological crisis of the subsistence sector was reflected in declining fallow cycles and soil fertility; deforestation, erosion, and watershed destruction; flash flooding and sedimentation of waterways; prolonged drought; wildlife scarcities; and poor water quality. Land degradation was so severe that the arable layer of soil had been eliminated on hillsides covering thousands of miles, particularly in the Matagalpa, Estelí, and Ocotal regions. Soil erosion was also quite severe on the steep slopes south of Managua.[30]

In coordination with many other government agencies and the agrarian reform, IRENA initiated a series of projects designed to restore, protect, and more rationally manage the ecological conditions of peasant *minifundio* production. Through the Western Erosion Control Project implemented in 1982, IRENA demonstrated a commitment to providing peasant communities with the education, technical assistance, and supplies needed to address problems of deforestation, erosion, and fertility loss. By the end of 1985, some 6,670 acres of achote, pine, and eucalyptus had been planted by the program to protect watersheds and provide windbreaks for crops, as well as the construction of 4,220 torrent-regulating dikes to control erosion and flooding.

In Managua, the Council of Environmental Quality promoted the cultivation of appropriate crops for soil conservation in the denuded Southern Managua Watershed, a project begun by IRENA in coordination with the area's small farmers. These efforts were extended in 1988 when the FAO and Dutch government supported a grassroots environmental education and restoration project (including reforestation and wildlife protection) called "Heroes and Martyrs of Veracruz." The project continued the work with peasant farmers to preserve some 500,000 acres of tropical dry forest and farmland in the degraded Pacific highlands, including the uppermost reaches of the rugged Marrabios watershed.[31]

Programs to reverse years of impoverishment and revitalize the subsistence sector were accompanied by a variety of national campaigns. By 1984, because of a massive vaccination campaign in which 70,000 Nicaraguan volunteer health workers participated, polio had been eliminated, cases of malaria decreased 40 percent, and cases of measles dropped from 3,784 to 104. By 1986, Nicaragua was allocating 14 percent of the national budget to health care, up from 3 percent in the days of Somoza. As a result, Nicaragua's infant mortality rate dropped from 120 per 1,000 live births in 1979 to 65 per 1,000 births by 1988, while the average life span increased from 53 to 60 years of age, despite the contra war. Improvements in health were so dramatic that Nicaragua won the 1982 World Health Organization prize for greatest achievement by a third world country.[32] Literacy campaigns reduced illiteracy from 58 percent to 12.9 percent.[33]

As part of the National Literacy Campaign of 1980, workers and peasants were also educated about the country's natural resources and environmental issues, such as erosion and deforestation. It was deemed essential that Nicaragua's popular classes understand the importance of these environmental programs if they were to be successfully integrated into the revolution. In 1981, IRENA established the Department of Environmental Education, which under the direction of Ruth Kelley introduced a highly successful environmental curriculum into the nation's school system. Elementary students participated actively in the department's programs, including tree planting, wildlife, and publicity projects. Many of these environmental education efforts received a much lower priority after the start of the contra war.[34]

Through "Campesino to Campesino," a community-based project supported by UNAG, small farmers initiated a process of environmental self-education, teaching communities throughout the country about soil conservation, biological control of agricultural pests, organic agriculture, and appropriate technology. The project's objective remains to promote and expand a campesino-led sustainable agricultural movement with its own vision of development, capable of forming national alternatives for food production and environmental preservation. This project was initiated in the context of numerous other projects in reforestation, solar ovens and more efficient wood stoves, soy and organic coffee, crop rotation and intercropping, tree planting, composting, landfills and improved latrines, agro-forestry, flood control, and windmills—all designed to restore the ecological conditions of subsistence production and promote a new model of sustainable peasant agriculture.[35]

Tropical Forest Management

The implementation of comprehensive agrarian reform in the early years of the revolution had an immediate impact on Nicaragua's rich tropical rainforests. By redistributing land to peasant families so that they could grow their own crops, the Ministry of Agriculture (MID-INRA) halted migrations from the Pacific coast to the agricultural frontier on the Atlantic side. By 1983, the government had halted all peasant colonization projects and removed state repression as a vehicle for cattle ranchers to displace peasants and destroy the forests.

While MIDINRA initially continued to encourage peasant families still living on the frontier to clear the rainforest for food production, the ministry soon came under fire from IRENA for implementing policies "against the principles of conservation."[36] MIDINRA responded in 1983 by limiting food production to subsistence farming and promoting ecologically sustainable permanent crops such as African palm, coconut, cocoa, and plantains. As a result, the annual rate of deforestation of Nicaragua's humid tropical rainforests had been cut in half to 194 square miles by 1985, compared to 386 square miles in the late 1970s, once the highest in Central America.[37]

Although foreign timber companies were no longer allowed to clear-cut the country's pine barrens in the north-central and northeast region, tree cutting for firewood, slash and burn agriculture, and development projects continued to claim large areas of forests elsewhere in the country. (More than 200 commercially viable varieties of trees exist among the 2,000-plus varieties known to grow there.) Deforestation and degradation of watersheds was particularly widespread along the Pacific coast and hillsides surrounding Managua and other western cities, contributing to severe soil erosion and flash flooding.[38] These dry tropical forests, already scarce, have disappeared almost totally from the Pacific volcanic ridge and coastal zones. In May of 1982, for instance, heavy rains in these fragile zones led to floods that destroyed almost all of the bridges in the León and Chinandega area, costing the government some $20 million to repair.[39]

To address critical environmental conditions caused by deforestation, IRENA launched four major reforestation projects (often with the assistance of voluntary environmental brigades from the United States). As high winds threatened to blow away valuable topsoil and cause other damage to communal and ecological conditions of agricultural production in both the export and subsistence sectors, the Western Erosion Control Project in the Pacific region of León built 745 miles of windbreaks in cotton-growing areas by planting some 3,000 trees a day over a two-year period.

In the watersheds surrounding both León and Managua, IRENA built thousands of minidams for erosion control, reforesting, and promoting permanent crop cultivation in order to stop mudslides that continued to damage low-lying areas. In the north-central Estelí region, IRENA replanted over 3,000 acres in an effort to restore the ocote pines that were decimated by transnational companies in the 1970s. The Northeast Forestry project did the same for the coastal pines that were clear-cut by the U.S. company NIPCO in the 1950s. Nurseries throughout the country grew two million trees annually for use in reforestation projects.[40]

National Parks

With the establishment of comprehensive agrarian reform policies in the early 1980s, many environmentalists hoped that IRENA's plans for a national park system would create a global model for rainforest conservation. In 1983, IRENA established a third national park and a new wildlife reserve and created plans for thirty-six forest preserves and protected areas. The plan, if fully implemented, would have given Nicaragua one of the highest percentages of protected areas and park lands (18 percent) of any country in the world—more than ten million acres. Many of these parks would have protected fragile rainforest areas.

By the mid-1980s, however, the contra war had militarized the wilderness. IRENA's plans were scaled back, now protecting areas comprising only 1.6 percent of Nicaragua's territory—although only 0.1 percent was managed in practice. These protected areas included the Zapatera Island National Park, Masaya Volcano National Park, and the Chacocente-Rio Escalante Wildlife Reserve, all located on the safer and less pristine Pacific coast. Protection of the few remaining pockets of wilderness on Nicaragua's Pacific side was especially crucial since the war forced other industries, such as forestry, to operate exclusively in this ecologically degraded region. By 1987, the Sandinistas had tripled the size of protected areas in the country from 0.5 percent under Somoza.[41]

One of Nicaragua's most pressing problems in wilderness conservation involved the polarizing tension that emerged between national park plans and indigenous land rights. In 1980, Lorenzo Cardenal, IRENA's director of national parks, declared Bosawas, the western hemisphere's largest tropical rainforest north of the Amazon Basin, a national reserve. Plans were made for national parks, wildlife refuges, biological reserves, and sustained-yield forestry within Bosawas' 4,250-square-mile boundaries.[42] The Bosawas reserve, according to Native American activists John Mohawk and Denis Shelton, was established with "the intent of benefiting indigenous communities and protecting the environment." Yet Miskito and Sumo Indians living there saw IRENA's park plans as an attempt to "nationalize" their lands.[43]

Aggravated by cultural insensitivity on the part of the Nicaraguan government, as well the contra war and political manipulations by the United States, military conflicts that foreclosed opportunities for establishing IRENA's plan for wilderness and cultural conservation soon developed. This clash would eventually give birth to a government-supported autonomy project for the entire Atlantic coast.[44]

Wildlife Conservation

In spite of the fact that the Somoza government signed the CITES Convention on International Trade in Flora and Fauna in 1973, Nicaragua was a Central American leader in the hunting and export of rare and endangered species during the 1970s. Spotted and other rare cat pelts brought high prices in both local and international markets, which devoured thousands of skins and birds annually. White-lipped peccaries, white-tailed deer, hawksbill turtles, crocodiles, caimans, freshwater otters, jaguars, ocelots, margays, and lobster were all extensively depleted or exterminated throughout Nicaragua.[45]

The green turtle (*Chelonia mydas*) suffered perhaps the greatest. In 1969, representatives from Costa Rica, Nicaragua, and Panama agreed to prohibit the exploitation and sale of green turtles and their eggs for three years. However, within a year Nicaragua opened two new turtle-processing plants, one in Puerto Cabezas and the other in Bluefields. Somoza and his associates owned "Tortugas SA" of Puerto Cabezas, while a foreign company owned "Frescamar" of Bluefields. Somoza's investment in turtle meat factories seriously threatened the already endangered green turtle and delivered a blow to the international movement to save this rare species. Between 1969 and 1975, the industry produced roughly 225 metric tons of turtle meat for export.[46]

After 1979, the Sandinista government moved vigorously to protect Nicaragua's diverse fauna population, which includes 750 bird species, 600 reptile and amphibian species, 200 mammal species, and 100 species of freshwater fish. When the Sandinistas nationalized the import/export banks, IRENA was able to ban the export of endangered species. By 1982, the environmental agency had established seasonal hunting bans for twenty-six endangered species of mammals, nineteen bird species and four reptile species, making Nicaragua one of the region's most strict compliers with the norms of CITES.[47]

The main challenge was to stop the contraband of wildlife sold to other countries, principally El Salvador and Honduras. IRENA launched extensive educational campaigns and initiated a system of marketplace and roadside inspection to make wildlife protection effective. To make up for shortages of border inspectors, the government organized local communities to democratically administer neighboring natural areas and resources, and protect these local ecological conditions of peasant production and consumption from illegal traders.

Most exemplary of IRENA's wildlife initiatives was the Sea Turtle Conservation Campaign. While government bans halted all green turtle exploitation on the Atlantic coast, except for subsistence hunting by Miskito Indians, the National Park Service initiated an elaborate program to save the Pacific coast's olive ridley (*Lepidochelys olivacea*), which nests on Nicaragua's sands by the thousands. The rapidly diminishing turtle eggs served as an important source of complementary income for many impoverished peasant communities near these beaches. IRENA's management and conservation program was able to organize and reduce the harvest of eggs, guaranteeing the conservation, incubation, and birth of sufficient young to repopulate the species. IRENA permitted only nearby local communities to gather the eggs under its direct supervision.

This effort, which included the creation of the Chococente-Rio Escalante Wildlife Refuge along the country's southwestern beaches, revolved around a broad-based environmental education campaign. Designed to allow local communities to democratically participate in the sustainable management of their own ecological conditions of subsistence production, including marine life, the model program quickly received worldwide attention for its innovation and success. Peasants who harvested the ridley's eggs, wholesalers and market vendors who sold the eggs as a delicacy, as well as consumers, were taught principles of conservation and laws regulating the eggs' sustainable appropriation, with harsh fines for anyone caught breaking the law.[48]

Energy and Appropriate Technology

In many third world countries, problems of deforestation, habitat destruction, and poverty are intimately connected to the peasantry's lack of access to alternative energy sources and appropriate technologies, as well as land, credit, and related social services.[49] Nicaragua is no exception.

Currently, approximately 50 percent of the energy consumed in Nicaragua is in the form of firewood, which is used predominately for cooking by the residential sector. Another 9 percent is in the form of vegetable residuals consumed in the agricultural and agro-industrial sectors. Most of the balance of the energy consumed in the nation, approximately 34 percent, is derived from petroleum. Of this amount, 35 percent is used as fuel in the transportation sector and 20 percent for electrical power production.[50]

Over 90 percent of all fuel used in the country's households and 25 percent in all industries is wood fuel. Some 1.1 million tons of firewood were consumed in Nicaragua's rural areas in 1982.[51] Therefore, efforts to lessen the social and ecological impoverishment of the peasantry required creating an appropriate technology program, especially in the area of renewable energy.

With the triumph of the revolution, the Nicaraguan Energy Institute (Instituto Nicaragüense de Energía, INE) worked with IRENA to promote alternative renewable energy technologies and other appropriate productive forces that would foster more democratic and equitable forms of sustainable rural development.[52] Small innovative programs in biomass, solar, wind, and microhydroelectricity were soon launched, including the development of three small hydroelectric plants in El Cuá and San José de Bocay (populations 2,000 and 4,000, respectively).

The Cuá-Bocay zone, in the northern portion of the country, was one of the hardest hit by the contra war. The Cuá-Bocay Project was designed in coordination with the Nicaragua Appropriate Technology Project (1984 to 1989) to generate electricity for the local town, including the health clinic and school, and to reduce a locally serious deforestation problem. It was there that the U.S. engineer Ben Linder was assassinated—shot at point-blank range—in April 1987 by the Contras, an act which served to further outrage and galvanize the U.S. environmental movement against U.S. policy in Nicaragua.

The first of the hydro facilities was completed in the town of El Cúa on May 1, 1986. Linder worked on the plant's design and construction during his employment at INE, from 1984 until his assassination. He was leading a site survey for the second plant on the river near San José de Bocay when he and his Nicaraguan coworkers were ambushed and killed. His colleagues have continued the work on the second plant.[53]

In coordination with the Center for Appropriate Technology Research (CITA-INRA)—a branch of the agricultural ministry—a series of other renewable energy projects were also initiated, including development of windmills, hand pumps, biogas and vehicle fuels, new agricultural equipment, and new cattle feeding methods. Working with the Center for Popular Education (CEPA), campesino communities sent elected representatives to the center outside of Estelí to work with technical advisors in the development and distribution of more appropriate technologies.

A number of projects supporting the use of more efficient woodstoves made of local materials were also initiated. These stoves reduced fuel consumption by up to 19 percent in many of these pilot projects.[54] The programs were important for reducing the hardships of rural women and children, who were often charged with the task of traveling great distances to search and haul firewood, experiencing many health problems related to the smoke from the older "open" stoves. According to Mira Brown, founder of the Nicaraguan Appropriate Technology Project (NICAT), damaged eyesight was one of the more common health problems related to the old stoves.

The Sandinistas also began exploring national energy conservation measures and experimenting with large-scale energy substitutes. The Office of Energy Conservation began an ambitious program to complete a series of national energy audits, as well as highly visible education campaigns for conservation. The government also developed plans to expand the nation's rail system as an alternative to the mostly unaffordable automobile. A rail line planned between Corinto and Managua saved the country an estimated fifteen to twenty million dollars annually in fuel imports.

In 1984, INE announced a goal of electricity self-sufficiency by the year 2000.[55] The aim of these "revolutionary energy programs" was to liberate the nation from its dangerous dependency on expensive international oil imports and technological inputs, which would in turn help free up foreign exchange for the purchase of more essential items such as medicines, etc.[56]

One such experiment with more economically and environmentally friendly productive forces involved the construction of the thirty-five-milliwatt Momotombo geothermal plant on the shores of Lake Managua, completed in August of 1983.[57] The first such plant in Nicaragua, it used steam heated by the magma underlying the Momotombo volcano to power its generators, a potentially limitless supply of cheap energy. Unfortunately, the plant emitted 8,640 cubic meters of hot residual water containing arsenic and highly concentrated salts, further contaminating Lake Managua with toxic and thermal pollution. Pollution control equipment was not included because the international credits that financed its construction did not cover environmental impact studies or funds to control ecological damage.[58]

Blessed with an extensive systems of lakes and rivers, the Sandinistas also initiated a series of large-scale hydro projects, including (with a loan from the Inter-American Development Bank) the construction of a pumping station at Asturias.[59] By the mid-1980s, renewable energy sources in the form of hydroelectric and geothermal power provided 42 percent of the country's total electricity.[60]

But perhaps the most innovative project was the construction of the controversial Tipitapa-Malacatoya (Timal) sugar complex, the largest in Central America.[61] As part of a sustainable energy project, eucalyptus and leucace trees were planted in between the circular sugar fields, where they would be harvested and burned along with cane wastes in the mill's boilers to generate electricity for both the plant and the national energy grid. Devotion of scarce state funds ($147 million, with an additional $103 million provided by Cuba) for the construction of the sugar refinery was considered highly risky by a number of observers because of the extremely low prices for sugar in the world market. By the mid-1980s, the sugar complex was producing some 3 percent of the country's total electric production.[62]

Biomass energy projects, or the use of crop wastes as solid fuel and fertilizer, were also developed in the cotton, coffee, livestock, and other agricultural sectors. In a project sponsored by Sweden, technology was employed to compress chopped-up cotton stalks into small briquette energy pellets.[63]

Water Quality and Lake Managua

Poor water quality poses an enormous environmental and human health problems in Nicaragua. A nationwide IRENA study in 1981 found that 50 percent of the water sources sampled were seriously polluted by sewage, 75 percent by agricultural residues, and 25 percent by highly toxic industrial contaminants.[64]

Lake Managua's southern watershed, the most highly developed and densely populated region of the country, is also the most polluted. Under the Somoza regime, Lake Managua (also referred to as Lake Xolotlán) was made into a chief dumping ground for Managua, receiving over 70,000 pounds of raw sewage from the capital daily. Soil erosion and sediment from the barren hillsides also contributed to the choking of the lake.[65]

Dozens of industries also looked to cut their environmentally related production costs and boost profits by polluting Lake Managua. Thirty-seven industrial plants located on the lake shore have freely dumped their waste there for years, including the U.S. corporation Pennwalt, Inc., which released an estimated forty tons of mercury into the lake between 1968 and 1981. (Mercury causes a series of neurologically related health problems ranging from birth defects to severe brain damage.)[66] An investigation by the Sandinista government and Pan American Health Organization found gross mercury contamination at the plant site, including mercury levels in the air of the facility six times higher than deemed permissible by the U.S. Occupational Safety and Health Administration (OSHA). As a result, 56 of the plant's 152 workers (37 percent) were found to have damaged central nervous systems—the result of mercury intoxication.[67]

When Pennwalt established operations in Nicaragua in order to supply Central America's growing market for chlorine and caustic soda, it was able to escape environmental regulations in the United States. Prior to the revolution, the plant was 40 percent owned by Pennwalt, 48 percent by a Nicaraguan business group, and 12 percent by the Somoza family. Free of stringent environmental and labor health and safety laws found in the United States, the operation yielded $1.2 million in dividends to stockholders between 1973 and 1978, as well as $5 million in profits on a $2 million initial investment.[68] Since the Somoza family owned 12 percent of Pennwalt's stock, the government looked the other way as mercury, sulfuric acid, toxaphene, chlordane, and many other toxic chemicals were dumped into the lake. This evasion of U.S. environmental law, however, inundated the once-sparkling blue Lake Managua with deadly poison.[69]

After the revolution, the Sandinista government faced an immediate problem. Aside from the contamination of fish sold in local markets, the contaminated water from Lake Managua had begun to seep into neighboring Asososca Lagoon, the capital city's most important reservoir of drinking water.[70] To combat mercury poisoning and other ecological costs of capitalist industrial production, the Sandinista government persuaded Pennwalt to reduce its effluents by two-thirds. In addition, millions of dollars worth of worker health and safety equipment and new pollution control technologies were also installed.[71]

However, the plant's key place in Nicaragua's devastated economy prevented it from being adequately overhauled or closed down. Pennwalt, which became nationalized in the late 1980s, produced a value amount equal to almost 25 percent of Nicaragua's annual industrial exports. In addition, twelve other industries in the country were dependent on the plant's products for its own inputs and would have been either severely damaged or crippled by its closure. For instance, the soft drink and beer industries needed its sodium hypochlorite for washing all reused bottles. Construction of a similar plant with the necessary environmental controls was estimated at more than $30 million, while temporary repairs of the existing plant were estimated at over $6 million. Since no international lending agencies or governments were willing to provide such "unproductive" capital, the pollution problem remains despite reduced effluent rates.[72]

A water rationing plan was also adopted. When the water level in Asososca lagoon dropped below a certain height, Lake Managua's contaminated waters began leaching into the lagoon. By closely monitoring the water table and shutting off water to different parts of the city two days a week—sometimes more in the dry season—the government was highly successful in maintaining the lagoon's water level and temporarily preventing a potentially serious human health hazard.

In 1983, the United Nations Environmental Program (UNEP) chose Lake Managua as one of three special priority lakes worldwide. UNEP earmarked $1 million to study Lake Managua and to modernize IRENA's water analysis capabilities. The French government also invested $400,000 in the watershed restoration program for Lake Managua's basin. Although the Sandinistas prioritized the construction of sewage treatment plants and restoration of the watershed, the growing economic crisis prevented the government from moving forward with these multimillion dollar projects.[73]

Getting Off of the Pesticide Treadmill

Pesticide abuse was probably the most serious of the environmental pollution problems inherited from the Somoza dictatorship by the Sandinista government. In the 1970s, Nicaragua consistently led the region in the sheer volume of pesticide applied and was one of the world's leading users of DDT. Pesticides drenched virtually the entire area along the fertile Pacific coast, entering the densely populated region's water table and food chain. A 1977 study revealed that mothers living in the city of León had forty-five times more DDT in their breast milk than the WHO deemed "safe." Hundreds of workers died of pesticide poisoning each year.[74]

The Sandinista government immediately established some of the most innovative regulations to control pesticide abuse ever introduced in Latin America. By nationalizing the banking and export/import systems, the government found itself with an effective means to regulate pesticides entering the country. Between 1979 and 1981, the Sandinista government banned the use of eight of the world's twelve most dangerous ("dirty dozen") pesticides, including DDT, BHC, endrin, dieldrin, Phosvel, and DBCP, replacing these chemicals with more expensive, but less harmful, synthetic pyrethroids. A product registration law was also established to prevent abuses, eliminating more than 1,400 undesirable products from the market.

In 1980, MIDINRA canceled all pesticide import permits granted by Somoza. After a review, only forty-four products were given permits. Long-neglected laws prohibiting the import of DBCP, lindane, and phosvel were also enforced for the first time. For cotton alone, the number of imported products was reduced 75 percent by 1982, although a number of other hazardous products, including toxaphene and paraquat, both of which were produced in the country, continued to be utilized.[75]

The Labor Ministry (MITRAB) also established a department of worker security, which initiated a workplace safety program to protect agricultural laborers from injury and pesticide-related hazards.[76] More than 4,000 training classes were conducted in cooperation with the Rural Workers Association. Growers and unions such as the Rural Workers' Association (Associación de Trabajadores del Campo, or ATC) were also closely involved in responding to health code and safety problems discovered by the Labor Ministry's worksite inspection program.

The Health Ministry (MINSA) and CARE International extended testing across the countryside and provided advice on protective measures to workers. In 1984 alone, 2,880 cotton workers were monitored for pesticide exposure.[77] The government also created the National Pesticide Commission (CNP). Composed of members from the public and private sectors, including environmentalists and union representatives, the CNP developed an innovative set of pesticide regulations to oversee imports and guard workers' health and safety. The commission developed, for the first time in Nicaragua's history, a new system of labeled warnings and instructions on pesticide products in Spanish, and they were color coded for those who could not read.[78]

Despite the increased regulation of pesticides, cotton pest problems on both state and privately owned farms continued to increase. In 1981 and 1982, foreign exchange losses to the boll weevil amounted to $42 million, or 16 percent of the total foreign exchange earnings in agriculture for that period. At the same time, the costs of pesticides applied to cotton increased dramatically to as much as $779 per acre, exceeding 26 percent of total production costs. As a result, average cotton yields were not enough to pay for expanded production expenses.[79] The ecological crisis of cotton was dealing a severe blow to the revolutionary process since the foreign exchange earned from agricultural exports such as cotton funded the reconstruction and social transformation of the country.

The Nicaraguan government began looking urgently for more effective alternatives to the pesticide treadmill. In 1980, MIDINRA resumed and strengthened what was formerly a United Nations test program in Integrated Pest Management (IPM). By 1982, the National Committee on Integrated Control, an advisory panel of IPM specialists, was formed.

The committee immediately recommended area-wide cotton pest management programs based on the IPM philosophy—an agricultural science that seeks to minimize the use of damaging pesticides by maximizing the use of more environmentally benign but economically effective, naturally occurring insect controls. These programs included the prescribed plowing under of cotton crop residues which sustained harmful pests between the harvest and planting seasons; more careful crop monitoring; and the use of trap cropping, bacterium, parasitic wasps (Trichogramma), and other beneficial insect predators of cotton pests.[80]

The IPM efforts stressed two separate but related goals: a long-term reduction in the use of expensive and highly toxic pesticides and the immediate or short-term reduction of the human poisonings and environmental contamination caused by their excessive and careless application. Both the short-term and long-term economic, ecological, and worker and community health gains would be considerable if these goals could be achieved.[81]

Under the Sandinista government, the IPM proved initially to be a huge success. During the first two years of testing in pilot projects, IPM reduced insecticide use to a record low of sixteen to seventeen applications per season, saving $2.02 million in 1982 and 1983.

Government implementation of regional IPM programs began in 1982 when MIDINRA approved a 41,500-acre pilot trap-crop program designed to suppress the boll weevil on more than half the cotton area of León—the largest single season mobilization of private and public resources for IPM in cotton ever undertaken in Nicaragua. The program trained 250 farmworker-scouts to supervise the management of 5,000 trap crops throughout the suppression area and relied on a network of several hundred trained workers to survey and control the boll weevil in the fields.[82]

IPM's success in 1982 combined with government pesticide regulations to lower the volume of pesticide imports by 45 percent lessened the environmental impact of insecticide use, while simultaneously bolstering the economic value of the country's cotton crop. In light of this success, MIDINRA expanded the IPM program to 83,000 acres in 1983. Under Decree Number 1226, grower participation in the program was mandatory, but the government subsidized 30 percent of the costs and insured growers against any financial loss. The 1983 efforts resulted in a net benefit of over $1.9 million from reduced pesticide use.[83] By 1985, the IPM program had expanded to cover about 45 percent of the nation's cotton crop, the largest such enterprise in Central America, and quite possibly in all of Latin America.[84]

In short, the Nicaraguan government's new emphasis on more "independent productive forces," such as IPM, successfully reduced the economic, social, and ecological costs of agricultural export production. Just as capitalist agriculture required technical innovation, or new productive forces, in the form of pesticides to overcome specific ecological barriers to capital accumulation during the 1960s, new productive forces in the form of IPM were needed in the 1980s to break the pesticide treadmill dependency and facilitate the process of social transformation through the production of export crops in a safe but profitable manner. Thus, an effort to safeguard environmental and human health had also increased economic productivity, making the Sandinista government's pesticide policy a model for "productive conservation" in the third world.

U.S. War Against the Nicaraguan Environment

Despite impressive social and environmental gains in the early years of the Nicaraguan revolution, the Sandinista government came under increasing military threat by the U.S. government and the contras, who were supported, organized and trained by the United States.

By December 1982, the contras had carried out their first major attacks in a war of harassment that targeted teachers, doctors, agricultural technicians, small farmers, and key economic installations. In the following year, the Reagan administration initiated what would become a seven-year campaign of socially and environmentally destructive, nonstop U.S. military maneuvers and build-up in neighboring Honduras, where the contras based their attacks. In fact, U.S. military assistance to the four countries surrounding Nicaragua (El Salvador, Honduras, Guatemala, and Costa Rica) comprised $5.2 billion between 1980 and 1987.

Eventually, the United States would spend nearly $1 billion and cause as much as $4 billion in damage in its war against Nicaragua—a war that would claim the lives of some 60,000 people, nearly 2 percent of the country's entire population.[85]

The Reagan administration's policy of "rolling back" the Nicaraguan revolution through the contra war of terror was accompanied by a series of economic reprisals as well. These included a financial blockade, which suspended U.S. bilateral aid in 1981, along with the pressuring of Latin American and Western European governments and international lending agencies like the World Bank and Inter-American Development Bank—through vetoes and direct threats to withdraw U.S. financing to those agencies—to stop all loans to Nicaragua. In 1983, the United States reduced sugar import quotas from Nicaragua, and on May 1, 1985, President Reagan announced a full commercial embargo, suspending all trade between the two nations.[86] By 1988, the International Court of Justice, ruling in favor of

Nicaragua's claims against military and economic U.S. aggression, calculated that the U.S. war had cost Nicaragua $15 billion.

Because of its centrality to the success of the revolution, environmentalism in Nicaragua came under direct fire from the U.S.-sponsored war. The contras attacked both natural resource projects and environmentalists themselves, killing or kidnapping more than seventy-five ecologists, including "internacionalistas" such as the West German biologist Regina Schememan, who was abducted and eventually released during the summer of 1985.[87]

In effect, to be an environmentalist in revolutionary Nicaragua was to be a target of the contras. One of the more notable environmental victims was Marvin José Lopez, formerly in charge of IRENA's projects in the northern city of Ocotal. Lopez was killed during a large-scale contra raid on June 1, 1984. He was ambushed as he left town at dawn to visit a reforestation project. In that same raid the contras attacked the Energy Ministry's offices, a lumber mill, and a hospital, and destroyed six grain silos.[88]

Forestry projects also became targets in the war. In 1983, retreating contras disabled all of the Northeast Forestry Project's fire-detecting and fire-fighting equipment and set fire to a reforested pine plantation which burned out of control for a month in the North Atlantic Autonomous Region, destroying more than 155 square miles. That same year, the contras attacked installations in Saslaya National Park, the first tropical wetland park in the country, kidnapping two rangers and the park director. Such attacks forced the government to put plans for a sustained-yield forestry industry on hold while concentrating forestry activity almost exclusively along the more environmentally degraded Pacific coast. Despite the government's high level of commitment, the war also severely limited other reforestation work. Nicaragua was the leader in a regional wood fuel reforestation project before the Reagan Administration ordered the project's sponsor, the U.S. Agency for International Development, to cut all funding for Nicaragua. Many other restoration and preservation projects were abandoned due to danger of contra attack, including the Bosawas National Park.[89]

The contra war damaged the government's pesticide programs as well. In 1983, a CIA-coordinated attack on the port at Corinto destroyed $7 million of methyl parathion that had just been unloaded on the docks. The attack occurred during a critical moment in the pest cycle, forcing the government to remove impounded organochlorine insecticides from warehouses and dealing Nicaraguan pesticide programs a serious setback.[90] The following year a daring attack destroyed the main seed storage warehouses.

With the establishment of the U.S. embargo, Nicaragua's access to the global seed market (including many varieties of seed which were once exclusively indigenous to the country) became highly restricted. Therefore, the new seed facilities were essential. The most successful, Enprosem, which developed three of its own bean varieties, was destroyed in that contra attack. The contras recognized that the Sandinista government's program for agricultural self-sufficiency depended on the recovery and development of indigenous seed varieties, many of which were under the exclusive control of the U.S. Department of Agriculture's global seed bank in Fort Collins, Colorado.[91]

The war also sapped human resources from environmental projects. Technicians and inspectors trained for environmental and human health programs were constantly being mobilized for the military. In 1983, nearly half of the forty workplace inspectors were mobilized for the war, greatly impeding MITRAB programs in worker health and safety. Often the targets of contra attacks, more than 100 workplace technicians and a dozen inspectors were killed.[92] Spare parts, vehicles and machinery were also in critically short supply. Environmentalists often had no means of getting out into the field.

The trade embargo and credit crunch also heightened the problem by cutting off access to an array of goods and replacement parts in the agricultural sector, including IPM technologies and less dangerous chemicals. By 1987, cotton production had declined to its lowest point since the revolution, as the difficulties of continuing mass-based IPM programs escalated.[93]

At the same time, the number of pesticide poisonings in basic grain production (particularly among small farmers) increased dramatically. The Ministry of Health reported an "epidemic" of 548 pesticide poisonings in the León area, principally by Furadan (a highly toxic carbamate pesticide) and methamidophos (a peripheral neurotoxin), although it is estimated that 3,700 poisoning cases actually occurred in 1987.[94]

Problems of growing pesticide abuse were magnified by ill-advised Sandinista policies. The government provided pesticides to producers at extremely cheap, subsidized prices in order to increase production, resulting in their overuse and abuse. Subsidizing the price of basic grains rather than pesticides would have been a much sounder economic and environmental program, although international credit policies posed difficulties for this strategy.[95]

Another equally severe ecological impact of the contra war involved the displacement of the population. Over 250,000 peasants were displaced by the war, moved out of zones of conflict to towns or cities (particularly Managua) with insufficient infrastructure or services necessary to guard their health and well-being.[96] As a result, pressures on resources in ecologically fragile areas of nearby cities, especially along the already degraded Pacific coast, increased dramatically.[97]

The Fall of Revolutionary Ecology

As Nicaragua's social fabric deteriorated under the weight of U.S. aggression and as the Sandinista government looked to increase economic production and export revenues in order to survive, programs concerning the social and ecological reconstruction of the country suffered. An opinion gradually developed within the FSLN leadership that there was increasingly less room to innovate and experiment with radical and comprehensive programs of "revolutionary ecology." IRENA steadily lost its direct regulatory control over natural resource sectors considered the most economically important to the war effort.

Between 1980 and 1982, responsibilities for the fishery sector had already been completely transferred into a newly created but separate institute, INPESCA (Instituto Nicaragüense de la Pesca). All mining activities had been centralized in another institute, CONDEMINA (Corporación Nicaragüense de Desarrollo Minero). Duties concerning the "exploitation" and processing of forest resources had been transferred to the Ministry of Industry. Oversight of *cuencas* (drainage basins) was transfered to the agricultural ministry MIDINRA. IRENA retained control of the Servicio Forestal, responsible for research and the cultivation of trees, national parks and wildlife, and environmental improvement.[98]

By 1985, the country had plunged into a deep economic crisis, forcing the Sandinistas to revise their development priorities by emphasizing increased short-term production over long-term environmentally sound development models. As part of a more general reorganization aimed at "compacting" the national government and cutting expenses, IRENA became a department within the Ministry of Agriculture and received a new director, Julio Castillo. In addition to the loss of institutional autonomy, IRENA's budget was slashed by 40 percent; an additional 10 percent was cut the following year in 1986. By 1988, more than 600 of IRENA's workers were laid off, while many others were transferred to other positions within MIDINRA. Most of its comprehensive development strategies were abandoned, unless supported by external funding.

Within a few brief years, IRENA had been transformed from an ambitious institute intimately linked to economically important sectors, such as mining and fishery, into an institute dependent on and accountable to the Ministry of Agriculture, with tasks limited to control, regulation, and supporting research. (With this move to a department status within MIDINRA, IRENA's acronym was changed to DIRENA. For purposes of simplicity, I refer to DIRENA as IRENA throughout the text, a title that was reestablished by the Chamorro government.)[99]

The growing conflict between production and protection was resolved in favor of maximized production and foreign exchange revenues and was reflected in the professional backgrounds of the successive directors of IRENA—anthropology, biology, and agronomy. IRENA even lifted some bans and resumed wildlife export of a few species, such as parrots. As personnel and budget cuts continued, enforcement of existing protection laws was made increasingly difficult. (As of 1990, permanent hunting bans remained in effect for six species, and seasonal bans for an additional eleven.)

Despite the assistance of international ecological brigades, IRENA was no longer able to provide sufficient personnel needed to guard sea turtle eggs on the beaches. By 1989, collectors and merchants once again began invading the La Flor and Chococente nesting areas, presenting a serious danger to the survival of the species. Programs under the control of other agencies, such as the numerous small-scale alternative energy programs common in the early years of the revolution under INE, were also abandoned as the economic crisis deepened.

The growing economic pressures on Nicaragua's government and the conflicting visions of development inside the government are best illustrated by the case of the San Juan River watershed in southeast Nicaragua, one of the wettest forests in Central America. Receiving up to six meters of rainfall annually, it is also one of the last and largest remaining stands of pristine tropical rainforest in the region, extending up the Atlantic coast and covering approximately 1,740 square miles. Virtually uninhabited and unexplored, only about 80 percent of the species of fauna and 45 percent of the species of flora have been identified. (The San Juan River area also comprises the smaller watersheds of the Indio, Maíz, and Punta Gorda Rivers.)[100]

In the early 1980s, three proposals emerged for developing the watershed. One called for damming the San Juan River for hydroelectric power, while another suggested reversing its flow toward Lake Nicaragua in order to irrigate the fertile Pacific coast during the dry season. Environmentalists suggested an integrated eco-development plan, targeting different areas for various forms of agricultural development, fisheries, and forestry, while setting aside wetlands south of Lake Nicaragua and a 1,160-square-mile tract of tropical rainforest in the country's southeast corner for conservation.[101]

With strong support from Nicaragua's growing environmental movement and the international community, President Daniel Ortega publicly announced his backing of the eco-development plan on World Environment Day in June of 1986. However, one month later, the Ministry of Industry and Nicaragua's State Forestry Corporation (CORFOP), in an effort to garner quick foreign exchange, granted the first forestry concession since the revolution to a Costa Rican logging company to clear-cut 1,235 square miles of virgin rainforest in the heart of the proposed reserve—almost the entire watershed.

An intense national debate erupted as the nongovernment Nicaraguan Association of Biologists and Ecologists (ABEN) called the concession comparable to the worst forestry concessions that Somoza used to give to transnational corporations. Environmentalists, combined with broad opposition in the larger society and pressure from the international environmental movement, eventually led President

Ortega to cancel the concession on June 19, 1987. In April of 1987, ABEN met with the directors of IRENA and the State Forestry Corporation, where it was agreed that ABEN would sit on the National Forestry Commission committee that would help develop a plan for the watershed.[102]

This popular-based support for social and ecological justice led to the approval of a new constitution in November of 1986, which included an article stating that "Nicaraguans do have the right to live in a healthy environment: it is the obligation of the state to preserve, conserve and rescue the environment and the natural resources."[103]

Having achieved this important victory, IRENA launched a conservation and sustainable development project known as SI-A-PAZ ("Yes-to-Peace") in the San Juan River area. With presidential backing, the "peace through parks" project proposed to create a five-million-acre international peace park between Nicaragua and Costa Rica, comprised of large reserves and refuges for scientific purposes and education, as well as quality of life improvements for the peasant population living on its periphery. Just as important, as then-National Parks Director Lorenzo Cardenal commented, the joint management of natural resources in the San Juan River Watershed "could serve as a bridge of reconciliation between our two governments."[104]

In early 1988, the ministers of natural resources from Costa Rica and Nicaragua signed a letter of intent to create SI-A-PAZ. The SI-A-PAZ plan, however, came under immediate challenge by other sectors of the government who were considering the building of a transoceanic canal in the embattled watershed as the only way to bring Nicaragua out of its deep economic crisis. Japan and other countries have expressed a strong interest in constructing a passage through the twelve-mile Rivas Strait on the Pacific end, into Lake Nicaragua, and then onto the San Juan River into the Caribbean Sea. The watershed is the original site proposed for the Panama Canal at the start of the century; the Canal is much too small to accommodate the modern supertankers, aircraft carriers, and warships that travel today's oceans.

Progress on SI-A-PAZ and other peace-park programs has been very slow, particularly given the political uncertainty surrounding the election of Violeta Chamorro. Sapped of financial and human resources, the country's once-ambitious national parks program has largely been abandoned. Today only a single national park—one-tenth of 1 percent of Nicaragua—is actually protected. By 1990, the staff of Nicaragua's National Park Service had dwindled from seventy to eight in 1980; none of the staff, including the Parks Director Jacinto Cedeno, were reimbursed for supplies or travel.[105]

Collapse of the Revolution

By the late 1980s, the U.S. siege, compounded by falling international prices for leading exports as well as a mounting foreign debt, had created the worst economic crisis in Nicaragua's history. More than 60 percent of the national budget went for defense, crippling the government's economic, social, and environmental programs. Between 1987 and 1990, the gross domestic product declined 11.7 percent, a per capita drop of 21.5 percent, while the trade balance showed a deficit of $1.2 billion and the balance of payments was a negative $2 billion. In 1989, despite the implementation of drastic austerity measures by the government, the foreign debt amounted to over $7.5 billion ($2,300 per capita).

Although hyperinflation was brought down from 33,000 percent in 1988 to around 1,700 percent in 1989, nearly 35 percent of the population was unemployed or underemployed. As agricultural production stalled and real wages tumbled, per capita food consumption dropped between 15 percent to 30 percent and family incomes by a third, resulting in dramatic increases in infant mortality rates and poverty. Real wages fell from an index of 29.2 in February 1988 (1980=100) to 6.5 in June 1989 and to 1 by December. During 1988, milk consumption fell by 50 percent, while tuberculosis and malaria spread widely.[106]

Illiteracy, which had been reduced from 50 percent to 12.5 percent, jumped back up to 22 percent. In June 1988, the Ministry of Education, facing shortages of classrooms, books, desks, and notebooks, estimated that 70 percent of Nicaraguan five-year-olds and 30 percent of ten-year-olds were not attending school.

According to the Report of the Economic Commission to the Government of Nicaragua in July of 1989, per capita output had fallen by 25 percent since 1980, while average living standards had been cut by more than 60 percent. The gross national production (GNP) had shrunk every year since 1983, with imports equal to four times the value of exports.

On top of all this, in 1988, the 120-mph winds of Hurricane Joan destroyed or severely damaged 1.2 million acres of the largest rainforest remaining in Central America (22 percent of Nicaragua's forested land), while causing $50 million in damage to farmlands and human settlements spanning the South Atlantic Region to Central Nicaragua. A detailed posthurricane study by the Research and Documentation Center of the Atlantic Coast (CIDCA) found that only 20 percent of the trees in sampled sites were left standing, while 27 percent had been completely uprooted and 53 percent snapped off at the trunk. (However, the study also found that although badly damaged, the forest was regenerating well through resprouting and seedlings and the diversity of tree species remains high.)[107]

In one hour, this natural disaster devastated a forest area equivalent in size to what had been deforested during those five long years of war with the contras, wood resources which could have been used for the benefit of the population.[108] The downed timber left by the hurricane led to a rash of fires, which by the end of the dry season in June of 1989 had burned 198,000 acres. In all, the hurricane wiped out more than 29,000 homes, while 114 people were killed and 178 injured.[109]

When one calculates the almost unbelievable economic destruction inflicted on this poor country over the past 20 years, it seems miraculous that the revolution could benefit the people at all while standing up to the most powerful nation on earth—the United States. In 1979, the Sandinista government inherited a country decimated by over $950 million in damage from the 1972 earthquake and the 1978–1979 revolution, as well as over $4 billion in economic losses (equivalent to two full years of the country's GDP) stemming from capital flight, lost income and export revenues, assumed foreign debt, and a looted national treasury.

Between 1982 and 1989, the contra war cost the Nicaraguan economy as much as $4 billion in direct and indirect losses, equivalent to almost twenty years of exports. At the same time, the country suffered from declining terms of trade in the world market and the U.S.-sponsored trade embargo: between 1981 and 1983, the prices Nicaragua received for exports fell by 11.9 percent, while import prices increased 35 percent. The 1985 trade embargo cost Nicaragua an additional $50 million in lost exports, as well as additional losses resulting from production problems associated with spare parts shortages. In 1987, ecological deterioration contributed to yet another severe drought, which affected 80 percent of basic grain production and caused losses of more than $100 million. (The 1982 drought caused $357 million in damage.)[110] Foreign aggression and natural disaster alone, however, did not fully account for the creation of Nicaragua's economic problems. The Sandinista government also contributed to the severity of the economic crisis, making a number of critical policy errors and strategic mistakes.[111] One of the most important elements of the revolutionary project was to encourage and promote popular participation and grassroots organizing through mass organizations—the basis for a revolutionary democracy.[112] But despite well-intentioned efforts to support and include the peasantry and agricultural workers as part of the revolutionary alliance, many of the structural problems and class privileges that gave birth to the revolution were not adequately addressed.

In particular, the agrarian reform and related marketing and support services did not go far enough.[113] Instead, the Sandinistas demonstrated a bias for large-scale investments in state agriculture in place of a comprehensive, long-term approach to the revitalization and transformation of the subsistence sector. The peasantry was never fully integrated into the FSLN's development strategy, giving the contras opportunities for making inroads into the country.[114]

This situation was also related to the FSLN's trust and "over-reliance" on the so-called patriotic sectors of the agricultural bourgeoisie in the export sector, which utilized massive government financial support and assistance in "unproductive" ways (instead of increasing production, as was hoped for by the FSLN). The financial costs of maintaining the political alliance with the wealthy agrarian bourgeoisie—who would gladly throw the Sandinistas out of power—was also a principal reason for the severe economic crisis. Subsidies to these growers resulted in massive state budget deficits, declining production and decapitalization of export operations, and capital flight—all at a heavy cost to other government programs. The Sandinistas financed these deficits primarily by printing money, substantially contributing to the outrageous inflation rates of the late 1980s.[115]

In some ways, Sandinista government policy served to recreate many of the more destructive aspects of the old model of disarticulated capitalist development. One of the principal aims of the Sandinista government was to end the exploitation of poor rural workers. However, comprehensive agrarian reform and revitalization of the subsistence sector threatened to create severe labor shortages for the state farms and agricultural exports estates, thereby undermining the FSLN's development strategy. This was one of many contradictions faced by the revolutionary government.[116] The Sandinistas subsidized capital flight by the agricultural bourgeoisie (their political adversaries) at the expense of poor peasants and workers (their political allies) and wasted scarce economic resources on unwise large-scale projects (sometimes the product of lower-level corruption). Many of these projects actually increased the country's vulnerability in the world market, particularly in terms of deepening dependencies on expensive inputs and imports. This led to short-term pressures for increased export production winning out over long-term sustainable development policies. Whether or not these errors were instrumental in the Sandinistas' collapse, they clearly reflected the need for even greater popular participation in the government's decision-making and planning processes.

Conclusion: The UNO Government

By the late 1980s, the harsh austerity programs adopted by the Sandinista government had severely undermined its ability to implement a broad agenda of social and environmental reform, leading to dramatic declines in the living standards of the people. In the months preceding the national elections scheduled for early 1990, the FSLN suffered diminished popular support. To many political observers, the election was a referendum on whether or not the Nicaraguan people were ready (as Ronald Reagan put it) to "cry uncle" in order to stop the death, social destruction, and severe economic deprivation caused by the contra war.

During the weeks before the election, President Bush and Secretary of State Baker made the choice clear by stating that an Ortega victory would result in a continuation of the war. The FSLN also restated the view that the U.S.-sponsored war was responsible for the country's growing economic crisis. Many Nicaraguans clearly saw a vote for Violeta Chamorro's U.S.-backed conservative National Opposition Union (UNO) as a vote to end the war and economic hardship. On February 25, 1990, the UNO won an unexpected victory with 54.7 percent of the vote for presidential candidate Chamorro, compared to 40.8 percent for FSLN incumbent Daniel Ortega.

The Chamorro campaign had accepted over $800,000 between 1984 and 1989 from the U.S. funded National Endowment for Democracy (NED), as did a number of other political parties, labor unions, business organizations, and media operations. In all, the United States spent some $17.5 million in government aid on the elections and UNO victory.[117]

Today, the UNO government remains a fragile coalition of fourteen divergent political factions: former contra leaders, Somocista business interests and the wealthy bourgeoisie, including the more liberal capitalist elements and traditional oligarchy. (Former contra leaders now in important government positions include National Assembly Secretary Alfredo César, Minister of Government Carlos Hurtado, Autonomy Institute Director Brooklyn Rivera, and Repatriation Institute Director Roberto Ferrey.)

There are two main camps. On the far right are those who desire a reversal of all revolutionary programs and a return to former political and economic structures characteristic of disarticulated capitalist development ("Somocismo without Somoza"). This hard-line faction includes the Superior Council of Private Producers, a right-wing association of the agricultural and industrial bourgeoisie; vice-president Virgilio Godoy; and the former contras (or *desmovilizados*).

The other wing is made up of more "moderate" elements, including President Violeta Chamorro and Presidential Minister Antonio Lacayo, who have indicated some willingness to reach a more "peaceful accommodation" with the Sandinistas as they implement a gradual dismantling of the revolutionary process. Rather than implementing a potentially explosive policy of taking away lands granted to peasants under the Sandinista agrarian reform, which would likely lead to a confrontation with the Sandinista army and perhaps civil war, Chamorro's approach initially seemed to favor more indirect economic measures, such as tougher credit policies. As more and more farmers face economic hardship, they would likely be forced to sell off their lands to many of their former owners.[118]

The new UNO government has enjoyed a number of advantages over its predecessor. The contras are almost entirely disarmed and, though highly critical of the Chamorro faction, are unlikely to take up arms against the government. The Sandinistas have not taken on COSEP's former role as an opposition party committed to sabotaging the new government. Indeed, the FSLN even asked the former Soviet Union and other nations to fulfill prior financial cooperation agreements made with the Sandinista government—not to cut off aid.

In the UNO's first year in power, President Bush lifted the trade embargo and restored Nicaragua's sugar quota immediately after UNO won the elections. While aid to Latin America is suffering due to changes in Eastern Europe, the U.S. Congress authorized $500 million in aid to Nicaragua for the next two years. Since the United States ended the financial blockade, the doors are open to far more foreign aid than the FSLN had access to. On September 25, 1991, the United States forgave Nicaragua's government debt to Washington, wiping $259.5 million of the country's $9 billion foreign debt ledger. This figure represented some 88 percent of Nicaragua's total debt with the United States. The action came a week after the Chamorro government had finally relented and dropped a World Court suit, filed in 1984 against the United States by the Sandinistas for the U.S. role in mining Nicaraguan ports and backing the contras.

A year later, however, President Chamorro began to succumb to pressure from Washington and the hard-right wing inside Nicaragua to speed up the counterrevolution. By September 1992, Republicans in Congress led by Senator Jesse Helms of North Carolina held up more than $100 million in U.S. aid, charging that the presence of Sandinistas in the Nicaraguan government was unacceptable, and demanding that 400 U.S.-owned businesses be returned to their previous owners. On September 9, 1992, Chamorro signed decrees that would return to their former owners properties that had been redistributed by the Sandinista government. About 16,000 properties, including businesses, homes, and ranches were involved in the transfer.

In spite of apparent advantages at its start, the new government is confronting a complex economic crisis, aggravated by continued social and political tensions throughout the country. The Chamorro administration inherited a $10.8 billion debt when it took office. Chamorro's economic program has shifted from an ambitious plan proposed by Central Bank president Francisco Mayorga, to the similar but more conservative and pessimistic "Stabilization and Structural Adjustment Plan for Nicaragua (1990–1993)." The new plan proposed an IMF-style program of short-term financial and monetary adjustments, whose goal is to rapidly reduce the fiscal deficit and inflation while promoting export production. The program has its political counterpart in the so-called *concertación*, or reconciliation between the different social and economic sectors.

But even after adopting the rhetoric of environmentalism and appointing ecologists such as Jaime Incer as the new Minister of IRENA, Chamorro has shown a willingness to sacrifice environmental quality and worker health and safety in favor of "structural adjustment" and neo-liberal economic policy. The UNO government has already voiced its intentions to encourage private investment in forestry projects; although requests for forest concessions have been rejected to date, this does not bode well for the future of Nicaragua's tropical forests.

The UNO government has also begun pushing the expansion of cotton production, even though the IPM program is crippled. Just days after UNO's electoral victory, Mayorga stated that UNO planned to redistribute 250,000 acres of land, giving one-third to increased cotton production, which would more than double the amount of cotton crop currently under cultivation.[119] In 1990, the Nordic Commission—representing Denmark, Sweden, Finland and Norway—threatened to withdraw aid from Nicaragua upon hearing the announcement from the World Bank of the long-term plan to expand cotton production.

On the other hand, the Chamorro government was sensitive from the start to the attention won by the Sandinistas in the international community, which put Nicaragua's environmental crisis and revolutionary social and ecological programs on the map. In 1989, for instance, Nicaragua hosted the internationally attended Fourth Biennial Conference on the Fate and Hope of the Earth, which noted that "the degradation of the people and natural resources of Nicaragua parallels the assault on the rest of the planet" and gave special support to the Sandinistas' ecological priorities.

Given the current government's desperate need for foreign lending and assistance, UNO has maintained many of the more symbolic (and less costly) vestiges of revolutionary ecology. The final version of the $300 appropriation of U.S. aid for the Nicaraguan government earmarked $8 million for "a variety of environmental concerns" including the "peace park" SI-A-PAZ.

These plans were complicated by the contras leaders, who disarmed in June 1990 in exchange for virtual political autonomy in two "development poles"—one in El Almendro and another near Waslala. Contra leaders insisted on resettlements en masse (as well as the establishment of a former contra "ecological police force") in "development poles" along the San Juan River and in part of Zelaya Sur— areas that include sections of unspoiled tropical rainforests in protected SI-A-PAZ park lands. Under the agreement, no government police or troops will be allowed inside these "sovereign" regions (the Southeastern enclave encompasses 7,722 square miles). Order will be maintained by armed "rural police" comprised of former contras under the command of strongman Israel Geleano.

The Chamorro government has publicly endorsed a number of other environmental initiatives. IRENA, previously under the auspices of MIDINRA, was reinstated as an autonomous ministry after March 1990. The UNO government has also so far rejected highly controversial solicitations for huge forestry concessions in Nicaragua's eastern rainforests, as well as proposals for toxic waste shipments from the United States. The majority of these financially attractive offers have been proposed by large North American corporations acting through Central American intermediaries.

Although some environmental programs will be maintained, it appears likely that the more far-reaching and comprehensive environmental programs initiated under the Sandinista government (which do not receive external funding) will be dismantled. UNO government policies of structural adjustment pose the greatest environmental threat. In order to boost export production (and revenues) while cutting the cost of imports, "unproductive expenditures" designed to safeguard environmental quality and worker health and safety will be reduced as much as politically possible.

In addition, anti-inflationary measures—including massive layoffs of agricultural and state workers, privatization of state properties and operations, exorbitant price hikes, and a severe contraction of credit for production—have produced a new national food, health, and energy crisis, principally affecting the poorest sectors of the population. This crisis is increasing pressure on natural resources, like firewood, timber, and wildlife, and deepening the vicious downward spiral of poverty and environmental deterioration. For the first time since the Sandinista revolution, land titles are now once again being held as collateral on bank loans—loans offered at very high interest rates.

In conclusion, under the Sandinista government, Nicaragua implemented one of the most comprehensive programs to restore and protect its environment and raise the quality of life for its popular classes yet seen in Latin America, if not the entire third world. Yet, United States intervention ended this unique experiment in revolutionary ecological and social transformation, pushing the country to the brink of collapse—creating conditions that contributed to the election of Violeta Chamorro. But having achieved its primary goal of "rolling back" the Sandinista revolution, the United States has largely abandoned the UNO government, showing little interest in fulfilling its promises to Chamorro and the Nicaraguan people for providing the financial assistance necessary to repair and reconstruct the country. By late 1992, the Bush administration had even begun to treat Chamorro with some of the same hostility it it had shown the Sandinistas, forcing her to fire a Sandinista police official and holding out on desperately needed aid in the wake of a disastrous Pacific Coast tidal wave in early September.

Lacking both popular support and a viable development strategy, it is likely that the Nicaraguan crisis will continue to worsen under the moderate wing of the Chamorro government. If the hard-line faction is successful in dismantling the heart and soul of the revolution, particularly the agrarian reform movement, civil war will likely return to Nicaragua. Whether the FSLN will become more democratic and continue the revolutionary struggle "from below" or follow a path of political moderation in order to gain U.S. acceptance and accommodation with the Chamorro government, remains to be seen. Nothing less than the future of the Nicaraguan people and their environment is at stake.

6

WAR AGAINST NATURE:
MILITARIZATION
AND THE IMPACTS OF U.S. POLICY

The massacres are destroying in a systematic manner all that sustains the life of the community, houses, woods, harvests, to the point that the water in the rivers is polluted to drive the people to desperation. The current wave of terror appears to have as a principal object to disarticulate the social life and the cultural inheritance of the Indian people and the peasant, to end the resistance of those that now won't support the weight of centuries of robbery, of maltreatment, and of persecution.

Dutch Catholic Congress Report on Guatemala
September 1982[1]

Since World War II, capitalist export agriculture and industry have besieged the environment in Central America. U.S. corporations and Central America's oligarchies, agrarian bourgeoisie, and military officers have been provided with virtually unrestricted and unregulated access to the region's rich natural resources. Lush tropical forest has been increasingly rolled back for vast plantations and cattle ranches.

This agro-export development model has also forced Central America's rapidly growing peasantry into farming the most ecologically fragile, least-productive land, such as steep mountain hillsides and nutrient-poor lowland tropical rainforests. Half of the region's rural families don't own enough land to support themselves—or they have no land at all.[2] As ecological degradation deepens the region's poverty, it feeds into the socioeconomic crisis, and conversely, as the socioeconomic crisis deepens, it exacerbates the environmental crisis.[3]

This vicious cycle has been accelerated by militarization and U.S. foreign policy. Over the course of the last decade, the United States has promoted a multitude of wars in the region: counterinsurgency campaigns in Guatemala and El Salvador; the proxy "contra war" in Nicaragua; the conversion of Honduras into an "armed camp" for purposes of supporting military operations in neighboring countries; and the bombing and invasion of Panama with 26,000 U.S. troops in 1989. At least 175,000 Central Americans have suffered war-related deaths since 1980, while Vietnam-style "scorched earth" operations and military maneuvers have obliterated vast agricultural lands and crucial ecosystems, pushing millions of refugees into overcrowded cities and overtaxed hillsides.

Perhaps even more important, U.S. militarization of Central America—in response to popularly based movements challenging socially unjust and ecologically unsound development practices—has blocked the potential long-term resolution of the social and environmental crisis, posing an incalculable threat to the health and security of the entire isthmus. In short, the United States appears to be following a contradictory and short-sighted military policy, which is destroying the region economically and ecologically in order to "save it" politically.

The Ecological Roots of Revolution

Over the course of the 1970s, growing poverty among Central America's popular classes began spurring a new wave of organizing by broad-based movements for a more equitable distribution and democratic management of social and natural resources. The deepening ecological and economic crisis of the region had contributed to untenable increases in the "rate of exploitation" and impoverishment of semiproletarian labor, breaking down the political viability of functional dualism and disarticulated capitalist development. Among workers, the ecological and economic crisis of the subsistence sector began invigorating movements for better wages, benefits, working and living conditions, and services.

This was exemplified in El Salvador in the late 1970s, when the Christian Federation of Salvadoran Peasants (FECCAS) and Union of Rural Workers (UTC) responded to the ecological crisis of the subsistence sector by organizing for better food and working conditions, as well as higher wages, on the export sector estates. In Guatemala, a series of bloody strikes by semiproletarian sugar and cotton workers resulted in a minimum wage increase in 1980 from $1.19 to $3.20 in U.S. currency (although the law was most often ignored). In short, as life for poor semiproletarian peasants became more difficult, struggles against the superexploitation of wage labor increased.[4] At the same time, the crisis also began invigorating peasant movements for agrarian and economic reform of the subsistence sector. When agricultural wages in El Salvador fell by 30 percent between 1973 and 1978, for instance, the Popular Revolutionary Bloc and other popular organizations stepped up their efforts for better land and wages by organizing land invasions and strikes.[5] Hardships became particularly magnified by the ecological crisis of cotton production, which led to the adoption of less labor-intensive crop substitutes, eliminating an important source of jobs and income for hundreds of thousands of migrant workers.

In Guatemala, cotton declined from 296,000 acres in the late 1970s to only 49,400 acres in 1985. Increased labor competition for scarce jobs resulted in wages falling far below the minimum of $1.20 a day during the 1980s. Considering that real wages for cotton, coffee, sugar, and banana workers dropped 20 percent between 1973 and 1979, it becomes easier to understand why so many Guatemalan families were pushed beyond the margins of survival.[6] The big drops in employment and wage income thus increased family dependence on a rapidly deteriorating resource base in the subsistence sector, and with it the growth of political organization by desperate peasant farmers.

By the late 1970s, popular struggles for agrarian and economic reforms, democratization of the state and political institutions, and respect for human rights were posing fundamental challenges to the traditional power structure. The intransigence of landed oligarchies and state officials, the escalation of repression against the popular movements, and the U.S. government's military and economic support of the existing class structure and development model, spurred the birth of revolutionary movements in El Salvador, Guatemala, and Nicaragua. It is in these three countries that functional dualism (see Chapter 2) had reached its ultimate expression, creating the largest and most intensely exploited agrarian working class (as well as the fastest-growing industrial working class and threatened artisanry) in the region.[7]

The development of popular-based revolutionary movements in Central America depended on the level of proletarianization and on the rate of exploitation of semiproletarian labor (in terms of total employment, wages, hours, and working conditions and the quantity and quality of agricultural land for the subsistence plot, credit rates, food prices, rents, etc.). Salvadoran, Guatemalan, and Nicaraguan peasants were superexploited as both migratory wage laborers in the capitalist export sector, and as socially and ecologically impoverished peasants in the rural subsistence and urban informal sectors. This is why the ecological and social conditions of subsistence and export production are key factors in the development of political movements and revolutionary struggles in Central America.[8]

In Honduras and Costa Rica, in contrast, political compromises were proving critical to submerging revolutionary tendencies. In the 1960s and 1970s, the most extensive land reforms in Central America occurred in Honduras. Peasant mobilization by organizations like the National Federation of Honduras Peasants (FENACH) in the late 1960s spurred government programs to lessen the marginalization of small farmers. These programs included colonization projects and deforestation of tropical rainforests, adjudication of land disputes and land occupations, redistribution of property, and titling of peasant landholdings. Between 1962 and 1980, for instance, about 36,000 rural families benefited from government agrarian reform measures.[9]

In Costa Rica, colonization projects, the security of land title, and the strategic location in the export sector of a "rich" segment of the peasantry, as well as a relatively advanced welfare state, defused any strategic alliance between urban labor and the rural working class and peasantry. Between 1962 and 1979, about 413,000 acres of land were distributed to 5,428 poor peasant families in Costa Rica.[10] In addition, relatively higher wages for agrarian and industrial workers also constrained rural income inequality and offset widespread social unrest in Costa Rica. Whether such reforms, which diminished considerably during the 1980s, will prove adequate to maintain "social stability" in Costa Rica and Honduras as the economic and ecological crisis grows during the 1990s, remains to be seen.[11]

U.S. Policy and the Assault on Central America

By the time the Reagan/Bush administration came into office in 1981, revolution was sweeping over the Central American isthmus. In Nicaragua, the Sandinista National Liberation Front (FSLN) had already overthrown the U.S.-backed Somoza dictatorship in July of 1979 and assumed control over the Government of National Reconstruction, implementing a process of social transformation oriented to the "logic of the majority."[12] Powerful guerrilla movements had emerged under the banners of the Salvadoran FMLN and (somewhat later) the Guatemalan UNRG to challenge the political domination of the coffee oligarchy and allied military officers. These popular revolutionary movements also presented a serious threat to the hegemony of the United States over a region that it had traditionally taken for granted as its own "backyard."[13]

These events were ill-timed, however, arising as the newly elected Reagan/Bush administration was expressing a commitment to defeating the "Vietnam syndrome," and reestablishing the United States as a "global policeman." Central America quickly became a test case for a renewed interventionist and militaristic foreign policy. Administration propaganda falsely attributed social turmoil in the region to interference by foreign powers, specifically the Soviet Union and Cuba, and the situation was presented to the American people as a threat to U.S. "national security."[14] With the return of the "domino theory" to the political discourse in Washington, both the Democratic and Republican Party majorities agreed that U.S. national interests were at stake in Central America, creating bipartisan backing for the Reagan/Bush administration's call for rapid increases in military and economic aid to the region.[15]

Central America became the proving ground for the emerging Reagan/Bush doctrine. This doctrine was aimed at defeating popular revolutions that might threaten the access of U.S. capital to cheap labor, natural resources, and markets in third world regions and countries.[16] Three major policy thrusts to the Reagan/Bush doctrine for the region quickly emerged: (1) to destabilize and roll back the Nicaraguan revolution; (2) to militarily defeat and therefore contain revolutionary movements in El Salvador and Guatemala, and (3) to utilize direct and massive intervention by U.S. military forces, in case options (1) or (2) were unsuccessful. In a nutshell, the policy sought to restore and/or preserve regimes sympathetic to U.S. business interests and to maintain disarticulated capitalist development.[17]

To implement these policies, the Reagan/Bush administration immediately increased economic and military aid to the Salvadoran, Honduran, and Guatemalan governments and began organizing, training, and financing a counterrevolutionary (contra) force against the Sandinista government in Nicaragua.[18] Direct U.S. security aid to Central America from 1980 to 1985 totaled $2.3 billion—ten times the amount spent in the region by the United States during the previous 30 years.[19] In fact, during the 1980s the region ranked second after Israel in per capita economic aid and received 65 percent of all U.S. aid to Latin America and the Caribbean.

U.S. taxpayers paid dearly for this presence in the region. In all, more than $9 billion in U.S. aid went to the militarization of Central America between 1981 and 1990. Of this figure, some $7.7 billion was in economic aid and $1.6 billion in military aid, although much of the economic aid was security related. According to the Arms Control and Foreign Policy Caucus of the U.S. Congress, for instance, three-quarters of the U.S. economic-aid package to El Salvador (the largest recipient) went to the military.[20]

The Vietnam War taught that prolonged U.S. military involvement against third world liberation struggles causes powerful dissent at home. The Reagan/Bush doctrine aimed to accomplish its counterinsurgency goals in Central America without directly involving U.S. troops. This strategy, commonly referred to as "low-intensity conflict" (LIC), relied on indigenous military forces under U.S. supervision. It employed tactics defined by the Pentagon as "a combination of military, paramilitary, political, psychological and civic action."[21]

The principal objective of the LIC strategy was (and remains) to exhaust revolutionary forces (whether guerrilla or governmental) and eliminate or isolate their popular base of support through military operations, civilian resettlement programs, etc. As such, the term "low-intensity conflict" is misleading, obscuring the brutality of these wars and the social and ecological destruction they bring.[22] Colonel John D. Waghelstein, former chief of the U.S. military group in El Salvador, summed up low-intensity conflict as "total war at the grassroots level."[23] In short, the U.S. strategy became to win the war without having to fight any battles.[24]

"Rollback": The Ecological Crisis of Honduras

With the implementation of the Reagan/Bush doctrine in the early 1980s, Honduran foreign policy became a mere reflection of the U.S. regional military strategy. Sharing key geopolitical borders with Nicaragua, El Salvador, and Guatemala, this mountainous country became a platform for U.S.-sponsored low-intensity conflict operations, serving as a staging ground for the contra war against Nicaragua, as well as the Salvadoran and Guatemalan armies.

U.S. military assistance to the Honduran government, which has been condemned by the Inter-American Court of Human Rights for abusing its citizens' rights, has rapidly increased, rising from $4 million in fiscal year 1980 to a high of $77 million in 1984. Between 1946 and 1980, Honduras received a total of $30.4 million in U.S. military loans and grants.[25] The United States continues to send over $21 million annually. As a result, the country's combined armed forces have expanded from just a few thousand in the 1970s to some 30,000 personnel.[26]

To prepare the U.S. armed forces for a possible invasion of Nicaragua or El Salvador, the Pentagon carried out more than six dozen military maneuvers in Honduras, involving tens of thousands of U.S. troops and national guardsmen. The United States has used the maneuvers to build a massive infrastructure of military bases, roads, port facilities, warehouse sites, and airfields. Eighteen U.S. military bases have emerged in the country since the early 1980s, leading Senator James Sasser (D-TN) to conclude that Honduras "is becoming an armed camp."[27] Much of the infrastructure was also used to house, arm, train and direct the contra army of over 15,000 men, a terrorist force which killed some 60,000 Nicaraguans and caused $4 billion in direct and indirect losses to their economy (as discussed in Chapter 5).

The impact of U.S. military and economic policy has been to worsen the hardships of the Honduran people. The large flow of U.S. economic and security assistance has enriched the Honduran military and the business establishment, resulting in dramatic increases in inequality, poverty, repression, and human rights abuses.[28] After over 214 political assassinations, 110 "disappearances," and 1,947 illegal detentions by the armed forces and the government death squad Battalion 3/16 between 1982 and 1984, government repression remains widespread. With the closing of "political space" in the country, the number of Hondurans living in poverty has risen to an alarming 68 percent of the population, 56 percent of whom cannot even cover basic food needs.[29]

Militarization has also worsened the country's ecological crisis. According to the Honduran State Forestry Corporation (COHDEFOR), the U.S.–Honduras joint maneuvers known as Cabañas '86 destroyed 10 percent, or 10,000 acres, of the country's pine forests on the savannas near the Nicaraguan border.[30] In the town of Villanueva, some people even suffered skin irritations when a U.S. aircraft reportedly flew over their community and released a toxic yellow substance.[31]

The United States is apparently ignoring the environmental impact of its activities in Honduras. Joseph G. Hanley, spokesman for the U.S. National Guard, which actively participates in U.S. military projects in Honduras, told the *Washington Post* on April 5, 1986, that engineering projects in Honduras are "less environmentally constrained" than in the United States. "If you're building a road," he said, "you don't have to worry about width of the culverts, about the Environmental Protection Agency or about the environmentalists. Those are not concerns down there."[32]

The direct and indirect effects of the U.S.-backed contra war on the country's natural and human ecology are equally extreme. A recent report to the president of Honduras by a number of government agencies asserts that the contra war has seriously impacted their second most important export base: forests. According to newspaper accounts of this confidential report and other documents, Nicaraguan refugees and contras have generated a wave of destruction in Honduran forests. In southern Honduras near the Nicaraguan border, hundreds of peasant coffee growers were forced from their traditional landholdings by the contras in the 1980s. With other arable land in the grip of the wealthy Honduran landowning elite, small farmer families and communities had nowhere else to go but into the nearby Mosquitia rainforest to subsist through slash-and-burn agriculture, destroying some 111,150 acres of rainforests in the process.[33]

While Salvadoran refugees on Honduras's southeastern border are kept in camps surrounded by soldiers, some 20,000 Nicaraguan refugees, according to the report, have been subject to little control. The resultant environmental destruction included deforestation for subsistence agriculture, land clearing to establish contra bases, black market export of parrots, and illegal exploitation of valuable tree species, including mahogany, cedar, and pine. Forest fires have also increased; one newspaper account claims that refugees have set over 110 square miles ablaze.[34] Many of these war refugees have moved into the UNESCO Río Plátano Biosphere reserve, doubling the population there.

(The Río Plátano reserve was also threatened by a road that USAID planned to build there in 1983. The road would have connected the capital city Tegucigalpa with a major new U.S. military base at Puerto Lempira on the east coast, tearing through "the Amazon of Central America." Apart from the direct impact of such construction, the road would have opened large tracts of forested land to colonization by landless peasants, timber removal by logging concerns, and resettlement by refugees. Pressure from U.S. environmental groups on the State Department, USAID, and members of Congress helped stop the road. It remains to be seen how permanent this decision is, but organized action did save this fragile ecosystem for the time being.)[35]

Deforestation is so severe, according to the Honduran Ecological Association (AHE), that within twenty years Honduras's forests will be gone, perhaps destroying the economic future of the country. Of the total 286,945 square miles that make up the total area of Honduras, only 25 percent has potential for agricultural use. Over 65 percent is suitable only for sustainable forestry or other nonagricultural uses.[36] The deforestation has already caused widespread damage to Honduras in the form of soil erosion, siltation, changing microclimate, and floods. In 1989, according to Honduran academics and campesinos, hundreds of people died in the massive flooding that ripped through villages in the rainy season.

Commenting on the causes of the environmental crisis and deforestation in Honduras, Dr. Juan Almendares, leader of the Coordinating Committee of Popular Organizations (CCOP) and former director of the National University of Honduras, stated in 1990:

> First is the lack of any policy. There is no policy over deforestation. Secondly, the push for the privatization of natural resources has accelerated; the government has sold all the forests to transnational corporations. And third, a very important cause is the military maneuvers and Contra activity. You have to understand that military maneuvers, military bases, and contra, they all move from one place to another place, they migrate, and with each migration they destroy the forests, causing soil erosion, siltation, flooding, and a change in our climate. And now there is some financial interest by people involved in U.S.-Honduran military policy, like [former Assistant Secretary of State under Reagan] Elliot Abrams. He's trying to negotiate a deal with the timber companies to do extractive hardwood harvests using army helicopters in remote areas of the rainforest previously unreachable.[37]

Although the contra war and Salvadoran civil war have apparently ended, the militarization of Honduran society continues, undermining the possibility for a democratic and equitable solution to the country's deepening economic crisis. In the early 1980s, a guerrilla alliance, National Unitary Direction of the Honduran Revolutionary Movement, did emerge, but has been weak and ineffective. Even as popular movements continue to grow in Honduras, they have yet to develop an effective political strategy for democratizing Honduran society. Without a dramatic shift in U.S. policy, poverty, repression, and ecological deterioration will probably continue to worsen.

"Containment": Scorched Earth in El Salvador

For decades, El Salvador's popular movements have faced brutal repression at the hands of state security forces and paramilitary "death squads." A renewed wave of government violence in the 1980s claimed the lives of tens of thousands, including four U.S. church-women and the country's archbishop, Oscar Romero—shot to death in his church while saying mass.[38] The United States has played a direct role in the repression. Beginning in the 1960s, under USAID's "Public Safety Program," Washington organized, equipped, and trained the Salvadoran police and security forces, and continues to arm, train, advise, and fund the Salvadoran military today.[39] According-ing to a 1988 report by Amnesty International, the "death squads" are "made up of regular army and policy agents, acting in uniform or plain clothes, under the orders of superior officers."[40]

Continuous repression against El Salvador's popular movements, particularly following the military coup of October 15, 1979, com-pelled many of those working for reforms to take up arms and fight for a revolutionary overthrow of the military regime. Thousands of Salvadorans joined the FMLN. Several political parties comprising the Democratic Revolutionary Front (FDR) also allied with the revolution-ary struggle. By the end of 1983, the FMLN had won widespread support, effectively controlling at least a third of El Salvador's national territory and had become one of the most powerful revolutionary armies in the history of Latin America.[41] The Salvadoran military, in turn, escalated the repression into a devastating "counterinsurgency" war, deepening the spiral of poverty and environmental deterioration.

The bloody civil war, which lasted for another eight years before ending (for now) with the peace agreements of January 16, 1992, has left El Salvador in a state of social and ecological disaster. Today, well over a million people (or one of every five Salvadorans) have been displaced from their homes, a greater percentage than the number of Vietnamese displaced during the U.S. war in Vietnam.[42] One-tenth of the population has fled the country, including some 500,000

Salvadorans to the United States. Money sent back to El Salvador by these immigrants are estimated to total as much as $1 billion annually and are now the country's principal source of foreign exchange. The economy is in ruins, hundreds of villages lie destroyed, more than 75,000 people have been killed and thousands more wounded. Virtually every Salvadoran family has been directly affected by the conflict.[43]

As in Nicaragua, the United States has promoted a policy designed to ecologically and economically destroy El Salvador in order to "save it" politically. Since the start of the conflict, the United States provided more than $6 billion in economic and security aid, accounting for more of the country's budget than provided by El Salvador itself.[44] In the 1980s, this aid to El Salvador became part of the low-intensity conflict strategy, combining a military effort to defeat the FMLN guerrillas with aid and limited economic reforms aimed at co-opting the broader movement for social transformation. The Salvadoran army used U.S. aid funds and relief assistance as part of "pacification" programs to control the civilian population and undermine opposition organizations. U.S. military advisors were stationed in El Salvador, and U.S. pilots regularly flew reconnaissance flights for army campaigns. The United States also intervened extensively in El Salvador's internal political processes, promoting "demonstration elections" and an image of "democracy" to maintain Congressional funding for the war.[45]

As part of the counterinsurgency, the Salvadoran military adopted an updated form of the "scorched earth" strategy once employed by the United States in Southeast Asia, aimed at crushing the FMLN by depriving them of their base of support—the peasantry and surrounding environment. Military analysts likened the civilian population and their local ecology to a "sea" in which the guerrilla "fish" swim. The military solution? A war against nature—to "drain the sea" by bombing and burning forests and fields where the guerrilla army could hide, razing croplands and villages, slaughtering wildlife and livestock, and conducting military sweeps (*guindas*) of peasant communities, to kill or drive out the population.[46]

Like the FMLN, the environment became the enemy of the Salvadoran military. In the words of Colonel Reynaldo García of the Salvadoran army:

It is a fairly typical low-intensity light infantry war. Take the population away from the guerrillas, that's the way you win. It's like malaria in this area. You can do two things: you can treat people with malaria for as long as you stay in the area, for the next 3,000 years maybe, or you can drain the swamp and not have to worry about malaria anymore ... killing guerrillas by itself is like killing mosquitoes.[47]

Central to this strategy of "ecocide" was the air war, which began in October of 1982. By the mid-1980s, the silhouettes of A-37 combat jets and the high-pitched rumble of "Huey" military helicopters had become commonplace in the skies above El Salvador. The air war in El Salvador—the bombing of villages, crop lands, and forests— reached levels unprecedented in Central America. The primary weapon in the massive air assaults against the FMLN and civilian population were the 250-pound, 500-pound, and 750-pound bomb. According to U.S. military sources, the Salvadoran air force dropped 2,829,000 pounds of bombs on the Salvadoran countryside in 1984 and 1985 alone.[48] Wide areas of Morazán, Cabañas, and Chalatenango provinces became virtual wastelands, the landscape scarred with bomb craters up to fifteen feet deep, crops destroyed, and burnt forests reduced to secondary growth scrub or rock.[49]

Emulating Vietnam-era "scorched earth" tactics, much of the bombing was designed to "soften up" an area of guerrilla and/or civilian occupation for army operations. As one Salvadoran villager described it:

They entered into the houses, burned the corn, clothes, fruit trees, the earth and the grass. They burned everything. The people left the village, those who didn't leave hid so they wouldn't be found. When they see people, they fire many rounds indiscriminately. We live with bombings too. They last for two hours each day. They drop twenty, thirty bombs, the large ones.[50]

In addition to heavy bombs, other weaponry of mass destruction used in Vietnam by the United States resurfaced in El Salvador. For instance, during the supposedly "peaceful" period during the March 1984 national election campaigns, the Salvadoran Air Force dropped 7.5 tons of explosives each day on rural targets, primarily peasant villages. On May 26, 1983, Colonel Rafael Bustillo of the Salvadoran Air Force first confirmed that "napalm incendiary weapons had been used against guerrilla forces."[51] Napalm is a jellied gasoline that sets an area equivalent to 1.5 football fields ablaze in a matter of seconds. White phosphorous rockets were also utilized to set forest fires and mark targets for bombing, including village schools and medical clinics. White phosphorous is a soft, pliable, gray metal that is so highly reactive, it burns spontaneously when it comes in contact with air. In water, it explodes. White phosphorous can prove lethal in as little as two days if inhaled or taken into the bloodstream. "When burning white phosphorous enters the body, it keeps on burning," according to Harvard University biochemistry professor Dr. Matthew Meselson. "It will burn under water and actually burns inside the body. It can be a horrible antipersonnel weapon."[52]

"Iron" bombs or "daisy cutters" also found a niche in the Salvadoran government's arsenal. These antipersonnel bombs explode just above ground level, blasting a horizontal force that clears the area not only of human beings, but shaves the forest floor, leaving thousands of charred stumps and splintered trees in many mountainous areas and erosion-endangered terrains.[53]

For the past twelve years, government repression has made scientific documentation of the social and ecological impacts of these deadly weapons extremely dangerous. In 1983, while investigating the Salvadoran army's use of white phosphorous and charges that the army used biological weapons, Salvadoran human rights official Marianella García-Villa was assassinated. Shortly before her death, she told an interviewer: "I have taken many photos of densely populated areas bombed with napalm. ... I have taken photos of children burned by white phosphorous, and we have proof that the government of El Salvador is using arms prohibited for conventional warfare."[54] Her findings were confirmed by Dr. John Constable, a leading U.S. burn surgeon who visited El Salvador in 1984 and witnessed "perfectly classical, clear-cut cases of napalm bombing of civilians."[55] In Cuscatlán, other investigators documented widespread damage to sugar cane plantations and coffee crops suffered from 200-pound bombs, as well as from the use of napalm and white phosphorus.[56] It remains unclear how extensively these weapons were utilized.

The impact of U.S.-sponsored low-intensity conflict has been to destroy (perhaps permanently) the ecological conditions of subsistence production for hundreds of rural communities, exacerbating the deterioration of an already ecologically overburdened Salvadoran countryside. From the coastal mangrove swamps to the high elevation cloud forests, virtually every original ecosystem is in ruins.

The destruction of El Salvador's forests is particularly alarming. A report on the causes and effects of drought in the eastern provinces of El Salvador, undertaken for the Lutheran World Federation, emphasizes the use of bombs and artillery as one of the prime causes of deforestation over the past decade. It describes "the indiscriminate burning of large expanses of vegetation and the uprooting and destruction of trees that the army and the air force carry out both in conflict zones and zones of dispute."[57] The National Parks Service reports that less than 7 percent of the country remains forested.[58]

Much of the bombing occurred during the dry seasons, provoking devastating fires in what little remained of the country's pine-oak forests. Many of these blazes were intentionally set by government infantry before entering an area as a way of flushing out guerrilla forces. Communities around the town of Perquín in northern Morazán province, an FMLN stronghold, saw at least 4,800 acres of pine forest destroyed by bombing and fires started by the Salvadoran army in the 1980s.

Extensive bombing of the countryside has also claimed some of the last wilderness areas in El Salvador. El Pital's mountain cloud forest was once selected to become a national park because it was home to the highest density of coniferous tree species in the country. But now, because of extensive bombing, there are only remnants of this national treasure. The Cerro Nejapa, once an important wildlife and fauna reserve, also lost its original forest cover to devastation by fire and bombs.[59] In the mountains of Chalatenango, bombing obliterated at least 12,200 acres of valuable pines. Fires started by bombing and artillery reduced 2,300 acres of pine forest in the Cordillera de Jucuaran to charred stumps. Even Guazapa Volcano, once an important wilderness area just twenty miles north of San Salvador, has been severely damaged by the war.[60]

Many of these forests have not regenerated from such burns, reverting to less productive forest scrub or grassland, and unleashing a process of ecological deterioration. In Morazán, Chalatenango, Cuscatlán, Cabañas, and San Miguel, army operations have severely damaged agricultural soils, aggravating problems of soil erosion, dust storms, siltation of waterways and reservoirs, water pollution, and the drying up of natural springs.[61] In San Francisco Gotera, in Morazán province, war-induced deforestation and soil erosion have reportedly caused river beds to dry and the water table to drop seventeen feet in recent years, causing problems of desertification.[62] In fact, the combination of repeated bombing, burning, and military incursions over the course of the decade destroyed vast areas of agricultural land, particularly in the most conflictive areas.[63]

The deterioration of El Salvador's watersheds has been further aggravated by the bombing of the country's mountainous cloud forests and volcanoes, which have been hit especially hard. Since they provided natural hiding places for the guerrillas, many volcanoes— Guazapa, Chicontepec, Chaparrastique, Santa Ana, Usulatán, Conchagua—today have largely denuded slopes. As major sources of fresh water, the elimination of vegetation (which permits as much as 30 percent of rainwater to filter into the soil) from the slopes of volcanic mountainsides is eroding millions of tons of fertile soil, creating severe water shortages, and posing a direct threat to the long-term viability of El Salvador's economy and environment.[64]

Large fluctuations and drought problems are now prevalent throughout El Salvador. As one study stated:

> Bare ground has one-twelfth the water filtration rate that has the same ground covered with vegetation and trees. This means that the military practice of bombing and burning of mountainsides, volcanos, and cloud forests is jeopardizing El Salvador's future supply of water. Instead of slowly filtering into the aquifers, huge amounts of water are rushing into the rivers and ending up in the ocean. It is no surprise that El Salvador's water table is falling rapidly.[65]

Increased flooding and landslides are another product left from the war. In 1988, heavy rains and sedimentation damage to major dam sites flooded 148,200 acres of agricultural land, killing some 20,000 animals while causing 20,000 people to lose their homes.[66] In 1982, the deforestation of Monte Bello by refugees from the war zones resulted in a massive landslide after a rainstorm. It is estimated that over 1,000 people were killed.[67] With the destruction of their habitats, many of El Salvador's wildlife populations have also suffered, including forest-dwelling sloths, howler monkeys, iguanas, and deer.[68] Moreover, as El Salvador is on the flyway for many migrating bird species, the civil war's environmental aftermath is also threatening the wintering habitats of some North American songbirds, such as tanagers, warblers, kingbirds, and vireos.[69]

The war-related problems of the National Park Service (NPS) over the past twelve years has further contributed to the decline of wildlife populations. In 1979, the army confiscated vital radio equipment donated to the NPS by the World Wildlife Fund—and then converted it to military use. When a new shipment of radios arrived at the airport, the military high command prevented its delivery without explanation. Subsequently, all of the country's park rangers, most working in remote areas, were disarmed. Without arms to protect the site from poachers, the effectiveness of these rangers was undermined.

The danger of travel in the countryside, as well as repeated war-related budget cuts, seriously set back NPS efforts. Environmental workers themselves became the target of repression. Several area reports indicate that in 1982 army paramilitary patrols killed four rangers at the Montecristo cloud forest, even though guerrillas were not active there. Apparently, the rangers were seen as an obstacle to the illegal trade in endangered species of Salvadoran wildlife, an activity in which a number of Salvadoran military officers were reportedly involved.

In December of 1990, Dago Aguirre, a University of El Salvador researcher working with the Environmental Project On Central America (EPOCA) to visually document the environmental impacts of the war, was murdered by right-wing death squads. He had been badly tortured. Twenty-six other victims found dead at the same time also showed evidence of severe torture. EPOCA's visual documentation project came to a halt with Aguirre's death, as did a reforestation program run by the University and the Association of Indigenous People of El Salvador.

With the signing of a United Nations-brokered cease-fire on January 16, 1992, in Mexico City, there is now hope that the twelve-year civil war in El Salvador has come to a permanent end. The fact that El Salvador's popular classes were able to win such a favorable agreement reflects their political and military strength and the failure of Reagan/Bush doctrine to create a viable alternative to the FMLN.

Maintaining this fragile peace will ultimately rest on a number of major breakthroughs, including reducing the 63,000-member armed forces by half and ending the repression; FMLN participation in a new civilian police force to replace the militarized police forces; economic and ecological adjustments, such as distribution and revitalization of land in guerrilla-held zones; and the logistics and security guarantees for the rebels' incorporation into civilian life, including open participation of the FMLN and the broad opposition Democratic Convergence coalition as political parties.

There are indications that the United States is working to obstruct the United Nations-negotiated peace agreement, having requested $65 million in 1992–1993 military aid for the Salvadoran army. (Joint military maneuvers were canceled after widespread protest.) In all probability, the U.S. government will attempt to weaken El Salvador's popular movements, especially through manipulation of economic aid. Already the Salvadoran government, with the encouragement of the United States, has failed to comply with many sections of the peace treaty, including economic reforms and the dissolving of security units. Without international support for a just resolution to these questions, and an end to military aid, El Salvador may once again become an environment under fire.[70]

Destructive Development: U.S. Economic Aid to El Salvador

In carrying out its "containment strategy," the United States also utilized economic aid while promoting limited reform. According to a report by the U.S. Congress Arms Control and Foreign Policy Caucus, 75 percent of U.S. aid to El Salvador during the 1980s was directly related to the war, even though most funds were labeled "economic support." This military spending overwhelmed the $1.5 million—or .005 percent—of U.S. aid annually spent on environmental protection during the same period. In 1988, the United States spent almost 200 times as much on waging war in El Salvador as it did to protect and restore the country's devastated environment.[71]

War-related aid in the 1980s also overshadowed the small percentage the United States spent on health (4 percent), education (4 percent), and agriculture (7 percent) in El Salvador.[72] But even this small amount of "development assistance" often had negative consequences. Since 1984, the USAID has greatly increased its support for export agribusiness and discouraged food production for domestic consumption, thus deepening problems of inequality in the country.[73]

While USAID does support some small farmer projects, most of these are promoting pesticide-intensive "nontraditional" export crops such as melons and berries, which come at the expense of basic food production. U.S. law requires environmental reviews of USAID programs, but these impact studies have little or no effect on project planning. Salvadoran sources familiar with USAID projects have noted that USAID's environmental reviews have failed to make major shifts in destructive practices. Although some steps have been taken to make development aid more environmentally sound, these efforts are far less than what is needed in a country whose state of environmental decay threatens to undermine any future development.[74]

The one USAID initiative aimed at addressing El Salvador's unequal control of land was the 1980 Agrarian Reform. The U.S.-designed-and-funded effort had three phases. In phase 1, a few large estates were nationalized and turned over to peasant cooperatives. In phase 2, the holdings of the large coffee growers were targeted for redistribution, and a small farmer program was initiated as phase 3.

Although many planners and organizers supported this land redistribution to address the unequal agrarian structure of the country, the reform's primary goal was to quell unrest in the Salvadoran countryside as part of the low-intensity conflict strategy. The land reform was seen by the U.S. embassy as an imperative to help prevent political collapse, strike a blow at the left, and help prevent further radicalization of the peasantry.

The aims of the land reform proved to be contradictory. By maintaining support for the Salvadoran oligarchy and military in order to oppose the revolutionary movement, the United States made it impossible to implement those aspects of the land reform that might profoundly change the country's agrarian structure. The oligarchy successfully stymied the key second phase of the reform, the break-up of coffee estates. Growers blocked implementation of much of the reform in the National Assembly and evaded laws by dividing land ownership between themselves and relatives—making their legal holdings too small to be redistributed.

As in the Philippines and South Vietnam, the military used the U.S.-designed agrarian reform as part of the counterinsurgency campaign to establish a network of pro-government informers and agents in the countryside and as cover for the wave of violence that saw more than 21,000 people killed from 1980 to 1981. One technician working with the Agrarian Reform Agency reported, "The troops came in and told the workers the land was theirs now. They could elect their own leadership and run the co-ops. The peasants couldn't believe their ears, but they had elections that very night. The next morning the troops came back and I watched as they shot every one of the elected leaders."[75]

Because the Salvadoran land reform failed to redistribute the best lands and reorient production, it turned out to be ecologically unsound. Phase 3, "land to the tiller," gave title to some peasant farmers renting the most marginal and degraded land in the country. But by locking them into the same plots for thirty years instead of using traditional shifting cultivation, the reform eliminated the crop rotation and fallow periods essential for recovery of the soil. According to an Oxfam America analysis, the program served to "exacerbate erosion, reduce yields of basic crops, and trap peasants in a vicious circle of increased inputs (fertilizer and insecticide) and decreased income." Oxfam correctly predicted that the reform would make El Salvador more dependent on expensive food imports and increase the number of landless peasants.[76]

While some nonproductive forest lands from large capitalist estates were incorporated into the National Park System under phase 1 of the reform, enormous debt and lack of technical assistance forced many farmers to further overexploit their land. USAID's Inspector General said that 45 percent of the land parceled out in phase 1 was nonproductive, and most of the remaining land was of poor quality. New small landholders and cooperative farms created under the measure have been denied access to the credit or technical assistance essential for farming—support that is instead reserved for the large export estates. Today an astonishing 95 percent of the beneficiaries under phase 1 cannot pay their debts. Roughly 500 cooperatives owe $800 million to their landlords.[77]

More than a decade after it was initiated, El Salvador's agrarian reform is in shambles. The Supreme Court is currently controlled by rightists aligned with the oligarchy and has been systematically dismantling the campesino cooperatives growing basic food crops on their own land. With their land repossessed, campesinos are being forced back onto marginal forested lands and hillsides. The Salvadoran government is justifying the land take-backs, by arguing that the new campesino cooperatives are not making payments on their debts—debts they were forced to acquire to compensate the previous landowners.

Because of the debt, along with the lack of government support for small farmers and sustainable food production, campesinos are unable to obtain credit for capital investment into their cooperatives. With productivity declining, cooperatives are forced to sell their land to the highest bidder, thus renewing concentration of land in the hands of the oligarchy and agrarian bourgeoisie. Once returned to the estate farms of the wealthy, the land is again used for export crops, increasing hunger and the division of wealth in Salvadoran society.

This rollback of the minimal land reforms attempted in El Salvador is exacerbating the social and environmental crisis. Whether the terms of the recent peace agreements will succeed in reversing this process and revitalize the peasant subsistence sector remains to be seen.

Guatemala: The Forgotten War

As in El Salvador, the social and ecological crisis of the peasantry and an unwillingness on the part of the traditional coffee oligarchy and military to respond with meaningful reforms gave birth to a new wave of revolutionary activity in Guatemala in the late 1970s.[78]

By the early 1980s, Guatemala's revolutionary movement had grown to 6,000 combatants and spread to most of the country, including major economic zones. The Ejército Guerrillero de los Pobres (Guerrilla Army of the Poor, EGP) was active on seven fronts, nominally covering two-thirds of the country's territory. The most important fronts were the Ho Chi Minh in Quiché, the Ernesto Che Guevara in Huehuetenango, and the Augusto César Sandino in Chimaltenango. The Organización del Pueblo en Armas (Organization of the People in Arms, ORPA) was active principally in the departments of San Marcos, Quetzaltenango, Sololá, and part of Retalhuleú and Suchitepéquez. The Fuerzas Armadas Rebeldes (Rebel Armed Forces, FAR) was active mainly in the lowland tropical rainforests of the Petén. All of the organizations carried out military actions in the capital city.[79]

The Guatemalan revolutionary struggle continues today under the banner of the Guatemalan National Revolutionary Unity (Unión Nacional Revolucionaria Guatemaltecal, UNRG). Consisting of about 1,500 to 2,000 guerrillas, the UNRG is made up of the four guerrilla organizations listed above, and is active in twelve departments and in the country's two largest cities.

In an effort to crush the revolutionary movement, along with Guatemala's many broad-based student, worker, peasant, women's, and church organizations, the army launched a brutal wave of repression. Civilians, activists, and leaders of popular movements have been systematically murdered and tortured. Over the last three decades, 100,000 civilians have been killed and 40,000 "disappeared" by Guatemala's brutal military dictatorship—half of all the *desaparecidos* in Latin America.[80] According to Amnesty International, "... the vast majority of peasants killed in the countryside have been non-combatant civilians extrajudicially executed by the Guatemalan army."[81]

Despite the supposed move toward "democratic civilian rule" in Guatemala under pressure from the Reagan and Bush administrations, the killing and kidnapping by the army and government-sponsored death squads has increased, averaging more than seventy people a month. In the last four years of President Vinicio Cerezo's Christian Democratic government, some 2,638 people were assassinated, 857 people "disappeared," and 655 wounded in right-wing attacks. Despite the wide use of death squads for the past thirty years, only one military officer has been prosecuted for human rights violations.[82]

"Scorched Earth" in Guatemala

Since 1981, the Guatemalan government has implemented a "total war" against the country's popular classes. As part of the army's counterinsurgency operations, the military has carried out a systematic program of "scorched earth" and depopulation in the countryside, focusing on the highland provinces of El Quiché, San Marcos, Huehuetenango, and Alta Verapaz. As in El Salvador and Vietnam, the military strategy is to "drain the sea"—to eliminate the social and natural resource base of the revolutionary movement.[83] Thousands of homes and communities have been destroyed, as well as vast areas of forests and peasant agricultural lands, particularly in the region of the Ixil Triangle.

During the first wave of army offenses in 1981 to 1982 (dubbed "Victory '82" under the Rios Montt regime), some 440 towns, villages, and hamlets were destroyed. Early estimates placed the number of deaths at 10,000 to 20,000, but it is now believed that as many as 50,000 to 75,000 people (mostly Mayan Indians) died or "disappeared" as a result of the counterinsurgency war in the *altiplano* in the 1980 to 1984 period.[84] By more conservative estimates, over 45,000 civilians were killed by the military in the last decade. Another million Guatemalans have become refugees, including 200,000 who have fled to neighboring countries, particularly Mexico and the United States.[85]

The military strategy of the counterinsurgency is thus one of both ecocide and genocide: to isolate and destroy the environment and traditional Indian communities that support the revolutionary movement. In late 1982, Americas Watch reported: "One of the 23 linguistic groups, the Ixil in El Quiché, has been all but wiped out as a cultural entity."[86]

In March of 1990, representatives and delegates from all the Communities of Population in Resistance of the Sierra, gathered at their first general assembly, commented on the violence:

> Since 1981 and 1982 when our people demanded their rights, the army unleashed a heavy wave of repression, massacres, human rights violations, destruction of crops and bombings against us which continues at present. Since this time, the army has invaded and occupied our lands, villages and towns. They pursue us, destroy our belongings and trample on all of our rights.[87]

As in El Salvador, scorched earth policies are threatening to create a permanent social and ecological crisis for the Guatemalan peasantry, magnifying the very conditions that gave rise to the revolutionary movement in the first place.[88] A delegation of European Parliament members recently reported that "entire areas have been totally burned," and that "in some regions, the countryside gives the impression of complete devastation." The delegation reported that in the Ixil "development pole," for instance, "One can see the ruins of the former village on a hilltop. The hill was stripped clear of vegetation and now there is a military post. To avoid surprise attacks by the guerrillas, the trees growing in the streets have been felled and the forests around the edges of the villages continue to be cut down."[89]

Military operations—which have included bombing, napalm and other chemical weapons, and setting fires—have destroyed forests and wood fuel, agricultural lands, wildlife populations, water sources, and other ecological conditions of peasant subsistence production. The destruction is further aggravated by the total disintegration of the cultural fabric that holds communities in a sustainable relationship with their resources, leading to further deforestation, soil erosion, and ecological deterioration.[90] One group of researchers with the Environmental Project On Central America stated in 1990:

> In conflict areas, in order to cut the guerrillas off from their rural bases of support, the army forbids farmers to go to their traditional *milpas* (cornfields) which are often far outside their villages. Instead, peasant farmers were told to plant close by where the army can keep watch over them. The result is increased pressure on that land still in cultivation, with increased poverty and ecological deterioration.[91]

Consequently, many economically productive and ecologically sustainable systems of traditional Indian agriculture, including the use of fallow periods, terraces, and contoured cultivation, are being replaced with more destructive forms of "slash and burn" agriculture.[92] Soil losses in some areas now average two to fourteen tons per acre a year.[93] Some 87 percent of the population is now living in poverty, up from 79 percent in 1980, and half of the country's families cannot even afford a minimally adequate diet, let alone other necessities.[94] Not since the Spanish conquest have the highlands seen such a general cultural breakdown.[95]

Again as in El Salvador, documenting the environmental and social impacts of the military's scorched earth strategy has proved extremely dangerous. Myrna Mack, a Guatemalan anthropologist working with the Association for the Advancement of Social Sciences (AVANCSO) in Guatemala, was murdered by a right-wing death squad outside her office on September 11, 1990. Before her death she had begun a significant project to document the environmental and human impacts of nontraditional agriculture, as well as the impact of the army's violence on indigenous highland communities.

The Drug War

U.S. support for the Guatemalan military is stronger now than at any time since 1976, when direct military aid was withdrawn by the Carter administration because of human rights violations. During the Cerezo government, U.S. military aid jumped from $5.4 million in the mid-1980s to more than $9 million by the end of the decade.

Although Congress approved only $2.8 million in military support for 1990 (which was later canceled by the State Department following the December 2 massacre in the town of Santiago Atitlán—and other human rights abuses, including the murder of U.S. citizen Michael Devine), other forms of military assistance are increasingly significant.[96] These include military parts and weapons, including a recent shipment of 16,000 M-16 automatic rifles.

A growing influx of advisors and trainers for the notorious *kaibiles* (counterinsurgency forces), National Guard troops, U.S. contract pilots, and Drug Enforcement Agency (DEA) officials with planes and machine-gun mounted helicopters are fulfilling Washington's priority to "stabilize" the country. Since 1987, the United States has provided logistical air support out of the Palmerola Air Base in Honduras for counterinsurgency and military-controlled refugee settlement operations (in which there have been numerous casualties of U.S. airmen).

In addition, Guatemala has become the seventh-largest recipient of U.S. economic aid in the world, which is often used to further strengthen the military. Title II Food Aid funnelled through USAID into military-controlled "food-for-work" programs, for example, is used to build the "strategic military hamlets" to control the civilian population. Between 1986 and 1990, nearly $2 billion in economic assistance has been provided to Guatemala by the United States and international financial institutions, representing 40 percent of the government's expenditures during this period.[97]

The U.S. government continues to support a model of capitalist development oriented to the interests of Guatemala's right-wing military, local oligarchy, and U.S. capital. This policy, once pursued under the banner of anticommunism, is now increasingly justified by "demonstration elections" and the rise of the drug trade in Guatemala and the rest of Latin America. As the military increasingly comes to dominate ownership of the economy itself, Washington has increasingly viewed the civilian administration as corrupt, ineffective, and implicated in the drug trade.[98]

On April 21, 1987, the United States and Guatemalan governments began a drug eradication program using U.S. pilots and planes to spray herbicides on allegedly burgeoning fields of opium and marijuana in the tropical rainforests of the northern Petén, an area denominated by the military as a "conflict zone." It then spread to the San Marcos, Huehuetenango, Quetzaltenango, and Quiché departments.[99]

In violation of both Article 3 of the 1949 Geneva Convention and Article 4 of Additional Protocol II (referring to the protection of the civilian population, indispensable resources for survival and cultural rights during a conflict of a noninternational character), this program continues into the 1990s. In pursuing the program, the DEA is working arm-in-arm with Guatemala's military intelligence division, the G-2, notorious for its death squad connections, but seen by U.S. agencies as essential for collecting information on the drug trade. A U.S. "drug expert," quoted in the *Los Angeles Times*, said that the DEA "couldn't have done 5 percent (of what it has accomplished here) without G-2's help ... as long as they keep doing good work, you don't ask."[100]

As noted in Chapter 4, the DEA claims to be using only the herbicide Glifosato (glyphosate), also known as Roundup, during aerial sprayings, although other sources have reported the use of extremely dangerous chemicals such as paraquat, 2,4-D and 2,4,5-T, an Agent Orange component used by the U.S. military to defoliate Vietnam.[101] The latter is considered to be particularly dangerous, as it often produces an end product containing dioxin, which is tetratogenic (causes deformation in the fetus) in very low concentrations.

Human deaths, deformed children, ulcerations of the mouth and throat from drinking sprayed water sources, an increase in infant mortality, deaths of whole herds of livestock and scores of endangered quetzals and other species, destruction of an entire season's corn and tomato crop as well as honey bees, and widespread defoliation and forest fires in Petén and San Marcos have all been reported as a result of the sprayings in the last five years.

In late 1987, for instance, coinciding with the fumigation program, an enormous fire developed in the Petén, suspiciously burning for more than thirty days. The fire destroyed over 580 square miles of tropical forests in a department that UNESCO calls the "fifth lung of the world," and threatened the Tikal National Park. The spraying was briefly stopped in early 1988 after environmental protests and more than a dozen poisoning-related deaths but resumed soon afterward. Most of these effects cannot be attributed to the use or overuse of Roundup, but they are consistent with poisoning by such chemicals as paraquat, 2,4,5-T, and 2,4-D.[102]

Evidence is now mounting that the major drug plantations in Guatemala are owned, operated, and protected by high-ranking military officials. For instance, marijuana grown in the eastern Petén near the border with Belize is on land belonging to army officers, according to one news service.[103] The sprayings are also reportedly concentrated in areas of guerrilla activity in the Petén, San Marcos, and Huehuetenango, and serve primarily to support the government's counterinsurgency policy rather than attack drug plantations.

More threatening than local opium and marijuana production, Guatemala may be serving as an alternative to Panama (since the U.S. invasion) as a transfer point for cocaine from Colombia to the United States. Last year, a Guatemalan news agency reported that "a judge in the southwestern province of Retalhuleu revealed that there are 28 clandestine airstrips in that province used to transport cocaine to the U.S. market. Most of the runways belong to cotton producers. Drug traffickers pay as much as $50,000 to use them as refueling stops." Guatemalan military officers, including military intelligence, are reported as some of the main drug traffickers.[104]

Militarization of the Guatemalan Countryside:
Model Villages and Development Poles

The economic and ecological disintegration of traditional peasant communities under the weight of state terrorism has broken many systems of support for the UNRG guerrillas.[105] With hundreds of thousands of peasant families forced off their homelands, starving in internal exile or abroad, the Guatemalan government has initiated a program designed to lure them back under the control of the military. Over the last ten years about 60,000 peasants, mostly refugees from the army counterinsurgency, have been forcibly relocated to some seventy so-called "model villages," particularly in the degraded northwestern highlands.

Constructed with "obligatory" Indian labor and modeled on the "strategic hamlets" of Vietnam, these villages have provided the Guatemalan army with the means to provide maximum military surveillance over the civilian population. At the same time, they promoted a development alternative that does not threaten the existing system of economic privileges. Peasant farmers and workers are required to have passes to enter and leave the villages. Whole areas have been completely emptied of inhabitants, only to be repopulated when the army prepared model villages to receive them.[106] In some cases, the new hamlets were built in the same places where original villages had been destroyed.[107]

Another half million peasants live within the boundaries of a network of "development poles," which the army defines as "organized population centers ... that guarantee the adherence of the population, and their support and participation with the Armed Institution against communist subversion."[108] Within the development poles, "civil patrol systems" (or Patrullas de Autodefensa Civil, PAC), organized by the military, require all men from the age of sixteen to provide unpaid labor on the average of one day a week for the military's counterinsurgency campaigns.

These involuntary paramilitary forces are favored over the development poles and model villages because of the oligarchies' unwillingness to fund the reconstruction and maintenance of destroyed villages. Model villages required capital investment and food supplies; the civil patrol system simply required forced peasant labor, which is easier to come by.[109] More than a million Guatemalan men participate in these patrols, wasting invaluable time, energy, and resources needed for their own farms and family.

The establishment of Vietnam-style model villages, development poles and civil patrols, and of the army's S-5 Civil Affairs section, which promotes rural development and dependency on military bureaucracies for aid and investment, have created a virtual gulag across the Guatemalan highlands.[110] These additional systems of repression and social control are further hastening the breakdown of viable subsistence practices that maintained both peasant communities and the environment on which they were dependent.

Since the inception of the model village program, Title II food of the U.S. PL480 Food for Peace program has been channeled through CARE and the Guatemalan government Committee for National Reconstruction. Dispossessed on their traditional lands and denied a means of livelihood, peasant refugees have become dependent on government "food-for-work" programs and other U.S. and Guatemalan government social service projects, as well as the army and model villages, for their existence.[111] Absent meaningful agrarian and economic reform measures to create greater access to better land and other natural resources, as well as cheaper credit and other social resources, this dependency continues to grow.

This system of social control, however, is highly precarious. One likely result of the military's program of systematically disrupting traditional systems of life and production in the *altiplano* region is to reduce the availability of *minifundista* land and thus accelerate the process of proletarianization.[112] But the superexploitation of Guatemala's workers requires the maintenance of a viable subsistence sector in order to insure their survival. In the words of researcher Gabriel Aguilera Peralta, "To assume that this drawback could be compensated for by raising agricultural pay rates and augmenting social benefits through services planned for development poles is to ignore the characteristics of the system of domination.... The basic contradiction between the reformist aspects of modern counterinsurgency and the refusal by dominant sectors to accept any reform for any reason has not yet been resolved."[113]

The effects of rural counterinsurgency in Guatemala could in fact turn out to be the opposite of those sought by the armed forces. The history of revolutionary movements has demonstrated that when the peasantry have been torn from their land and traditional forms of life, but not incorporated into alternative forms of work and life, they join revolutionary movements most readily and with the strongest determination.[114]

For hundreds of thousands of internally displaced families who refuse to be resettled into the army's militarized zones, life goes on clandestinely in the forest highlands and the lush tropical rainforests of the Petén, where they grow food for their own consumption in small scattered fields, and struggle to keep ahead of the army's troops. These Communities in Resistance, as they are called, are noncombatant civilians being pursued by the army (which labels them as guerrilla sympathizers).

All together, some 85 percent of Guatemalans lack minimal consumer goods—housing, education, and health—and about 72 percent of the population does not have an adequate diet. While the Guatemalan military has maintained its dominance, it has yet to win the war.

Conclusion

To overcome the root causes of the social and ecological crisis in Central America, a new development path that is both socially just and ecologically sustainable is envisioned. Throughout the region, popularly based movements and political parties are struggling for goals necessary for this transformation to occur, including human rights, democratization, a negotiated settlement to regional conflicts, authentic agrarian and economic reforms which include democratic control of natural resources, a nonaligned foreign policy and an end to U.S. military intervention. In response, Washington's bipartisan "national security rationale" has aimed at preserving the traditional development model and class privileges of the landed oligarchy, agrarian bourgeoisie, military officers, and U.S. business interests.

In this respect, the U.S. counterinsurgency doctrine has achieved its primary goals—rollback and containment of revolutionary movements, at least for now. In Nicaragua, the Sandinista-led government has been defeated at the polls, and the revolution is in shambles; the Guatemalan revolutionary movement has been severely crippled; and in El Salvador, the United Nations has brokered a peace agreement, bringing an end to the civil war without placing the FMLN in political power. However, the U.S. government has continued to discourage the substantive economic and political reforms needed to fundamentally address the social inequalities and ecological problems that have created the Central American crisis.

Without a major shift in U.S. policy, the region will inevitably continue on its path towards further social, political, economic, and ecological destabilization.

CONCLUSION:
THE STRUGGLE FOR SOCIAL
AND ECOLOGICAL JUSTICE

It's about time that the U.S. environmental movement recognized that it has a crucial role to play in resolving the Central American environmental crisis.

Steve Sawyer
Executive Director, Greenpeace International

For centuries the diverse peoples and environments of Central America have suffered exploitation at the hands of imperialist powers, principally Spain and the United States, and their local client ruling classes, providing abundant sources of cheap natural resources for the world economy. But with the internationalization of capitalist-based agriculture and industry since World War II and the consequent development of more profitable yet more dangerous production processes, consumer and capital goods, and methods of waste disposal, ecological destruction, and human misery have become more profound. In Central America, as well as throughout much of Latin America and the third world, the unparalleled degradation and destruction of the ecological conditions necessary for the healthy reproduction of human beings (labor-power) and profitable capitalist production has reached crisis proportions.[1]

The ecological crisis has become a life-and-death issue, especially for the poor family farmers and workers who make up the vast majority of the population. U.S.-financed wars and scorched earth campaigns against the Sandinista government in Nicaragua, as well as against popular-based revolutionary movements in El Salvador and Guatemala, have devastated much of what little remains of the region's once lush forests and fields. Hundreds of thousands of people have been killed, and millions more displaced. More than two-thirds of the rainforests have been destroyed, taking with them invaluable plant and animal species. Erosion eats away at most of the agricultural lands, destroying the ecological basis for continued subsistence farming. Dangerous health and safety hazards pervade the workplace. Thousands of workers are poisoned each year by deadly pesticides. Massive deforestation, habitat and watershed destruction, agricultural and industrial pollution, and toxic dumping plague the region.[2] Some 50 percent of all Central Americans lack access to safe drinking water.[3] As a result, infant diarrhea and dehydration, malaria, polio, chronic parasitosis, and perinatal problems related to poor water and environmental quality, malnutrition, and a lack of social services remain leading causes of death. Women, children, and the elderly are hit the hardest.

As demonstrated by the case of the U.S. corporation Pennwalt, which dumped an estimated forty tons of lethal mercury into Lake Managua between 1968 and 1981 (rather than installing costly pollution control equipment), the economic prosperity of the United States in the post-World War II era has been based, in part, on the "externalization" of the social and ecological costs of capitalist production to the third world, including Central America. And in this era of "free trade" pacts and a "new world order," ecological imperialism is being intensified. Compelled by the deepening economic crisis of the United States and other advanced capitalist countries, a growing number of multinational corporations and banks are seeking to cut costs and boost sagging profits by investing in countries where regulations and enforcement of expensive environmental protection and worker health and safety is minimal. In short, the internationalization of capitalist production and the consequent export of further environmental degradation and health problems to Central America and the third world is creating an international ecological crisis, which, as in the case of rainforest destruction, is posing new threats to the integrity of the globe's climate, oceans, and atmosphere.[4]

Fueled by the innovations that have occurred in communication and transportation technologies, which now allow multinational corporations to do business anywhere in the world, this process is taking a number of disturbing forms.

First of all, in the *money circuit of capital*, U.S. corporations are now pursuing a more destructive scramble for cheaper sources of renewable and nonrenewable resources from Central America and the third world. These schemes to gain access to new oil fields, forests, agricultural lands, etc., which are leading to the export of massive natural-resource degradation, are motivated less by oil, food, or timber shortages than by capital's need to bring in lower costs for oil, food, timber, and other fuels and raw materials—lower costs that become generalized throughout the economy and help to fight the U.S. recession.[5]

For instance, Honduras, a country strapped for foreign capital since the end of the U.S.-sponsored Contra War, recently considered a proposal that would have destroyed most of its remaining forests, along with its indigenous cultures. According to the Task Force on Multinational Resource Corporations, Stone Container Corporation—the Chicago-based world leader in paper bag and cardboard boxes—pushed for exclusive rights to cut and manage the legendary La Mosquitia wilderness, a vast area in the northeastern part of the country, where savannas of lowland Caribbean pine are surrounded by lush hardwood forest and coastal communities.

Under a preliminary agreement signed in September 1991, the Honduran government would have allowed the company to cut, with virtual impunity, about 1,544 square miles or 988,000 acres of woodlands over a forty-year period in return for building a pulp mill in the fishing town of Puerto Lempira that would employ more than 1,000 Hondurans. Even though the agreement limited logging to the country's last remaining pine forests, instead of its more valuable tropical hardwoods, the roads projects into La Mosquitia would have resulted in much wider deforestation of the area by land-hungry peasants, cattle ranchers, and land speculators, as well as large-scale soil erosion, sedimentation of rivers and lakes, loss of diverse flora and fauna, and a drastic change in the indigenous cultures of the Mosquito Coast.

According to the Task Force on Multinational Resource Corporations, Stone Corporation would then have replanted clear-cut forests with the exotic gmelina, a pine species from India. The hope was that this fast-growing species could then be cut every five years, further degrading soil and species diversity. Stone's appetite for resources stems from its need to pay off its enormous debts (currently around $3 billion in junk bonds). Fortunately, massive local and international opposition has led the Honduran government to shelve the agreement, at least for now.

Multinational corporations based in countries other than the United States are also looking to exploit Central America's tropical forests. In Nicaragua, across the Coco River from Stone Corporation's contract area, lies a sprawling area encompassing 926,000 acres where Equipe de Nicaragua, a subsidiary of the Taiwanese firm Equipe Enterprise Co., Ltd., planned to cut tropical hardwoods over a twenty-year period. Under Equipe's preliminary contract, signed with the United National Opposition (UNO) government in August 1991, timber from cedar, ceiba, and rosewood trees would have been used for laminated veneer and plywood for the Asian market. In exchange, Nicaragua would have received a $30 million Taiwan loan. Under the proposed plan, the project would be tax-exempt for the first five years of operation, with an 80 percent exemption for the remaining period. Company representatives indicated that the UNO government would, however, recoup any losses "from the income taxes the workers will pay."[6]

Although economics minister Silvio de Ranco has called the firm's proposal a model for the future utilization of Nicaragua's natural resources,[7] a popular campaign led by the Nicaraguan Environmental Movement (MAN) has apparently forced President Chamorro to reject the concession. Whether the UNO government has really learned the economic and ecological lessons from the Somoza era, when such forest concession ripoffs were typical of the dictatorship, remains to be seen.

Another manner in which the United States is further threatening Central America's environment is through the export of pollution, occupational health and safety abuses, and other dangers in the *productive circuit of capital*. For instance, the escalating costs arising from the EPA's regulation of the disposal of toxic wastes has led some companies, as well as financially strapped local and state governments, to employ organized crime and other shady operations to handle and dispose of their wastes in the third world, including Central America.[8] In Panama, a plan developed in the late 1980s to send the local government of Bocas del Toro 250,000 tons of extremely dangerous dioxine-laden fly ash from Philadelphia (at $37 a ton, a bargain compared to dumping fees at home). This money would have been used to build a road through 3,000 acres of pristine wetlands—the last remaining Panamanian habitat for the Manatee, as well as home for tapirs, the white-collared peccary, sea turtles, ducks, and a variety of wildcats such as jaguars. The toxic fly ash could have also seriously affected the region's coral reefs, already significantly degraded due to soil runoff from nearby banana plantations. The plan was eventually rejected under pressure by the Panamanian and international environmental movements.[9]

According to Guatemala's National Environmental Commission, similar offers were also made in Guatemala by Applied Recovery Technologies Inc. (ART), a company representing the cities of Boston, New York, Washington, and Philadelphia, which proposed a twenty-year plan to send 10,000 tons a day of sewage sludge, contaminated with heavy metals, dioxin (one of the most carcinogenic chemicals known), and bacteria, to be used as "organic fertilizer" on the Atlantic coast and in Puerto Quetzal on the Pacific coast. The commission noted that if Guatemala, a country of eight million people, had accepted the plan, it would have been the recipient of "the daily waste of a population of approximately twenty million people."[10] The commission eventually succeeded in getting this plan rejected.

Honduras has been the target of "garbage imperialism" as well.[11] When Guatemala rejected the sewage sludge proposal, Los Angeles tried to buy a permit with Honduras. The plan to dump at least seven million tons of waste each year (at eight dollars per ton) in a pristine wetland along the country's Pacific coast, was also eventually rejected after public protest. A new plan by a U.S. firm, International Asphalt and Petroleum, to build an industrial waste incinerator in the isolated rainforest of Gracias a Dios, was also proposed. This plan, which has been defeated (for now), threatened to pose significant risks, both chronic and acute, to the public and the environment through the transport, storage, and incineration of toxic and potentially toxic wastes. If approved, the waste would have arrived in Honduras in one to four ships per month, each carrying 20,000 to 80,000 barrels weighing 450 pounds each.

Pat Costner of Greenpeace USA estimated that at maximum efficiency, which involves burning 403 million pounds of waste per year, "more than four million pounds of unburned wastes will be blown into the air. ... Once airborne, the toxic or potentially toxic wastes may be inhaled by the local people, farm animals and wildlife, or deposited in water resources, onto existing food crops, and onto soils where food crops will be grown."[12] Since 1985, Greenpeace has documented at least eighteen different schemes on the part of multinational corporations to dump hazardous waste in Central America.[13]

Finally, in the *commodity circuit of capital*, the United States is dumping and/or introducing more profitable but also more dangerous foods, drugs, pesticides, technologies, and other consumer/capital goods in Central America and the third world.[14] Every year U.S. chemical manufacturers export approximately 400 to 600 million pounds of toxic pesticides worth over $4 billion. A loophole in the current law allows U.S. manufacturers to produce and export pesticides that have been banned or severely restricted for use in the United States, because of health hazards and negative environmental impacts.[15]

For instance, even though the EPA banned the domestic use of

DBCP in 1979, because of evidence linking it to cancer and sterility, the Standard Fruit Company in Costa Rica continued using the chemical in the 1980s. According to a number of reports, thousands of Standard Fruit banana workers in Costa Rica and Honduras exposed to the chemical have been sterilized (see Chapter 3). In addition to massive fish, lobster, and shrimp kills, thousands of acres of former banana lands have been rendered irreversibly damaged by excessive chemical contamination.[16]

Although DBCP is no longer used in Costa Rica or manufactured in the United States, other pesticides banned or severely restricted in the United States are still being dumped around the world in a vicious "circle of poison." In June of 1991, residues of the Rhone Poulenc insecticide aldicarb (brand name Temik) were discovered at up to ten times the U.S. legal tolerance level on Latin American bananas. The pesticide treadmill and circle of poison is even reappearing in the new wave of nontraditional food crops, currently being promoted in Central America by USAID.[17] The Food and Drug Administration reports that in 1989, forty-five shipments of cantaloupe and snow peas from Guatemala were rejected for entry into the United States, due to pesticide contamination.[18] One Central American farm survey found the amount of the pesticide aldrin on cabbage to be nearly two thousand times the level allowed in food sold in the United States.[19]

Although ecological awareness and political mobilization has increased in response to the growing threats posed by the export of first world hazards (deforestation, toxic dumping, and dangerous consumer and capital goods such as pesticides) to Central America, governments throughout the region are nevertheless reducing environmental and human health programs as a way of attracting foreign capital investment, reducing a growing debt burden, and addressing the economic crisis. The debt crisis is particularly problematic because it is increasing the pressure on Central American governments to exploit greater reserves of natural resources as quickly as possible, to pay principal, interest, and interest-on-interest to the international lending agencies. During the 1980s, the external debt doubled, reaching $25 billion in 1990, with annual debt service (interest plus principal repayments) representing 30 percent to 40 percent of annual export income in most countries.[20]

As Central American nations become unable to meet their debt payments, changes in their national economic plans are being increasingly dictated by the U.S. government and international banks, such as the World Bank and the International Monetary Fund (IMF). These changes are innocuously called "structural adjustments" and are designed to increase the availability of foreign exchange to service the international debt. There are two main components to structural adjustments. First, the debtor nation is forced to cut imports and reduce government spending, particularly in the areas of environmental protection, health and safety, essential food and energy subsidies, and social welfare programs. These cuts hit hardest at the living standards of the working poor, particularly women and children. Over 65 percent of all Central Americans, some 15.3 million people, now live in poverty, unable to afford even an adequate minimum diet.[21]

Secondly, structural adjustment requires debtor Central American nations to boost production of traditional and nontraditional export commodities and foreign-exchange earnings. This is typically achieved through the intensified exploitation of both human labor-power and natural resources, further exacerbating the social and ecological crisis that lies at the root of the economic crisis in the first place. In Honduras, as well as in Costa Rica, which possesses one of the highest per capita debts of any country in the world, the IMF, USAID, and other lending agencies have pressured the government into promoting the substitution of basic grain production with nontraditional, chemical-intensive export crops, such as melons and pineapples.[22]

These crops are termed *agricultura de cambio* in Costa Rica, because they are meant to generate valuable foreign exchange to service the country's external debt. This policy is concentrating more and more land under export production, since the peasantry is unable to afford its expensive high-tech requirements. The country's once stable class of small farmers is losing their traditional land as a result, and is forced to migrate to the urban barrios and tropical rainforests in order to eke out an existence.[23] As stated by Josh Karliner, "Without a change in policy, Costa Rica could find itself moving along the same violent path that other countries in the region have trod."[24]

In summary, U.S.-imposed structural adjustments are forcing Central American governments to cut social and environmental protection programs at precisely the moment they are becoming most critical. But the so-called "debt-for-nature" swaps, where a lender nation forgives part of a debtor nation's debt in exchange for the debtor's agreement to protect part of its remaining wilderness, such as tropical forest lands, offer no solution—despite their popularity among some international environmental organizations.

Most commonly, a debt-for-nature swap is initiated when a northern environmental organization purchases debt at a substantial discount from a private bank and converts the debt into local currency to be administered by an in-country conservation organization. However, the debt swaps fail to address the systemic roots of ecological crises in Central America, and in many circumstances, actually worsen the problem.[25] Only with a major transformation of the current development model and U.S. policy in Central America can the fundamental sources of poverty and ecological deterioration be addressed.

Toward A New International Environmental Politics

The export of ecological hazards by U.S. corporations to Central America is becoming increasingly typical of the manner in which first world economic crises are being displaced to the third world in the form of social and environmental crises. This form of ecological imperialism poses an increasingly serious challenge to not only Central America and the third world, but also to the U.S. environmental and labor movements. Many of the national legislative battles waged by U.S. workers and environmentalists in the 1960s and 1970s to safeguard the health of America are being directly contradicted in the 1980s and 1990s by the export of jobs, industries, capital investment, and consequent ecological degradation and health problems, to Central America and the third world.

How can victories against ecological destruction at home not be undermined by the threats being shipped abroad? It is becoming increasingly clear that the U.S. environmental movement (not to speak of the labor movement) has weakened itself by its failure to revive the struggle to democratize the state and the workplace; to fight against ecological racism and sexism, and incorporate oppressed minorities and broader segments of the working class; and in particular, to develop solidarity with those movements and governments in the third world that know that capitalist economic development, ecological degradation, and human poverty are different sides of the same general problem.

The growing ability of multinational corporations and transnational financial institutions to evade and dismantle unions, environmental safeguards, and worker/community health and safety regulations in the United States, is being achieved by crossing national boundaries into politically repressive and economically oppressive third world countries. As a result, peoples and governments of the world are increasingly being pitted against one another in a bid to attract capital investment, leading to one successful assault after another on labor and environmental regulations seen as damaging to profits. And as I have attempted to demonstrate in this book, the absence of ecological and labor internationalism in opposition to capitalist exploitation is proving particularly disastrous for Central America, where labor and environmental protection is weakest.

As the crisis of world capitalism deepens and global ecological conditions worsen, the need for a mass-based international movement, which unites the struggle for both social and ecological justice, will become more pressing. The environmental and other social movements in the United States must be made to realize that they need strong environmentalism and worker health and safety in Central America, and throughout the third world, in order to protect local initiatives and gains. We no longer can afford the potentially self-negating strategy of protecting local and national gains at the expense of the third world. U.S. environmentalists, health activists, and trade unionists must internationalize and unite their movements. This is one of the major challenges facing the left.

This is not to say environmental organizing across borders to address the "internationalization" of ecological problems is not occurring. When news of the Philadelphia ash shipment plant to Panama got out, for instance, the Environmental Project On Central America (EPOCA) and Greenpeace built an international coalition between the United States and Panama that stopped the project.

As seen in the Global Forum at the United Nations Conference on Environment and Development (UNCED) in Brazil in the summer of 1992, there are signs that a progressive international ecology movement, perhaps even a self-consciously socialist or radical ecology movement, may develop in the future. In the United States, major environmental organizations such as Greenpeace, Earth Island Institute, Earth First!, National Toxics Campaign, and Friends of the Earth have periodically joined with the Rainforest Action Network, the Pesticide Action Network, and other organizations to oppose the capitalization and degradation of nature in the third world, especially in Central and South America. Many of these same organizations supported the Sandinista government's initiatives in revolutionary ecology and joined efforts with the solidarity movement to call for an end to U.S. domination in El Salvador and Guatemala on both human rights and ecological grounds.

Similarly, some 1,200 activists from seventy different countries and indigenous nations, representing hundreds of grassroots organizations around the world, attended and supported the Fourth Biennial Congress on the Fate and Hope of the Earth, held in Managua in the summer of 1989. Such international support is crucial for the many organizations and popularly based movements in Central America now struggling for a more socially just and ecologically sustainable model of development.

Summary

There are no easy answers to the social and environmental crises in Central America because solutions must address the fundamental question of power. A new social order that raises the standard of living for all citizens is essential to comprehensively address problems of poverty, injustice, and environmental destruction. Central American history has shown us that further "development" rooted in economic inequality will only worsen the already existing environmental crisis. A primary obstacle to achieving this new social order, however, has been, and continues to be, U.S. foreign policy and military intervention.

The human and ecological impacts of this intervention necessitate coalition building within, and between, the United States and Central American environmental, labor, and solidarity movements, as well as other movements for social and ecological justice. The U.S. and international environmental movements must inject their perspective into the public debate on Central America.

The United States must be made to support a long-term development strategy for the region, which is both ecologically sustainable and socially just. To achieve this goal, the United States must be pressured to support popular-based movements for social and ecological justice, instead of attempting to crush their struggles. Instead of viewing popular movements as a threat to its national security, U.S. foreign policy must be made to recognize these movements as the foundation of a new democratic order in the third world—a fundamental prerequisite for achieving the ecological security of the planet.

This environmental perspective can bring us beyond rhetoric to examine the real causes of conflict in the region. When we see how current U.S. policy carves a path to social and ecological disaster in Central America, as well as in other parts of the world, we can recognize the environmental imperative for social change. With informed analysis, we can begin to take environmental action at home.

The hamburger connection and circle of poison directly affect all citizens of the world. Although we can be somewhat effective at home, our environmental action must go hand in hand with support for fundamental social change in Central America, as new initiatives for structural transformation emerge in the region. We must also be aware that Central American efforts to address the root causes of environmental destruction face stiff opposition by those who benefit most from injustices in the region. As demonstrated in Nicaragua, revolution elicits counterrevolution; and again it is the poor and the environment that suffer most. We must join hands with others working for social and ecological justice, in Central America and throughout the world.

NOTES

1: A Legacy of Ecological Imperialism

1. In El Salvador, "the cumulative ecologic pressures of hunting, the use of fire, and the selective subsistence activities...significantly altered the early ecology of much of El Salvador." For a discussion, see Howard E. Daugherty, "Man-Induced Ecologic Change in El Salvador" (Ph.D. diss., University of California at Los Angeles, 1969), pp. 70–96.

2. Ibid., pp. 92–93.

3. See Robert M. Carmack, *The Quiché Mayas of Utatlán: The Evolution of a Highland Guatemalan Kingdom* (Norman: University of Oklahoma Press, 1981), p. 82.

4. See Jeffrey Leonard, *Natural Resources and Economic Development in Central America: A Regional Environmental Profile* (New Brunswick, NJ: Transaction Books, 1987), p. 10.

5. See Norman Myers and Richard Tucker, "Deforestation in Central America: Spanish Legacy and North American Consumers," *Environmental Review* (Spring 1987), 55–57.

6. Ibid.

7. Leonard, *Natural Resources and Economic Development*, p. 2.

8. Myers and Tucker, "Deforestation in Central America," p. 57.

9. Ibid.

10. See Steve C. Ropp and James Morris, *Central America: Crisis and Adaption* (Albuquerque: University of New Mexico Press, 1984), p. 1.

11. See Andrew Goudie, *The Human Impact on the Natural Environment* (Cambridge: MIT Press, 1986), p. 27.

12. See David Browning, *El Salvador: Landscape and Society* (Oxford: Clarendon Press, 1971), p. 19.

13. Goudie, *The Human Impact*, p. 27.

14. See Adrian Forsyth and Ken Miyata, *Tropical Nature: Life and Death in the Rain Forests of Central and South America* (New York: Charles Scribner's Sons, 1984), pp. 7–15.

15. For a historical review, see Murdo J. MacLeod, *Spanish Central America: A Socioeconomic History, 1520–1720* (Berkeley: University of California Press, 1973), pp. 23–45.

16. Myers and Tucker, "Deforestation in Central America": 58.

17. Leonard, *Natural Resources and Economic Development*, p. 4.

18. Browning, *Landscape and Society*, p. 10.

19. For geological descriptions of Central America, see Richard Weyl, *Geology of Central America*, 2nd ed. rev. (Berlin: Gebruder Borntraeger, 1980); and Robert C. West and John P. Augelli, *Middle America: Its Lands and Peoples* (Englewood Cliffs, NJ: Prentice-Hall, 1966).

20. Leonard, *Natural Resources and Economic Development*, p. 21.

21. Ropp and Morris, *Crisis and Adaptation*, pp. 8–13.

22. See Eduardo Galeano, *Open Veins of Latin America: Five Centuries of the Pillage of a Continent*, trans. Cedric Belfrage (New York: Monthly Review Press, 1973).

23. See Jan L. Flora and Edelberto Torres-Rivas, "Historical Origins of Social Structure and Class Formation: Introduction," in *Central America: Sociology of "Developing Countries"* (New York: Monthly Review Press, 1989), p. 5.

24. For a discussion of ecological imperialism and the restructuring of the "new world" environment as a means of conquest by "old world" powers, see Alfred Crosby, *Ecological Imperialism: The Biological Expansion of Europe, 900–1900* (Cambridge: Cambridge University Press, 1986). See also the North American Congress on Latin America's special issue, "The Conquest of Nature: 1492–1992," *Report of the Americas* 25, no. 2 (September 1992): 1–40.

25. See Linda Newson, "The Depopulation of Nicaragua in the Sixteenth Century," *Journal of Latin American Studies* 14, no. 2 (1982): 253–86.

26. See Browning, *Landscape and Society*, p. 42; and Newson, "The Depopulation of Nicaragua," pp. 284–86.

27. Browning, *Landscape and Society*, p. 31.

28. See H.F. Dobyns, "Estimating Aboriginal American Populations: An Appraisal of Techniques with a New Hemispheric Estimate," *Current Anthropology* 7 (1966): 395–449. For a discussion and dispute with these figures, see Newson, "The Depopulation of Nicaragua": 254–55.

29. Myers and Tucker, "Deforestation in Central America," p. 58.

30. Browning, *Landscape and Society*, pp. 41–50.

31. See Linda Newson, *The Cost of Conquest: Indian Decline in Honduras Under Spanish Rule* (Boulder: Westview Press, Dellplain Latin American Studies 20, 1986), pp. 89–165.

32. See Jan L. Flora, Douglas K. Benson, and Cornelia B. Flora, "Central America: Cultures in Conflict," in Flora and Torres-Rivas (eds.), *Central America: Sociology of "Developing Societies"* (New York: Monthly Review Press, 1989), p. 19.

33. See Jan L. Flora and Edelberto Torres-Rivas, "Historical Origins of Social Structure and Class Formation: Introduction," ibid., p. 5.

34. Flora, Benson, and Flora, "Cultures in Conflict," p. 19.

35. Browning, *Landscape and Society*, p. 32.
36. For a comprehensive study of Spanish colonialism, see MacLeod, *Spanish Central America: A Socioeconomic History, 1520–1720.*
37. Newson, *The Cost of Conquest*, pp. 116–262.
38. See MacLeod, *Spanish Central America*, pp. 80–95; and Browning, *Landscape and Society*, p. 52.
39. Browning, *Landscape and Society*, p. 134.
40. MacLeod, *Spanish Central America*, pp. 206–98.
41. Browning, *Landscape and Society*, p. 134.
42. Ibid., pp. 70–77.
43. Myers and Tucker, "Deforestation in Central America," pp. 58–60.
44. Browning, *Landscape and Society*, p. 32.
45. Myers and Tucker, "Deforestation in Central America," pp. 58–60.
46. Flora and Torres-Rivas, "Historical Origins" in *Central America: Sociology of "Developing Countries,"* p. 9.
47. Daugherty, "Man-Induced Ecologic Change in El Salvador," p. xiii.
48. See O. Nigel Bolland, *Colonialism and Resistance in Belize: Essays in Historical Sociology* (Belize City: Cubola Productions, 1988), pp. 15–25.
49. Myers and Tucker, "Deforestation in Central America," pp. 58–60.
50. Ropp and Morris, *Central America: Crisis and Adaptation*, pp. 13–16.
51. Browning, *Landscape and Society*, pp. 155–57.
52. See Ralph Lee Woodward, Jr., *Central America: A Nation Divided* (London: Oxford University Press, 1985), pp. 160–72.
53. Browning, *Landscape and Society*, p. 158.
54. See George Black, *Triumph of the People: The Sandinista Revolution in Nicaragua* (London: Zed Press, 1981), pp. 3–15.
55. For the most concise discussion of regional variations in the class dynamics of coffee, see Jeffery M. Paige, "Coffee and Politics in Central America," in Richard Tardanico (ed.), *Crisis in the World Economy* (Beverly Hills: Sage Publishers, 1987).
56. Flora and Torres-Rivas, "Sociology of Developing Societies: Historical Bases of Insurgency in Central America" in *Central America: Sociology of "Developing Societies,"* p. 35.
57. Paige, "Coffee and Politics," p. 145.
58. See Liisa North, *Bitter Grounds: Roots of Revolt in El Salvador*, 2nd ed. (Toronto: Between The Lines, 1985), p. 17.
59. See Michael McClintock, *The American Connection: State Terror and Popular Resistance in Guatemala*, vol. 2 (London: Zed Books, 1985b), p. 8; and Julio Castellanos Cambranes, *Coffee and Peasants: The Origins of the Modern Plantation Economy in Guatemala, 1853–1897* (Stockholm: Institute of Latin American Studies, 1985).

60. See Jaime Wheelock, *Imperialismo y Dictadura: Crisis de una Formación Social* (Mexico: Siglo Veintiuno Editores, 1980), pp. 108–10.

61. See Paige, "Coffee and Politics," p. 145; and Browning, *Landscape and Society*, pp. 174–207.

62. See John A. Booth, *The End of the Beginning: The Nicaraguan Revolution* (Boulder: Westview Press, 1985), p. 21. For El Salvador, see North, *Bitter Grounds*, p. 19.

63. Browning, *Landscape and Society*, p. 219.

64. See J. Edward Taylor, "Peripheral Capitalism and Rural-Urban Migration: A Study of Population Movements in Costa Rica," *Latin American Perspectives* 7, no. 2–3 (Spring-Summer, 1980): 76–77.

65. Paige, "Coffee and Politics," pp. 144–45.

66. Taylor, "Peripheral Capitalism," p. 78.

67. Ibid., p. 79.

68. Daugherty, "Man-Induced Ecologic Change," p. 51.

69. Ibid., pp. 122–204.

70. Ibid., pp. 205–06.

71. Booth, *The End of the Beginning: The Nicaraguan Revolution*, p. 21.

72. Browning, *Landscape and Society*, pp. 162–63.

73. North, *Bitter Grounds*, p. 19.

74. McClintock, *The American Connection*, vol. 2, p. 8.

75. Taylor, "Peripheral Capitalism," p. 79.

76. See Mitchell A. Seligson, *Peasants of Costa Rica and the Development of Agrarian Capitalism* (Madison: University of Wisconsin Press, 1980), p. 27.

77. Taylor, "Peripheral Capitalism," p. 78.

78. See David McCreery, "An Odious Feudalism: *Mandamiento* Labor and Commercial Agriculture in Guatemala, 1858–1920," *Latin American Perspectives* 13, No. 1 (Winter 1986): 99.

79. Ibid., p. 105.

80. Ibid., pp. 103–04.

81. McClintock, *The American Connection*, pp. 10–11.

82. See Jim Handy, *Gift of the Devil: A History of Guatemala* (Boston: South End Press, 1984), pp. 65–75.

83. McCreery, "An Odious Feudalism," p. 110.

84. See Robert L. Woodward, *Class Privilege and Economic Development: The Consulado Comercial de Guatemala, 1793–1871* (Chapel Hill: University of North Carolina Press, 1966).

85. McCreery, "An Odious Feudalism," p. 111.

86. Ibid., pp. 112–13.

87. Booth, *The End of the Beginning*, p. 23.

88. Flora and Torres-Rivas, "Historical Bases of Insurgency" in *Central America: Sociology of "Developing Societies,"* p. 36.
89. See John Weeks, *The Economies of Central America* (New York: Holmes and Meier, 1985), p. 22.
90. Booth, *The End of the Beginning,* pp. 23–27; and Weeks, *The Economies of Central America,* p. 23.
91. See Jenny Pearce, *Under the Eagle: U.S. Intervention in Central America and the Caribbean* (Boston: South End Press, 1982), p. 52.
92. Daugherty, "Man-Induced Ecologic Change," pp. 155–57.
93. See *Libro Azul de El Salvador* (San Salvador: Latin American Publicity Bureau, 1916), p. 54, cited in Browning, *Landscape and Society,* p. 216.
94. Daugherty, "Man-Induced Ecologic Change," pp. 158–60.
95. Browning, *Landscape and Society,* p. 167.
96. Daugherty, "Man-Induced Ecologic Change," pp. 204–05.
97. Browning, *Landscape and Society,* p. 224.
98. Daugherty, "Man-Induced Ecologic Change," p. 205.
99. North, *Bitter Grounds,* p. 18.
100. See Richard Lapper and James Painter, *Honduras: State for Sale* (London: Latin America Bureau, 1985), pp. 18–20.
101. Flora and Torres-Rivas, "Historical Bases of Insurgency" in *Central America: Sociology of "Developing Societies,"* pp. 33–38.
102. Lapper and Painter, *Honduras: State for Sale,* p. 20.
103. See Antonio Murga Frassinetti, "The Liberal Reform," in Nancy Peckenham and Annie Street (eds.), *Honduras: Portrait of a Captive Nation* (New York: Praeger, 1985), pp. 29–34.
104. Flora and Rivas-Torres, "Historical Origins," p. 13.
105. Lapper and Painter, *Honduras,* p. 22.
106. See Walter LeFeber, *Inevitable Revolutions: The United States in Central America* (New York: W.W. Norton and Co., 1983), pp. 42–46; and ibid., p. 22.
107. Flora and Torres-Rivas, "Historical Origins," p. 13.
108. Seligson, *Peasants of Costa Rica,* pp. 58–63.
109. See Victor Bulmer-Thomas, *The Political Economy of Central America since 1920* (Cambridge: Cambridge University Press, 1987), pp. 34–35.
110. Myers and Tucker, "Deforestation in Central America," p. 61.
111. McClintock, *The American Connection,* vol. 1, p. 25.
112. Bulmer-Thomas, *The Political Economy of Central America,* pp. 34–38.
113. Lapper and Painter, *Honduras,* p. 22.
114. Bulmer-Thomas, *Political Economy,* p. 33.
115. For data on declining terms of trade in Central America during the depression from 1929 to 1939, see Bulmer-Thomas, *Political Economy,* pp. 51–58.

116. Whether or not *real* wages for coffee workers actually declined remains uncertain, but it seems likely that unemployment posed the greatest economic threat to Central American workers. See ibid., pp. 58–60.

117. Booth, *The End of the Beginning*, pp. 21–62.

118. Ibid., p. 62.

119. Bulmer-Thomas, *Political Economy*, p. 66.

120. Daugherty, "Man-Induced Ecologic Change," p. 205.

121. See Leon Zamosc, "Class Conflict in an Export Economy: The Social Roots of the Salvadoran Insurrection of 1932," in Flora and Torres-Rivas (eds.), *Central America: Sociology of "Developing Societies,"* p. 61.

122. North, *Bitter Grounds*, pp. 29–35.

123. See Thomas P. Anderson, *Matanza: El Salvador's Communist Revolt of 1932* (Lincoln: University of Nebraska Press, 1971).

124. Farabundo Martí was executed on February 1, 1932. See North, *Bitter Grounds*, p. 39.

125. Lapper and Painter, *Honduras*, p. 28.

126. See Mitchell A. Seligson, "Agrarian Policies in Dependent Societies," *Journal of Interamercian Studies and World Affairs*, May 1977, p. 216.

127. Production relations on the coffee haciendas and banana plantations were mostly capitalist; workers were salaried, not peons. See Flora and Torres-Rivas, "Historical Bases of Insurgency," pp. 35–38.

128. Bulmer-Thomas, *Political Economy*, pp. 58–76.

129. Taylor, "Peripheral Capitalism," p. 81.

130. Ibid.

131. For a concise political history, see John A. Booth, "Representative Constitutional Democracy in Costa Rica: Adaptation to Crisis in the Turbulent 1980s," Steve C. Ropp and James A. Morris (eds.), *Central America: Crisis and Adaptation* (Albuquerque: University of New Mexico Press, 1984) pp. 153–87.

132. Bulmer-Thomas, *Political Economy*, p. 60.

133. Lapper and Painter, *Honduras*, p. 27.

134. McCreery, "An Odious Feudalism," p. 114.

135. McClintock, *The American Connection*, vol. 1, p. 25.

136. For a discussion, see Jim Handy, *Gift of the Devil: A History of Guatemala* (Boston: South End Press, 1984), pp. 103–27.

137. McClintock, *The American Connection*, vol. 2, p. 26.

138. Ibid., p. 29.

139. For a good summary, see James Painter, *Guatemala: False Hope, False Freedom* (London: Latin America Bureau, 1987).

2: Poverty, Injustice, and the Ecological Crisis

1. Quoted from a leaflet entitled *The Committee for Peasant Unity to the People of Guatemala*, circulated at the 1978 May Day demonstrations in Guatemala City by the mass organization Comité de Unidad Campesina (Committee for Peasant Unity); cited in Michael McClintock, *The American Connection: State Terror and Popular Resistance in Guatemala*, vol. 2 (London: Zed Books, 1985b), p. 146.

2. See Jonathan Evan Maslow, *Bird of Life, Bird of Death: A Naturalist's Journey Through a Land of Political Turmoil* (New York: Laurel, 1986); and Thomas Belt, *The Naturalist in Nicaragua* (Chicago: University of Chicago Press, 1985).

3. In Nicaragua, where gold remained an important export, the share was less than 50 percent. See Victor Bulmer-Thomas, *The Political Economy of Central America since 1920* (Cambridge: Cambridge University Press, 1987), p. 111.

4. See Michael A. Webb, "Economic Opportunity and Labor Markets in Central America," in Kenneth M. Coleman and George C. Herring (eds.), *The Central American Crisis: Sources of Conflict and the Failure of U.S. Policy* (Wilmington: Scholarly Resources Inc., 1985), p. 19.

5. See Albert Szymanski, *The Logic of Imperialism* (New York: Praeger Press, 1981), p. 181.

6. See Walter LeFeber, *Inevitable Revolutions: The United States in Central America* (New York: W.W. Norton and Company, 1983); and Robert Henriques Firling and Luis Goldring, "U.S. Strategic Interests in Central America: The Economics and Geopolitics of Empire," in Stanford Central America Action Network (ed.), *Revolution in Central America* (Boulder: Westview Press, 1983), pp. 186–205.

7. Alain de Janvry uses Lenin's concept of the "junker road" to describe national agricultural development based on large-scale estates (as in El Salvador, Guatemala, and to a lesser extent Nicaragua), and "farmer road" to describe development based on smaller family farms (as in Honduras and Costa Rica). I prefer the terms "*latifundio* road" and "*minifundio* road" to describe capitalist development in Latin America because of the greater cultural, historical, and political-economic specificity which these terms imply. See Alain de Janvry, *The Agrarian Question and Reformism in Latin America* (Baltimore: Johns Hopkins Press, 1981); and Jan L. Flora and Edelberto Torres-Rivas, "Sociology in Developing Societies: Historical Bases of Insurgency in Central America," in Jan L. Flora and Edelberto Torres-Rivas (eds.), *Central America: Sociology of Developing Countries* (New York: Monthly Review Press, 1989).

8. See Georgeanne Chapin and Robert Wasserstrom, "Pesticide Use and

Malaria Resurgence in Central America and India," *The Ecologist* 13, no. 4 (1983): 115–17; and Robert Williams, *Export Agriculture and the Crisis in Central America* (Chapel Hill: University of North Carolina Press, 1986), p. 21.

9. See Howard Daugherty, "Man-Induced Ecological Change in El Salvador" (Ph.D. diss., University of California at Los Angeles, 1969), p. 202; Howard Daugherty, Charles A. Jeannert-Grosjean, and H.F. Fletcher, *Ecodevelopment and International Cooperation: Potential Applications for El Salvador* (Ottawa: CIDA and Advanced Concepts Center of the Environment, 1979), pp. 32–34; USAID-Nicaragua I, *Environmental Profile of Nicaragua*, prepared by Steven L. Hilty (Tucson: Arid Lands Information Center, University of Arizona, 1981), p. 5; and USAID-Guatemala I, *Draft Environmental Profile of Guatemala* (Athens: Institute of Ecology, University of Georgia, 1981), pp. 5–19.

10. See Charles Brockett, *Land, Power, and Poverty: Agrarian Transformation and Political Conflict in Central America* (Boston: Unwin Hyman, 1988), pp. 68–69.

11. See Williams, *Export Agriculture*, pp. 13–32; ICAITI, *An Environmental and Economic Study of the Consequences of Pesticide Use in Central American Cotton Production: Final Report* (Guatemala City: Instituto Centroamericano de Investigación y Tecnología Industrial, 1977), p. 177; and Loria Ann Thrupp, "The Political Ecology of Pesticide Use in Developing Countries: Dilemmas in the Banana Sector of Costa Rica" (Ph.D. diss., University of Sussex, England, 1988), pp. 198–203.

12. See Tensie Whelan, "Rebuilding A Tropical Forest," *Environmental Action*, November/December 1987, p. 16.

13. Williams, *Export Agriculture*, p. 223.

14. See H. Jeffrey Leonard, *Natural Resources and Economic Development in Central America: A Regional Environmental Profile* (New Brunswick, NJ: Transaction Books, 1987), p. 7.

15. See James Nations and H. Jeffrey Leonard, "Grounds of Conflict in Central America," in Janet Welsh Brown (ed.), *Bordering on Trouble: Resources and Politics in Latin America* (Bethesda: Adler and Adler, 1986), p. 72.

16. Ibid.

17. Leonard, *Natural Resources*, p. 99.

18. See John Weeks, *The Economies of Central America* (New York: Holmes and Meier, 1985), pp. 96–98.

19. Flora and Torres-Rivas, "Historical Bases of Insurgency," p. 37.

20. De Janvry, *The Agrarian Question and Reformism in Latin America*, pp. 32–49.

21. For a discussion of the Central American economy, see Xabier

Gorostiaga and Peter Marchetti, "The Central American Economy: Conflict and Crisis," in Nora Hamilton, Jeffrey A. Frieden, Linda Fuller, and Manuel Pastor, Jr. (eds.), *Crisis in Central America: Regional Dynamics and U.S. Policy in the 1980s* (Boulder: Westview Press, 1988), pp. 119–36.

22. Bulmer-Thomas, *Political Economy*, p. 189.

23. Weeks, *The Economies of Central America*, pp. 55–86.

24. Ibid., pp. 59–60.

25. See Tom Barry, *Roots of Rebellion: Land and Hunger in Central America* (Boston: South End Press, 1987), pp. 43–65.

26. For a theoretical discussion of negative externalities, see Narindar Singh, *Economics and the Crisis of Ecology* (London: Oxford University Press, 1976), pp. 26–30.

27. In Costa Rica under the *minifundio* development model, a majority in the coffee-growing areas of the Central Valley around San José enjoy the best rural social services (paved roads, piped water supplies, electricity, etc) in Latin America. According to Weeks, *The Economies of Central America*, pp. 41–43, virtually 100 percent of the country's urban dwellers have access to piped water, compared to 66 percent of the rural population. No country in Latin America or the Caribbean supplies a larger potion of its rural population with piped water.

28. See USAID-Honduras II, *Honduras: Country Environmental Profile* (McLean, VA: JRB Associates, 1982).

29. See Morris J. Blachman and Kenneth E. Sharpe, "Things Fall Apart: Trouble Ahead in El Salvador," *World Policy Journal*, Winter, 1988, p. 111.

30. See USAID-El Salvador I, *Environmental Profile of El Salvador*, prepared by Steven L. Hilty (Tucson: Arid Lands Information Center, University of Arizona, 1982), pp. 91–92.

31. USAID-Honduras II, *Honduras: Country Environmental Profile*, p. 23.

32. See USAID-Costa Rica I, *Costa Rica: Country Environmental Profile*, prepared by Gary Hartshorn et al. (San Jose: Tropical Science Center, 1982), pp. 7–10.

33. See David Michaels, Clara Barrera, and Manuel G. Gachara, "Occupational Health and the Economic Development of Latin America," in Jane H. Ives (ed.), *The Export of Hazard: Transnational Corporations and Environmental Control Issues* (Boston: Routledge and Kegan Paul, 1985), pp. 94–114; and Joshua Karliner and Daniel Faber, with Robert Rice, *Nicaragua: An Environmental Perspective*, Green Paper no. 1 (San Francisco: Environmental Project on Central America, 1986).

34. See IRENA (Instituto Nicaragüense de Recursos Naturales y del Ambiente), *Planificación de Cuencas Hidrográficas: Plan de Ordenamiento y Manejo* 3 (Managua, 1983), p. 170.

35. For a discussion of worker health and safety problems related to pesticide exposure and programs launched in revolutionary Nicaragua to combat this problem, see Douglas L. Murray, "Pesticides, Politics and the Nicaraguan Revolution," *Policy Studies Review* (November 1984); and Sean L. Swezey and Daniel Faber, "Disarticulated Accumulation, Agroexport, and Ecological Crisis in Nicaragua: The Case of Cotton," *Capitalism, Nature, Socialism: A Journal of Socialist Ecology* no. 1 (Fall 1988): 47–68.

36. See USAID-Costa Rica I, *Country Environmental Profile*, p. 7.

37. Thrupp, "Political Ecology," pp. 157–74.

38. For a discussion, see Chapter 3; and Daniel Faber, "Imperialism and the Crisis of Nature in Central America," Ph.D. dissertation (Santa Cruz: University of California, 1989), pp. 251–94.

39. ICAITI, *Consequences of Pesticide Use*, p. 2; and Sean L. Swezey, Douglas L. Murray, and Rainer G. Daxl, "Nicaragua's Revolution in Pesticide Policy," *Environment* 28, no. 1 (January/February 1986): 29–30.

40. See Jeffery M. Paige, "Cotton and Revolution in Nicaragua," presented at *The Eighth Conference on the Political Economy of the World System* (Brown University, 1984); and Laura Enríquez, *Harvesting Change: Labor and Agrarian Reform in Nicaragua, 1979–1990* (Chapel Hill: University of North Carolina Press, 1991).

41. On the average, the price of labor power will be the difference between the cost of subsistence for the worker and his/her family and the production of use values or petty commodities that can be obtained from the land plot. See de Janvry, *The Agrarian Question*, pp. 80–83.

42. Ibid.

43. See James Painter, *Guatemala: False Hope, False Freedom* (London: Latin American Bureau, 1987), p. 40.

44. See Carmen Diana Deere, "Rural Women's Subsistence Production in the Capitalist Periphery" in Robin Cohen, Peter Gutkind, and Phyllis Brazier (eds.), *Peasants and Proletarians: The Struggle of Third World Workers* (New York: Monthly Review Press, 1979), p. 138.

45. See William Durham, *Scarcity and Survival in Central America: The Ecological Origins of the Soccer War* (Stanford: Stanford University Press, 1989). Durham terms this process "competitive exclusion," and goes the furthest in exploring various ecological and demographic contradictions of functional dualism in El Salvador. See also Alain de Janvry and C. Garramon, "The Dynamics of Rural Poverty in Latin America," *Journal of Peasant Studies* 4 (1977): 206–16.

46. Bulmer-Thomas, *Political Economy*, pp. 222–23.

47. Ibid., pp. 115–28.

48. See Peter Dorner and Rodolfo Quiros, "Institutional Dualism in Central

America's Agricultural Development," Stanford Central America Action Network (ed.), *Revolution in Central America* (Boulder: Westview Press, 1983), pp. 222–23.

49. Ibid., p. 221.
50. Williams, *Export Agriculture*, p. 58.
51. See James J. Parsons, "Forest to Pasture: Development or Destruction?," *Revista de Biologia Tropical* 24 (1976): 121; and Williams, *Export Agriculture*, p. 113.
52. See Charles D. Brockett, *Land, Power, and Poverty: Agrarian Transformation and Political Conflict in Central America* (Boston: Unwin Hyman, 1988), pp. 73–82. See also Nations and Leonard, "Grounds of Conflict," p. 72; and Joshua Karliner, "The Ecological Destabilization of Central America," *World Policy Journal*, Fall 1989, p. 790.
53. See James Nations and Daniel Komer, "Rainforests and the Hamburger Society," *Environment*, April 1983.
54. Brockett, *Land, Power, and Poverty*, p. 73.
55. See Monica Ewert, "Human Impact on the Aquatic Ecosystem of the Rio Lempa, El Salvador" (M.A. thesis in environmental studies, York University, 1978), p. 77.
56. See USAID-Honduras II, *Country Environmental Profile*, p. 37.
57. See USAID-Panama II, *State of the Environment and Natural Resources* (Washington, DC: International Science and Technology Institute, 1980), p. 61.
58. Brockett, *Land, Power, and Poverty*, p. 75.
59. Dorner and Quiros, "Institutional Dualism," p. 225; and Enríquez, *Harvesting Change*, p. 51.
60. See USAID-Nicaragua I, *Environmental Profile*, pp. 56–57.
61. Dorner and Quiros, "Institutional Dualism," p. 224.
62. Michaels, Barrera, and Gachara, "Occupational Health," in Ives (ed.), *The Export of Hazard*, pp. 96–97.
63. ICAITI, *An Environmental and Economic Study of the Consequences of Pesticide Use.*
64. Paige, "Cotton and Revolution in Nicaragua."
65. Williams, *Export Agriculture*, pp. 64–65; Dorner and Quiros, "Institutional Dualism," pp. 223–24; and Lester Schmid, *The Role of Migratory Labor in the Economic Development of Guatemala* Research Paper no. 22 (Madison: Land Tenure Center, 1967), p. 12.
66. See Jeffery M. Paige, *Agrarian Revolution: Social Movements and Export Agriculture in the Underdeveloped World* (New York: Free Press, 1975), p. 361; and Washington Office on Latin America, *Guatemala: The Roots of Revolution* (Washington, DC: WOLA, 1983), p. 3.
67. Dorner and Quiros, "Institutional Dualism," p. 224.

68. See Williams, *Export Agriculture*, pp. 64–65.

69. See Carlos M. Vilas, *The Sandinista Revolution: National Liberation and Social Transformation in Central America* (New York: Monthly Review Press, 1986), pp. 63–66.

70. See Jaime Biderman, "The Development of Capitalism in Nicaragua: A Political Economic History," *Latin American Perspectives* 36 , no. 1 (1983).

71. See David Kaimowitz, "Agrarian Structure in Nicaragua and its Implications for Policies Towards the Rural Poor" (Ph.D. diss., University of Wisconsin, Madison, 1986).

72. Flora and Torres-Rivas, "Historical Bases," p. 50.

73. Ibid., p. 37.

74. For a pathbreaking discussion of these concepts, see James O'Connor, "Capitalism, Nature, Socialism: A Theoretical Introduction," *Capitalism, Nature, Socialism: A Journal of Socialist Ecology* No.1 (Fall 1988): 11–38.

75. De Janvry, *The Agrarian Question*, pp. 85–87.

76. For an excellent critique of de Janvry's work as it relates to Central America versus South America, see Timothy Wise, "The Current Food Crisis in Latin America: A Discussion of de Janvry's *The Agrarian Question*," *Latin American Perspectives* 14, no. 3 (Summer 1987). For an analysis of functional dualism and agroecology in Latin America, see Frederick H. Buttel, "Toward a Rural Sociology of Global Resources: Social Structure, Ecology, and Latin American Agricultural Development," in Kenneth A. Dahlberg and John W. Bennet, eds., *Natural Resources and People: Conceptual Issues in Interdisciplinary Research* (Boulder: Westview Press, 1986).

77. For a discussion, see David Browning, *El Salvador: Landscape and Society* (Oxford: Clarendon Press, 1971).

78. For example, see USAID-Honduras II, *Country Environmental Profile*, p. 37.

79. For instance, see P.F. Barlett, "Labor Efficiency and the Mechanism of Agricultural Evolution," *Journal of Anthropolitical Research* 32, no.2 (1976): 124–40; P.F. Barlett, "Adaptive Strategies in Peasant Agricultural Production," *Annual Review of Anthropology* 9 (1980): 545–74; D. Windsor and R. Stanley, *Evidence of Climatic Change in the Rainfall Records of Panama and Costa Rica* (Panama: Smithsonian Research Institute, 1984); and Steve Lustgarden, "El Salvador: The Political Economy of Environmental Destruction," unpublished manuscript (EPOCA, 1984).

80. USAID-Honduras II, *Country Environmental Profile*, pp. 47–48.

81. Leonard, *Natural Resources and Economic Development*, pp. 82–128; and Brockett, *Land, Power, and Poverty*, p. 80.

82. USAID-Costa Rica I, *Country Environmental Profile*, pp. 55–58.

83. Ibid., pp. 6–64.

84. See Susan E. Place, "Ecological and Social Consequences of Export Beef Production in Guanacaste Province, Costa Rica" (Ph.D. diss., University of California, Los Angeles, 1981), pp. 114–16.

85. Leonard, *Natural Resources and Economic Development*, p. 82.

86. USAID-Costa Rica I, *Country Environmental Profile*, pp. 3–35.

87. See Billie R. DeWalt, "Microcosmic and Macrocosmic Processes of Agrarian Change in Southern Honduras: The Cattle Are Eating the Forest," in Billie DeWalt and Pertti J. Pelto (eds.), *Micro and Macro Levels of Analysis in Anthropology: Issues in Theory and Research* (Boulder: Westview Press, 1985), pp. 226–34.

88. USAID-Honduras II, *Country Environmental Profile*, p. 93.

89. See Jefferson Boyer, "Agrarian Capitalism and Peasant Praxis in Southern Honduras" (Ph.D. diss., University of North Carolina, Chapel Hill: 1983).

90. Leonard, *Natural Resources and Economic Development*, p. 82; and USAID-Honduras II, *Country Environmental Profile*, p. 37.

91. Brockett, *Land, Power, and Poverty*, p. 80.

92. See Florence Gardner, with Yaakov Garb and Marta Williams, *Guatemala: A Political Ecology*, Green Paper No.5 (San Francisco: Environmental Project On Central America, 1990); and UNICEF, *Dimensions of Poverty in Latin America and the Caribbean* (Washington, DC: 1982).

93. USAID-Guatemala I, *Draft Environmental Profile*, p. 18.

94. See USAID-Guatemala II, *Perfíl Ambiental de la República de Guatemala* (Guatemala City: Universidad Rafael Landivar, 1984).

95. See Gardner, Garb, and Williams, *Guatemala*, p. 3.

96. For a review of El Salvador's ecological crisis, see Bill Hall and Daniel Faber, *El Salvador: Ecology of Conflict*, Green Paper no. 4 (San Francisco: Environmental Project On Central America, 1989).

97. See Weeks, *The Economies of Central America*, p. 112; and Brockett, *Land, Power, and Poverty*, p. 74.

98. See OAS, El Salvador: Zonificación Agricola, Fase I (Washington, DC: 1974); Howard Daugherty, Charles A. Jeannert-Grosjean, and H.F. Fletcher, *Ecodevelopment and International Cooperation: Potential Applications for El Salvador* (Ottawa: CIDA and Advanced Concepts Center of the Environment, 1979), p. 40; Howard Daugherty, "Man-Induced Ecological Change in El Salvador" (Ph.D. diss., University of California, Los Angeles: 1969); and Leonard, *Natural Resources and Economic Development*, pp. 128–29.

99. See USAID-El Salvador I, *Environmental Profile* p. 89.

100. Blachman and Sharpe, "Things Fall Apart," p. 111.

101. Lustgarden, "Environmental Destruction," p. 45.

102. See Jeffrey R. Jones, "The Central American Energy Problem: Anthro-

pological Perspectives on Fuelwood Supply and Production," *Culture and Agriculture* 22 (1984): 6–9.

103. Ibid., pp. 6–7; and Leonard, *Natural Resources and Economic Development*, p. 62.

104. USAID-Honduras II, *Country Environmental Profile*, p. 61.

105. See Ariane van Buren, "An Analysis of the Commercial Woodfuel System in Nicaragua" (Ph.D. diss., University of Sussex, England, 1988), pp. 1–97.

106. Jones, "The Central American Energy Problem."

107. See Place, "Ecological and Social Consequences," pp. 173–76; and Daugherty et al., *Ecodevelopment*, p. 32.

108. See Place, "Ecological and Social Consequences," p. 177.

109. USAID-El Salvador I, *Environmental Profile*, pp. 89–90.

110. For a discussion of wildlife exploitation, see Leonard, *Natural Resources and Economic Development*, p. 155.

111. Ibid., pp. 155–58.

112. Hall and Faber, *Ecology of Conflict*, p. 7.

113. Gardner, Garb, and Williams, *Guatemala*, p. 3.

114. See Jane McAlevey, "Honduras: Multi-Nationals, Military and Ecological Crisis," *EPOCA Update*, Spring 1990, pp. 1–13.

115. For a discussion, see Michael McClintock, *The American Connection: State Terror and Popular Resistance in El Salvador* vol. 1 (London: Zed Books, 1985); Rigoberta Menchú, *I, Rigoberta Menchú: An Indian Woman in Guatemala*, edited by Elizabeth Burgos-Debray (London: Verso Books, 1984); and Amnesty International, *Guatemala: Human Rights Violations Under the Civilian Government* (New York: Amnesty International Publications, 1989).

116. See Jim Handy, *Gift of the Devil: A History of Guatemala* (Boston: South End Press, 1984), p. 260.

117. See Washington Office on Latin America, *Guatemala: The Roots of Revolution* (Washington, DC: WOLA, 1985).

118. Cited in Gardner, Garb, and Williams, *Guatemala*, p. 9.

119. Blachman and Sharpe, "Things Fall Apart," p. 111; and Arms Control and Foreign Policy Caucus of the U.S. Congress, *Bankrolling Failure: U.S. Policy in El Salvador and the Urgent Need for Reform* (Washington, DC: U.S. Congress, 1987).

120. USAID-El Salvador I, *Environmental Profile*, p. 23.

121. Hall and Faber, *Ecology of Conflict*, p. 9.

122. For instance, see Edward J. Taylor, "Peripheral Capitalism and Rural-Urban Migration: A Study of Population Movements in Costa Rica," *Latin American Perspectives* 7, no. 2–3 (1980): 75–90.

123. See William Durham, *Scarcity and Survival in Central America: The Eco-*

logical Origins of the Soccer War (Stanford: Stanford University Press, 1979).

124. Brockett, *Land, Power, and Poverty*, pp. 133–34.

125. Weeks, *Economies*, pp. 145–96.

126. See Billie DeWalt, "Economic Assistance in Central America: Development or Impoverishment?," *Cultural Survival Quarterly* 10, no. 1 (1986): 17; Marcelo Alonso, Central America in Crisis: Washington Institute Task Force Report (Washington, DC: Institute for Values in Public Policy, 1984), p. 101; and Xabier Gorostiaga and Peter Marchetti, "The Central American Economy," p. 133.

127. USAID-El Salvador I *Environmental Profile* p. 94.

128. USAID-Guatemala I, *Draft Environmental Profile*, p. 31.

129. Leonard, *Natural Resources and Economic Development*, p. 47. For a review of health indicators in Central America, see Alonso, *Central America in Crisis*.

130. See Beatriz Manz, *Refugees of a Hidden War: the Aftermath of the Counterinsurgency in Guatemala* (New York: State University of New York Press, 1988).

131. De Janvry, *The Agrarian Question*, p. 88; Pearce, *Promised Land*, pp. 64–79; and Daniel Fogel, *Revolution in Central America* (San Francisco: Ism Press, 1985).

132. Deere, "Rural Women's Subsistence Production," pp. 133–34.

133. Ibid, p. 139.

134. In the United States, the decision by most working and middle class parents to raise children is economically similar to consumer rationality for purchasing durable consumer goods. The increased commoditization of goods and services formerly produced by women and children within the family household, as well as the growing separation from subsistence production and exchange in favor of the wage and/or salary, has transformed children from "production agents" into "consumption items." Children no longer produce extra income, which serves as a powerful economic incentive for families in advanced capitalist countries to have less births. As a result, the first world is reaching birth levels close to zero population growth. For a discussion, see William W. Murdoch, *The Poverty of Nations: The Political Economy of Hunger and Population* (Baltimore: John Hopkins University Press, 1980), pp. 15–58; Maria Mies, *Patriarchy and Accumulation on a World Scale: Women in the International Division of Labour* (London: Zed Press, 1986), pp. 112–43; June Nash and Maria Patricia Fernandez-Kelly (eds.); *Women, Men, and the International Division of Labor* (Albany: State University of New York Press, 1983); and de Janvry, *The Agrarian Question*, p. 88.

135. De Janvry, *The Agrarian Question*, pp. 89–91.
136. Durham, *Scarcity and Survival;* and Barry, *Roots of Rebellion*, pp. 174–76.
137. Leonard, *Natural Resources and Economic Development* pp. 37–45.
138. USAID-Honduras II, *Country Environmental Profile*, p. 37.
139. De Janvry, *The Agrarian Question*, pp. 90–91.
140. Leonard, *Natural Resources and Economic Development*, pp. 37–41.
141. De Janvry, *The Agrarian Question*, pp. 85–93; and James M. Malloy and Silvia Borzutzky, "Politics, Social Welfare Policy, and the Population Problem in Latin America," *International Journal of Health Services* 12, no. 1 (1982): 77–98.
142. Weeks, *The Economies of Central America*, pp. 102–15. For a devastating critique of the neo-Malthusian perspective of overpopulation as the source of El Salvador's ecological crisis, see Durham, *Scarcity and Survival*, pp. 18–51.
143. Weeks, *Economies*, pp. 102–15.
144. See Lawrence Simon et al., *El Salvador: Land Reform 1980–81: Impact Audit* (Boston: Oxfam America, 1981).
145. See Tom Barry and Deb Preusch, *The Central America Fact Book* (New York: Grove Press, 1986), p. 140; and Tom Barry and Deb Preusch, *The Soft War* (New York; Grove Press, 1988), p. 188.
146. Barry, *Roots of Rebellion*, p. 175; and Durham, *Scarcity and Survival*, pp. 18, 34–51.
147. Leonard, *Natural Resources and Economic Development*, p. 39.
148. Weeks, *Economies*, pp. 39–40.
149. Daugherty et al., *Ecodevelopment*, p. 13. For additional figures, see USAID-Guatemala I, *Draft Environmental Profile*, pp. 12–16); and USAID-Honduras II, *Country Environmental Profile*, pp. 37–40.
150. For a discussion, see Durham, *Scarcity and Survival*, p. 18.
151. De Janvry, *The Agrarian Question*, pp. 91–93.
152. See Gorostiaga and Marchetti, "The Central American Economy," pp. 133–34.
153. See John W. Ratcliffe, "Population Control Versus Social Reorganization: The Emergent Paradigm," *International Journal of Health Services* 8, no. 3 (1978): 558. See also Bonnie Mass, *Population Target: The Political Economy of Population Control in Latin America* (Brampton, Ontario: Charter's Publishing, 1976), p. 2.
154. See *St. Louis Post-Dispatch*, 22 April 1977.
155. See Marilyn Thomson, *Women of El Salvador* (United Kingdom: Ishi Press, 1986), p. 37.
156. Mass, *Population Target*, pp. 209–12.
157. See USAID-Costa Rica I, *Country Environmental Profile*, p. 18.
158. For a discussion, see Barry Commoner, "How Poverty Breeds Over-

population," in Rita Arditti, Pat Brennan, and Steve Cavrak (eds.), *Science as Liberation* (Boston: South End Press, 1980), p. 80.

159. For excellent analyses of the population question, see Betsy Hartmann, *Reproductive Rights and Wrongs* (New York: Harper and Row, 1987); and William W. Murdoch, *The Poverty of Nations: The Political Economy of Hunger and Population* (Baltimore: John Hopkins University Press, 1980).

160. See USAID-Costa Rica I, *Country Environmental Profile*, p. 2.

161. Barry, *Roots of Rebellion*, p. 175.

162. Leonard, *Natural Resources and Economic Development*.

163. For a pathbreaking discussion of this concept, see James O'Connor, "Capitalism, Nature, Socialism: A Theoretical Introduction," *Capitalism, Nature, Socialism* 1, no. 1 (Fall 1988): 11–38; and James O'Connor, *The Meaning of Crisis: A Theoretical Introduction* (New York: Basil Blackwell, 1987), p. 53. For a discussion of external barriers in Central America, see Daniel Faber, "Imperialism and the Crisis of Nature in Central America," *Capitalism, Nature, Socialism* 1, no. 1 (Fall 1988): 39–46.

164. USAID-Costa Rica I, *Country Environmental Profile*, pp. 51–66.

165. Leonard, *Natural Resources and Economic Development*, p. 135.

166. See James Hester, "Is Central America Taking Mother Nature for Granted?," *Horizons* (Washington, DC: U.S. Agency for International Development, 1986), p. 82; and Stanley Heckadon (ed.), "La Colonización Campesina de Bosques Tropicales en Panama," *Estudio Rurales Latinoamericanos* 4, no. 3 (1981).

167. USAID-Honduras II, *Country Environmental Profile*, pp. 12–95.

168. See IRENA, *Proyecto Heroes y Martires de Veracruz Nicaragua, C.A.: Resumen Ejecutivo* (Managua: Instituto Nicaragüense de recursos Naturales y del Ambiente, 1988).

3: Poisoning for Profit

1. An account by Nicaraguan Minister of Culture Ernesto Cardenal of his return from exile in Costa Rica on the eve of the July 19, 1979 triumph of the Nicaraguan Revolution. See Ernesto Cardenal, "Lights," in *Zero Hour and Other Documentary Poems* (New York: New Directions Publishing, 1980).

2. See Peter Dorner and Rodolfo Quiros, "Institutional Dualism in Central America's Agricultural Development," in Stanford Central America Action Network (ed.), *Revolution in Central America* (Boulder: Westview Press, 1983), p. 228.

3. Cited in David Browning, *El Salvador: Landscape and Society* (Oxford: Clarendon Press, 1971), pp. 227–28.

4. See Robert Williams, *Export Agriculture and the Crisis in Central America* (Chapel Hill: University of North Carolina Press, 1986), p. 53.

5. See Georgeanne Chapin and Robert Wasserstrom, "Pesticide Use and Malaria Resurgence in Central America and India," *The Ecologist* 13, no. 4 (1983): 115–17.

6. Williams, *Export Agriculture*, p. 21.

7. Ibid., pp. 23, 53, 215.

8. See USAID-Guatemala I, *An Environmental Profile of Guatemala: Assessment of Environmental Problems and Short- and Long-Term Strategies for Problem Solution* (Prepared for USAID, University of Georgia: Institute of Ecology, 1981), pp. 5–19; and Williams, *Export Agriculture*, pp. 23–53.

9. See Howard Daugherty, "Man-Induced Ecological Change in El Salvador" (Ph.D. diss., University of California, Los Angeles, 1969), p. 202; Howard Daugherty, Charles A. Jeannert-Grosjean, and H.F. Fletcher, *Ecodevelopment and International Cooperation: Potential Applications for El Salvador* (Ottawa, Canada: CIDA and Advanced Concepts Center of the Environment, 1979), pp. 32–34; USAID-Nicaragua I, *Environmental Profile of Nicaragua*, prepared by Steven L. Hilty (Tucson: Arid Lands Information Center, University of Arizona, 1981), pp. 5–45; USAID-Guatemala I, 1981, pp. 5–19; Ernesto López Zepeda, "The Ecological Impact of Cotton Cultivation in El Salvador: The Example of Jiquilisco," (M.A. thesis, York University, 1977), pp. 16–43; and USAID-El Salvador I, *Environmental Profile of El Salvador*, compiled for USAID by Steven Hilty (Tucson: Arid Land Information Center, University of Arizona, 1982), pp. 55–67.

10. Browning, *Landscape and Society*, pp. 241–47.

11. Ibid., p. 236.

12. Dorner and Quiros, "Institutional Dualism," p. 228.

13. See Charles D. Brockett, *Land, Power, and Poverty: Agrarian Transformation and Political Conflict in Central America* (Boston: Unwin Hyman, 1988), pp. 68–69.

14. For example, sesame exports produced in the Pacific frontier of Chinadega, Nicaragua reached $4 million in 1952 (7.9 percent of total exports). See Victor Bulmer-Thomas, *The Political Economy of Central America Since 1920* (Cambridge: Cambridge University Press, 1987), p. 113.

15. See Sean L. Swezey, Douglas L. Murray, and Rainer G. Daxl, "Nicaragua's Revolution in Pesticide Policy," *Environment* 28, no. 1 (January-February 1986): 8; and Dorner and Quiros, "Institutional Dualism," p. 229.

16. Swezey et al., "Nicaragua's Revolution," pp. 8–31; and Williams, *Export Agriculture*, pp. 23–55.

17. Ibid.
18. See Leo Caltagirone, Merlin Allen, Walter Kaiser, Jr., and Joseph Or-senigo, *The Crop Protection Situation in Guatemala, Honduras, Nicaragua, Costa Rica, Panama, and Guyana,* study prepared by AID (University of California at Berkeley, 1972), p. 13; and Brockett, *Land, Power, and Poverty,* p. 70.
19. See James Painter, *Guatemala: False Hope, False Freedom* (London: Latin America Bureau, 1987), pp. 5–19.
20. Browning, *Landscape and Society,* p. 234.
21. Bulmer-Thomas, *Political Economy,* pp. 115–16.
22. See Jacques M. May and Donna L. McLellan, *The Ecology of Malnutrition in Mexico and Central America* (New York: Hafner Publishing, 1972). p. 69.
23. Williams, *Export Agriculture,* pp. 31–32.
24. Ibid.; Dorner and Quiros, "Institutional Dualism," p. 223; and Browning, *Landscape and Society,* pp. 230–35.
25. See Daniel Faber, "Imperialism, Revolution, and the Ecological Crisis of Central America," *Latin American Perspectives* 19, no. 1 (Winter 1992): 17–44; and Faber, "Imperialism and the Crisis of Nature in Central America," *Capitalism, Nature, Socialism: A Journal of Socialist Ecology* 1, no. 1 (Fall 1988): 39–46.
26. Tensie Whelan, "Rebuilding A Tropical Forest," *Environmental Action,* November/December 1987, p. 16.
27. See ICAITI, *An Environmental and Economic Study of the Consequences of Pesticide Use in Central American Cotton Production: A Final Report.* (Guatemala City: Instituto Centroamericano de Investigación y Tecnología Industrial, 1977), p. 177; and Williams, *Export Agriculture,* pp. 31–32.
28. See Victor Bulmer-Thomas, "Central American Economic Development Over the Long Run: Central America Since 1920," *Journal of Latin American Studies* 15 (November 1983): 288.
29. See Lori Ann Thrupp, "The Political Ecology of Pesticide Use in Developing Countries: Dilemmas in the Banana Sector of Costa Rica" (Ph.D. diss., University Sussex, August 1988), p. 199; Caltagirone et al., *Crop Protection,* p. 18; and Charles D. Brockett, "The Commercialization of Agriculture and Rural Economic Insecurity: The Case of Honduras," *Studies in Comparative International Development* 22, no. 1 (Spring 1987).
30. Browning, *Landscape and Society,* pp. 246–47.
31. Ibid., pp. 241–47.
32. López, "The Ecological Impact of Cotton Cultivation," p. 55.
33. See ICAITI, *Consequences of Pesticide Use,* p. 187.
34. See Joshua Karliner, "The Ecological Destabilization of Central America," *World Policy Journal,* Fall 1989, pp. 787–810.

35. Browning, *Landscape and Society*, p. 244.
36. Translated from Mario Payeras, *Latitud de la Flor y el Granizo* (Mexico: Joan Boldó i Climent, 1988), p. 50; cited in Florence Gardner, with Yaakov Garb and Marta Williams, *Guatemala: A Political Ecology*, Green Paper no. 5 (San Francisco: Environmental Project On Central America), October 1990.
37. For an excellent historical account, see Swezey et al., "Nicaragua's Revolution," p. 9.
38. Ibid.
39. ICAITI, *Consequences of Pesticide Use*, p. 29.
40. See D.A. Wolfenberger, M.J. Lukefahr, and H.M. Graham, "A Field Population of Bollworms Resistant to Methyl Parathion," *Journal of Economic Entomology* 64 (1971): 755–56, cited by Swezey et al., "Nicaragua's Revolution," p. 9.
41. For a discussion, see ICAITI, *Consequences of Pesticide Use*."
42. For Nicaragua figures, see M. Vaughn and G. Leon, "Pesticide Management in a Major Crop with Severe Resistance Problems," *Proceedings of the XV International Congress of Entomology* (Washington, DC: 1977), pp. 812–15. For Guatemala figures, see USAID-Guatemala I, Draft Environmental Profile, p. 24.
43. See ICAITI, *Consequences of Pesticide Use*, pp. 27–30.
44. See López, "Ecological Impact," p. 33; Swezey et al., "Nicaragua's Revolution," p. 9; and USAID-Guatemala I, *Draft Environmental Profile*, p. 24.
45. Vaughn and Leon, "Pesticide Management," pp. 812–15.
46. López, "Ecological Impact," p. 53.
47. See ICAITI, *Consequences of Pesticide Use*, p. 29; and López, "Ecological Impact," p. 34.
48. See Williams, *Export Agriculture*, p. 66; Browning, *Landscape and Society*, p. 240; and William H. Durham, *Scarcity and Survival in Central America: The Ecological Origins of the Soccer War* (Stanford, CA: Stanford University Press, 1979), p. 32.
49. See Williams, *Export Agriculture*, pp. 60–68; and Leo Caltagirone, Merlin Allen, Walter Kaiser, Jr., and Joseph Orsenigo, *The Crop Protection Situation in Guatemala, Honduras, Nicaragua, Costa Rica, Panama, and Guyana*, study prepared for the U.S. Agency for International Development, University of California at Berkeley (October-November 1972), p. 18.
50. Durham, *Scarcity and Survival*, pp. 32–33.
51. Williams, *Export Agriculture*, pp. 60–61.
52. Cited in Swezey et al., "Nicaragua's Revolution," pp. 8–9. See also

Centro Experimental del Algodon, *Informe de las Labores de la Seccion de Entomologia* (Managua: Comisión Nacional del Algodón, 1968–1975).

53. Vaughn and Leon, "Pesticide Management," pp. 812–15.

54. See David Weir and Mark Schapiro, "The Circle of Poison," *The Ecologist* 11, no. 3 (May-June, 1981): 120.

55. For a discussion, see Daniel Faber, with Joshua Karliner and Robert Rice, *Central America: Roots of Environmental Destruction*, Green Paper no. 2 (San Francisco: Environmental Project on Central America, August 1986), p. 5; and Swezey et al., "Nicaragua's Revolution," p. 8.

56. ICAITI, *Consequences of Pesticide Use*, pp. 30–141.

57. See López, "Ecological Impact," p. 33; Daugherty et al., *Ecodevelopment*, p. 30; and Sean Swezey and Daniel Faber, "Disarticulated Accumulation, Agroexport, and Ecological Crisis in Nicaragua: The Case of Cotton," *Capitalism, Nature, Socialism* 1 (Fall 1988): 53.

58. See Chapin and Wasserstrom, "Pesticide Use," p. 120; and ICAITI, *Consequences of Pesticide Use*, pp. 31, 143.

59. See Caltagirone et al., *Crop Protection*, p. 15. These death figures are very high in comparison to other government-sponsored studies. For example, a 1983 report by the Guatemalan Institute for Social Security reported a total of 765 poisonings in 1983, with only two deaths. See Jeffrey Leonard, *Natural Resources and Economic Development in Central America: A Regional Environmental Profile* (New Brunswick, NJ: Transaction Books, 1987), p. 149.

60. Weir and Schapiro, "The Circle of Poison," p. 123.

61. See Swezey, Murray, and Daxl, "Nicaragua's Revolution," p. 8; and ICAITI, *Consequences of Pesticide Use*, pp. 252–54.

62. ICAITI, *Consequences of Pesticide Use*, pp. 143–49.

63. Thrupp, "Political Economy of Pesticide Use," pp. 79–80.

64. See Swezey, Murray, and Daxl, "Nicaragua's Revolution," p. 31; and Swezey and Faber, "Disarticulated Accumulation," pp. 61–62.

65. The world's largest seed enterprise is Shell, which alone controls some thirty seed outfits in Europe and North America. See Jack Kloppenburg, Jr., and Daniel Lee Kleinman, "Seed Wars: Common Heritage, Private Property, and Political Strategy," *Socialist Review* 17, no. 5 (September-October 1987): 7–41; and Weir and Schapiro, "The Circle of Poison," p. 127. For a short political analysis of how multinational chemical companies such as Shell, Dupont, Ciba-Geigy, and Bayer have worked with the Food and Agricultural Organization and other international agencies to subvert IPM and other, more democratically based productive forces, in favor of chemical solutions, see Chapin and Wasserstrom, "Pesticide Use," pp. 123–25.

66. For a discussion of this point, see Richard Levins and Richard Lewontin, *The Dialectical Biologist* (Cambridge: Harvard University Press, 1985).

67. See Thrupp, "Political Economy of Pesticide Use," pp. 88–90.

68. See ICAITI, *Consequences of Pesticide Use*, p. 29; and Thrupp, "Political Economy," pp. 79–82.

69. See René Méndez, "Informe Sobre Salud Ocupacional de Trabajadores Agrícolas en Central America y Panama" (Washington, DC: Pan-American Health Organization, May 1977); and Leonard, *Natural Resources and Economic Development*, pp. 148–49.

70. See FAO, "The Development of Integrated Pest Control in Agriculture: Formulation of a Co-operative Global Programme," 1975, Rome: Report on Ad Hoc Session, October 15-25, 1974, Appendix B; and E.M. Corrales, *Relación entre Aplicaciónes de Insecticidas y Numero de Intoxicaciónes en Zonas del Occidente durante el Período 1970–78* (León, UNAN Monografía, Departamento de Biología, 1980); cited in Swezey, Murray, and Daxl, "Nicaragua's Revolution," p. 29.

71. For a review, see ICAITI, *Consequences of Pesticide Use*.

72. This estimate assumes an annual rate of 7,323 pesticide poisonings reported each year in the 1970s (1,486 cases a year in El Salvador; 1,377 in Guatemala; 3,000 in Nicaragua; 907 in Honduras; and 553 in Costa Rica). These numbers should be considered reasonable because of the level of suspected underreporting of actual cases. For a discussion, see Daniel Faber, "Imperialism and the Crisis of Nature in Central America" (Ph.D. diss., University of California at Santa Cruz, 1989). The World Health Organization estimates that one-half million people are poisoned and 5,000 die worldwide from direct contact to pesticides each year. See Ruth Norris, *Pills, Pesticides, and Profits* (New York: North River Press, 1982), p. 15.

73. See Meg Wilcox and Daniel Faber, "Pesticide Use: What Goes Around Comes Around," *Central America Reporter*, May-June 1992, p. 5.

74. See Gardner, Garb, and Williams, *Guatemala*, p. 6.

75. See Catharina Wesseling, Judith Appel, and Luisa Castillo, "Programa Regional de Plaguicidas: Confederación Universitaria Centroamericano," manuscript (Universidad Nacional de Costa Rica, Programa de Plaguicidas, Octubre 1990), pp. 1–3.

76. See David Bull, *A Growing Problem: Pesticides and the Third World Poor* (Oxford: Oxfam, 1982), p. 42.

77. See Norris, *Pills, Pesticides, and Profits*, p. 35.

78. For a brief discussion, see Tom Barry, *Roots of Rebellion: Land and Hunger in Central America* (Boston: South End Press, 1987), pp. 92–93.

79. See ICAITI, *Consequences of Pesticide Use*, pp. 190–94.

80. See Wilcox and Faber, "Pesticide Use," p. 5.

81. See Bill Hall and Daniel Faber, *El Salvador: Ecology of Conflict*, Green Paper no. 4 (San Francisco: Environmental Project On Central America, 1989), p. 4.

82. Ibid.

83. Barry, *Roots of Rebellion*, p. 93.

84. See statement of Catharina Wesseling before the Committee on Agriculture, Nutrition and Forestry (U.S. Senate, 5 June 1991), p. 6.

85. See Amnesty International, *El Salvador's Death Squads: A Government Strategy* (London: Amnesty International Publications, 1988), p. 27.

86. For a discussion, see Daniel Faber, with Joshua Karliner and Robert Rice, *Central America: Roots of Environmental Destruction*, Green Paper no. 2, (San Francisco: Environmental Project On Central America, August 1986), pp. 5–7.

87. See Martin Wolterding, "The Poisoning of Central America," *Sierra* 66 (September/October 1981): 64; and ICAITI, *Consequences of Pesticide Use*.

88. ICAITI, *Consequences*, pp. 91, 189.

89. See Swezey et al., "Nicaragua's Revolution," p. 29; A.C. Delgado, "Determinición de Pesticidas Clorinados en leche Materna del Departmento de León" (Monografía, Depto. de Biología, Facultad de Ciencias y Letras, Universidad Nacional Autonoma de Nicaragua, León, 1978); and Gardner, Garb, and Williams, *Guatemala*, p. 6.

90. ICAITI, *Consequences of Pesticide Use*, p. 190.

91. Ibid., p. 91.

92. Norris, *Pills, Pesticides, and Profits*, p. 16.

93. Ibid., p. 16.

94. ICAITI, *Consequences of Pesticide Use*.

95. Ibid., pp. 2–129; and Thrupp, "Political Economy of Pesticide Use," p. 254.

96. See Mark Schapiro, "The Toxic Double-Standard," *Multinational Monitor*, May 1983, p. 17. See also Swezey, Murray, and Daxl, "Nicaragua's Revolution," pp. 29–30; and Sociedad Alemán de Cooperación Técnica, "Reporte del Laboratorio Ecotoxicológico del GTZ, DGTA" (Managua: MIDINRA, 1980).

97. Chapin and Wasserstrom, "Pesticide Use," pp. 115, 331.

98. Norris, *Pills, Pesticides, and Profits*, p. 24; and López, "Ecological Impact," p. 63.

99. Chapin and Wasserstrom, "Pesticide Use," p. 117.

100. ICAITI, *Consequences of Pesticide Use*, p. 3; and Chapin and Wasserstrom, "Pesticide Use," p. 115.

101. See J. Georghiou, "Resistance to Insects and Mites to Insecticides and Acaracides and the Future of Pesticide Chemicals," in J. Swift (ed.),

Agricultural Chemicals: Harmony or Discord for Food, People and Environment (Berkeley: University of California, Agricultural Sciences, 1981).

102. ICAITI, *Consequences of Pesticide Use*, p. 127.
103. Thrupp, "Political Economy of Pesticide Use," p. 202; and Swezey et al., "Nicaragua's Revolution," p. 30.
104. Thrupp, "Political Economy of Pesticide Use," p. 202.
105. Cited in Barry, *Roots of Rebellion*, p. 100.
106. Ibid.
107. ICAITI, *Consequences of Pesticide Use*, pp. 30, 189.
108. Wolterding, "The Poisoning of Central America," p. 64.
109. Washington Post wire story, "Dark clouds: Air currents wend pollution worldwide," *New Orleans Times-Picayune*, 20 March 1988.
110. See Daugherty et al., *Ecodevelopment*, p. 39; and López, "Ecological Impact," p. 44.
111. Leonard, *Natural Resources and Economic Development*, pp. 157–58; and J. Millington, *The Effect of Land-Use Changes in Central America on the Population of Some Migratory Bird Species* (Washington, DC: The Nature Conservancy, 1984).
112. López, "Ecological Impact," p. 44.
113. Barry, *Roots of Rebellion*, p. 100.
114. See G.D. Peterson, "The Quiet Crisis in Nicaragua" (USAID-CIPP Project Library, Berkeley, 1969); C.C. Peterson, J. Sequeira, and F. Estada, "Principios y Problemas de Control Integrada de Plagas del Algodón en Nicaragua" (Managua: Ministerio de Agricultura y Ganadería, Programa de Control Integrado de Plagas, 1969); A. Van Huis, "Integrated Pest Management in the Small Farmer's Maize Crop in Nicaragua" (Mededelingen Landbouwhogeschool Wageningen, Nederland, vol. 81, no. 6, 1981); and L. Lacayo, "Especies Parasíticas de *Spodoptera Frugiperda, Diatraea Lineolata, Trichoplusia* ni en la Zona de Managua, Estelí, y Masatepe," (León: UNAN Monografía, 1976); cited in Swezey and Faber, "Disarticulated Accumulation," p. 54.
115. Leonard, *Natural Resources and Economic Development*, p. 148.
116. López, "Ecological Impact," pp. 47–52; and Leonard, *Natural Resources and Economic Development*, p. 147.
117. López, "Ecological Impact," pp. 47–52.
118. Barry, *Roots of Rebellion*, p. 148.
119. See Daugherty et al., *Ecodevelopment*, p. 33.
120. See Shelley A. Hearne, *Harvest of Unknowns: Pesticide Contamination in Imported Foods* (New York: Natural Resources Defense Council, 1984), p. 21; and Michael Satchell, "A Vicious 'Circle of Poison,'" *U.S. News and World Report*, 10 June 1991, p. 31.
121. For an excellent summary of this phenomenon on an international scale,

see David Weir and Mark Schapiro, *Circle of Poison: Pesticides and People in a Hungry World* (San Francisco: Institute for Food and Development Policy, 1981).

122. Thrupp, "Political Economy of Pesticide Use," p. 250.

123. ICAITI, *Consequences of Pesticide Use*, pp. 178–86.

124. Weir and Schapiro, "The Circle of Poison," p. 13; ICAITI, *Consequences of Pesticide Use*, pp. 67–75; and Swezey, Murray, and Daxl, "Nicaragua's Revolution," p. 29.

125. ICAITI, *Consequences*, pp. 75–151; Thrupp, "Political Economy," p. 250; Leonard, *Natural Resources and Economic Development*, p. 152; USAID-El Salvador I, *Environmental Profile*, p. 92; and Swezey, Faber and Daxl, "Nicaragua's Revolution," p. 7.

126. These figures on total number of pounds rejected exclude transpotation damage, water damage, and missing shipping marks. See U.S.D.A. Meat and Poultry Products, *Report on Lots and Pounds Presented, Inspected, and Rejected by Year and by Country* (6 June 1992), pp. 1–7.

127. Norris, *Pills, Pesticides, and Profits*, p. 27.

128. Weir and Schapiro, "The Circle of Poison," p. 122.

129. See Sandra Marquardt, *Exporting Banned Pesticides: Fueling the Circle of Poison* (Washington, DC: Greenpeace USA, August 1989), p. 21.

130. See L.A. Falcon and Rainer G. Daxl, "Informe al Gobierno de Nicaragua sobre Control Integrado de Plagas de Algodonero" (Organización de la Naciónes Unidas para la Agricultura y la Alimentación (FAO), Programa de las Naciónes Unidas para el Desarrollo (PNUD), Managua, 1977).

131. See John Weeks, *The Economies of Central America* (New York: Holmes and Meier, 1985), pp. 180–81.

132. Thrupp, "Political Economy of Pesticide Use," p. 199.

133. See James Painter, *Guatemala: False Hope, False Freedom* (London: Latin America Bureau, 1987), p. 22.

134. Weeks, *Economies*, p. 189.

135. For figures on cotton acreage, see FAO, "Centroamerica: Estudio Regional del Algodon" (Rome: Centro de Inversiónes Programa de Cooperación FAO/Banco Mundial, 6 December 1990), p. 3.

136. See Scott Alan Lewis, "Bad News Bananas: The Economic Dream Becomes an Ecological Nightmare in Costa Rica," manuscript (1991), p. 5.

137. See Satchell, "A Vicious 'Circle of Poison,'" p. 31; and Wesseling, statement, p. 10.

138. See Wessling, statement, pp. 11–12.

139. See Lewis, "Bad News Bananas," p. 7.

140. Thrupp, "Political Economy of Pesticide Use," pp. 157–263.

141. For some excellent analyses of this process, see Douglas Murray, "Recurring Contradictions in Agrarian Development: Pesticide Problems in Caribbean Basin Non-Traditional Agriculture," *World Development* 20, no. 4 (April 1992): 597–608; Douglas Murray, "Export Agriculture, Ecological Disruption and Social Inequity: Some Effects of Pesticides in Southern Honduras," *Agriculture and Human Values* 8, no. 4 (Fall 1991): 19–29; and Peter Rosset, "Sustainability, Economy of Scale, and Social Instability: The Achilles Heel of Non-Traditional Export Agriculture?," *Agriculture and Human Values* 8, no. 4 (Fall 1991): 30–37.

142. See Murray, "Export Agriculture," p. 20.

143. For a discussion of the ecological impact of non-traditional crops in Guatemala, see Gardner et al., *Guatemala*, pp. 8–11.

144. Weir and Schapiro, "The Circle of Poison," p. 121.

145. See U.S. General Accounting Office, "Pesticides: Better Sampling and Enforcement Needed on Imported Food," (GAO/RCED, September 1986), pp. 86–219.

146. See Barry, *Roots of Rebellion*, p. 96; and Weir and Schapiro, "The Circle of Poison," p. 121.

147. For more information, contact the Circle of Poison Working Group, 1436 U Street NW, Suite 305, Washington, DC 20009.

148. For a discussion, see Lori Ann Thrupp, "Pesticides and Policies: Approaches to Pest-Control Dilemmas in Nicaragua and Costa Rica," *Latin American Perspectives* 15, no. 4 (Fall 1988).

4: Revolution in the Rainforest

1. Active in the Guerrilla Army of the Poor in Guatemala, Payeras is the author of numerous works on ecology, short stories, poetry, and children's literature. The above citation is from Mario Payeras, *Days of the Jungle: The Testimony of a Guatemalan Guerrillero, 1972–1976* (New York: Monthly Review Press, 1983), p. 19.

2. The story of the León family, a composite of Costa Rican peasants, is taken from Daniel Faber, with Joshua Karliner and Robert Rice, *Central America: Roots of Environmental Destruction*, Green Paper no. 3 (San Francisco: Environmental Project On Central America, 1986), p. 1. It is based on the personal experiences of the authors.

3. For a comprehensive discussion, see James Nations and H. Jeffrey Leonard, "Grounds of Conflict in Central America," pp. 78–81, in Andrew Maguire and Janet Welsh Brown (eds.), *Bordering on Trouble: Resources and Politics in Latin America* (Bethesda: Adler and Adler, 1986); James Nations and Daniel Komer, "Rainforests and the Hamburger

Society," *Environment*, April 1983, p. 12; and Joshua Karliner, "Central America's Other War," *World Policy Journal*, Fall 1989, pp. 787–810.

4. See Norman Myers, "The Hamburger Connection: How Central America's Forests Become North America's Hamburgers," *Ambio* 10, no. 1 (1981): 6.

5. See USAID-Costa Rica I, *Country Environmental Profile: A Field Study*, Prepared for USAID by Fary Hartshorn et al. (San Jose: Tropical Science Center, 1982), pp. 3–28; and Food and Agriculture Organization of the United Nations, *Production* vol. 42, Statistics Series no. 88 (1988). See also Table I in this chapter.

6. See Norman Myers, *The Primary Source: Tropical Forests and Our Future* (New York: W.W. Norton, 1984), p. 142.

7. See Steven Lyons, "Research Pact May Help Rain Forests Pay For Their Keep," *Boston Globe*, 4 November 1991, pp. 25–27.

8. See Douglas Shane, *Hoofprints on the Forest: Cattle Ranching and the Destruction of Latin America's Tropical Forests* (Philadelphia: Institute for the Study of Human Issues, 1986), p. 38.

9. For an excellent discussion of this process, see Robert Williams, *Export Agriculture and the Crisis in Central America* (Chapel Hill: University of North Carolina Press, 1986), p. 223.

10. The World Bank is composed of three major institutions: (1) the International Bank for Reconstruction and Development (IBRD); (2) the International Development Association (IDA); and (3) the International Finance Corporation (IFC). See J. Edward Taylor, "Peripheral Capitalism and Rural-Urban Migration: A Study of Population Movements in Costa Rica," *Latin American Perspectives* 7, no. 2–3, (Spring/Summer 1980): 82.

11. For a discussion, see Williams, *Export Agriculture*, p. 78.

12. Ibid., p. 223.

13. See James J. Parsons, "Forest to Pasture: Development or Destruction?," *Revista de Biología Tropical* 24 (1976): 130.

14. Williams, *Export Agriculture*, p. 80.

15. Nations and Komer, "Rainforsts and the Hamburger Society."

16. For a further elaboration, see USAID-Costa Rica I, *Country Environmental Profile*, p. 26.

17. Williams *Export Agriculture*, p. 26.

18. For an analysis of subsistence production and export beef production in Choluteca, see Billie R. DeWalt, "Microcosmic and Macrocosmic Processes of Agrarian Change in Southern Honduras: The Cattle are Eating the Forests," pp. 165–86 in Billie DeWalt and Pertti J. Pelto (eds.), *Micro and Macro Levels of Analysis in Anthropology: Issues in Theory and Research* (Boulder: Westview Press, 1985).

19. See Taylor, "Peripheral Capitalism," pp. 83–86.
20. Guanacaste contains a little under 38 percent of Costa Rica's pasture land and about 37 percent of the nation's cattle. See Susan Place, "Ecological and Social Consequences of Export Beef Production in Guanacaste Province, Costa Rica" (Ph.D. diss., University of California, Los Angeles, 1981), pp. 68–90; and Williams, *Export Agriculture*, p. 113.
21. See Susan E. Place, "Ecological and Social Consequences of Export Beef Production in Guanacaste Province, Costa Rica" (PhD. diss., University of California, Los Angeles, 1981), pp. 124–31, 145–87.
22. Ibid., pp. 29–187. For a discussion of ecological protection and restoration efforts in Guanacaste, see Tensie Whelan, "Rebuilding a Tropical Forest," *Environmental Action*, November-December 1987, pp. 15–17.
23. See Shane, *Hoofprints*, p. 19; Elbert E. Miller, "The Raising and Marketing of Beef in Central America and Panama," *Journal of Tropical Geography* (Singapore), no. 41 (1975): 68; and Williams, *Export Agriculture*, p. 106.
24. Williams, *Export Agriculture*, pp. 126–27.
25. Ibid., pp. 129–34.
26. See George Black, *Triumph of the People: The Sandinista Revolution in Nicaragua* (London: Zed Press, 1981), pp. 78–82.
27. Williams, *Export Agriculture*, p. 129.
28. The northeastern region of Nicaragua's Caribbean lowlands is dominated by lowland wet forests. See USAID-Nicaragua I, *Environmental Profile of Nicaragua* (Tucson: Arid Lands Information Center, University of Arizona, 1981), pp. 34–37.
29. See James Nations and H. Jeffrey Leonard, "Grounds of Conflict in Central America," in Janet Welsh Brown (ed.), *Bordering on Trouble: Resources and Politics in Latin America* (Bethesda, MD: Adler & Adler, 1986), pp. 55–100.
30. See Parsons, "Forest to Pasture," p. 124; and James D. Nations and Daniel I. Komer, "Tropical Rainforests in Post-Revolution Nicaragua" unpublished manuscript (Austin: Center for Human Ecology, 1983b), p. 11.
31. Williams, *Export Agriculture*, p. 106.
32. Nations and Komer, "Tropical Rainforests," p. 8.
33. Williams, *Export Agriculture*, p. 135.
34. See Jim Handy, *Gift of the Devil: A History of Guatemala* (Boston: South End Press, 1984), pp. 323.
35. According to then vice-president Clemente Marroquin Rojas, American pilots flew napalm attacks on suspected guerrilla strongholds from a U.S. airbase in Panama. See Ibid., pp. 218–33; and Williams, *Export Agricuture*, pp. 134–38.

36. Ibid.; and Handy, *Gift of the Devil*, pp. 218–22.

37. For a discussion, see James Painter, *Guatemala: False Hope, False Freedom* (London: Latin America Bureau, 1987), pp. 47–57.

38. See USAID-Guatemala I, *Draft Environmental Profile of Guatemala* (Athens: Institute of Ecology, University of Georgia, 1981), p. 5.

39. Williams, *Export Agriculture*, pp. 141–42.

40. See Michael McClintock, *The American Connection: State Terror and Popular Resistance in Guatemala* vol. 2 (London: Zed Press, 1985), pp. 132–36.

41. See also Rigoberta Menchú, *I, Rigoberta Menchú: An Indian Woman in Guatemala*, edited by Elizabeth Burgos-Debray (London: Verso Books, 1984); and George Black, *Garrison Guatemala* (London: Zed Books, 1984).

42. Williams, *Export Agriculture*, p. 143.

43. McClintock, *The American Connection* vol. 2, p. 136.

44. See Florence Gardner, with Yaakov Garb and Marta Williams, *Guatemala: A Political Ecology*, Green Paper no. 5 (San Francisco: Environmental Project On Central America, 1990), pp. 9, 12.

45. Ibid.

46. Ibid.

47. Handy, *Gift of the Devil*, pp. 219–20.

48. Gardner, Garb and Williams, *Guatemala*, p. 7; and Guatemala News and Information Bureau, "CELGUSA: An Environmental Disaster in the Making," *Report on Guatemala* (Oakland: GNIB, Spring 1990).

49. See Karen Parker, *Fumigation Programs in Guatemala* (San Francisco: Association of Humanitarian Lawyers, 1989); and Gardner et al., *Guatemala*, p. 13.

50. For a discussion, see Chapter Two. See also Daniel Faber, "Imperialism, Revolution, and the Ecological Crisis of Central America," *Latin American Perspectives* 19, no. 1 (Winter 1992): 17–44.

51. Nations and Komer, "Tropical Rainforests," pp. 13–14.

52. Parsons, "Forest to Pasture," p. 122.

53. For descriptions of this process, see Jefferson Boyer, "Agrarian Capitalism and Peasant Praxis in Southern Honduras" (Ph.D. diss., Chapel Hill: University of North Carolina, 1983); and Nations and Komer, "Rainforests and the Hamburger Society," pp. 13–14; Parsons, "Forest to Pasture," p. 122, and Williams, *Export Agriculture*, p. 114.

54. See USAID-Honduras II, *Country Environmental Profile: A Field Study*, prepared by Paul Campanella et al. (McLean, VA: JRB Associates, 1982), pp. 61–76.

55. Nations and Leonard, "Grounds of Conflict," pp. 78–81.

56. USAID-Guatemala I, *Draft Environmental Profile*, pp. 17–18.

57. Nations and Komer, "Rainforests and the Hamburger Society," p. 14.

58. For example, see Paul D. Lopes, "The Agrarian Crisis in Modern Gua-

temala" (Master's thesis, University of Wisconsin, Madison, 1986), pp. 68–77.

59. Faber, Karliner, and Rice, *Roots of Environmental Destruction*, p. 3.
60. Nations and Komer, "Tropical Rainforsts," p. 10.
61. See Laura Enríquez, *Harvesting Change: Labor and Agrarian Reform in Nicaragua, 1979–1990* (Chapel Hill: University of North Carolina Press, 1991), pp. 50–51.
62. Nations and Leonard, "Grounds of Conflict," p. 61.
63. See James Nations and Daniel Komer, "Indians, Immigrants and Beef Exports: Deforestation in Central America," *Cultural Survival Quarterly* 6, no. 2 (Spring, 1982): 12.
64. For an excellent discussion of this account, see Enríquez, *Harvesting Change*, pp. 51–53; and Black, *Triumph of the People*, p. 89.
65. See Nancy Peckenham, "Land Settlement in the Petén," *Latin American Perspectives* 7 (Spring-Summer, 1980): 169–77; and John L. Fielder, "Commentary on Land Settlement in the Petén: Response to Nancy Peckenham," *Latin American Perspectives* 10, no. 1 (Winter 1983): 120–23.
66. For an excellent discussion, see Handy, *Gift of the Devil*, pp. 213–18.
67. For an excellent discussion, see McClintock, vol. 2, pp. 324–44.
68. See Myers, "The Hamburger Connection," p. 4; and Myers and Tucker, "Deforestation in Central America: Spanish Legacy and North American Consumers," *Environmental Review*, Spring 1987, p. 66.
69. Nations and Leonard, "Grounds of Conflict," 72.
70. See Jeffrey Leonard, *Natural Resources and Economic Development in Central America: A Regional Environmental Profile* (New Brunswick, NJ: Transaction Books, 1987), p. 7.
71. Myers and Tucker: "Deforestation," p. 31; and Williams, *Export Agriculture*, p. 99.
72. Myers and Tucker, "Deforestation," p. 65.
73. Parsons, "Forest to Pasture," p. 124; and Nations and Komer, "Tropical Rainforests," p. 11.
74. Nations and Komer, "Rainforsts and the Hamburger Society."
75. Shane, *Hoofprints*, p. 91; Williams, *Export Agriculture*, pp. 84–100; and Robert H. Holden, "Central America is Growing More Beef and Eating Less, as the Hamburger Connection Widens," *Multinational Monitor*, October 1981, p. 17.
76. Nations and Komer, "Rainforests," p. 18. See also Shane, *Hoofprints*, pp. 91–93, and Myers, "The Hamburger Connection," p. 4.
77. Shane, *Hoofprints*, p. 77; Myers and Tucker, "Deforestation," p. 67; and U.S. Department of Agriculture, *U.S. Agricultural Imports—Period: Jan. 1990–Dec. 1991* (17 June 1992), p. 001.

78. Parsons, "Forest to Pasture," pp. 121–31; and Williams, *Export Agriculture*, p. 113.

79. Leonard, *Natural Resources and Economic Development*, p. 99.

80. There are at least 112 species of mammals, over 700 birds, and 196 reptiles and amphibians in Honduras. See USAID-Honduras II, *Country Environmental Profile*, pp. 141–44; USAID-Guatemala I, Draft Environmenta; Profile, pp. 10–11; and James Nations and Daniel Komer, *Conservation in Guatemala*, unpublished manuscript (Austin: Center for Human Ecology, 1984), p. 31.

81. Myers, "The Hamburger Connection," pp. 3–8.

82. See Table I. See also Steven A. Sader and Armond T. Joyce, "Deforestation Rages and Trends in Costa Rica, 1940 to 1983," *Biotropica* 20, no. 1 (1988), p. 14.

83. See USAID-Costa Rica I, *Country Environmental Profile*, pp. 42–50.

84. See Al Buchanan, "Costa Rica's Wild West," *Sierra* (July/August 1985). For a discussion of national parks and wildlife conservation in Central America, see Faber, Karliner, and Rice, *Roots of Environmental Destruction*, pp. 3–5.

85. Shane, *Hoofprints*, p. 11.

86. See Charles D. Brockett, *Land, Power, and Poverty: Agrarian Transformation and Political Conflict in Central America* (Boston: Unwin Hyman, 1988), pp. 133–34.

87. For an elaboration, see Parsons, "Forest to Pasture," p. 127.

88. Nations and Leonard, "Grounds of Conflict," pp. 73–74.

89. Williams, *Export Agriculture*, 73.

90. USAID-Costa Rica I, *Country Environmental Profile*, pp. 6–64.

91. USAID-Guatemala I, *Draft Environmental Profile*, pp. 6–64.

92. See Rexford Daubenmire, "Some Ecological Consequences of Converting Forest to Savanna in Northwestern Costa Rica," *Tropical Ecology* 13, no. 1 (1972): 40; Charles F. Bennett, "Human Influences on the Zoogeography of Panama," *Ibero-Americana* vol. 51 (Berkeley: University of California Press, 1968), cited in Place, "Ecological and Social Consequences," pp. 101–16.

93. See USAID-Guatemala I, *Draft Environmental Profile*, pp. 17–18.

94. Nations and Leonard, "Grounds of Conflict," pp. 73–74; and Adrian Forsyth and Ken Miyata, *Tropical Nature: Life and Death in the Rain Forests of Central and South America* (New York: Charles Scribner's Sons, 1984), pp. 7–15.

95. Place, "Ecological and Social Consequences," p. 97.

96. Nations and Leonard, "Grounds of Conflict," pp. 80–81.

97. See John Lee and Ronald Taylor, "Ravage in the Rain Forests," *U.S. News and World Report*, 31 March 1986.

98. Leonard and Nations, "Grounds of Conflict," pp. 80–81.

99. USAID-Nicaragua I, *Environmental Profile,* p. 61.

100. See Charles Hall, R.P. Detwiler, Philip Bogdonoff, and Sheila Underhill, "Land Use Change and Carbon Exchange in the Tropics: I. Detailed Estimates for Costa Rica, Panama, Peru, and Bolivia," *Environmental Management* 9, no. 4 (1985): 313–34.

101. See James D. Nations, "Bearing Witness: The Lacandon Maya's Traditional Culture Survives in the Images of Gertrude Blom," *Natural History* 94, no. 3 (March 1985); and Nations and Komer, "Rainforests and the Hamburger Society," p. 15.

102. Parsons, "Forest to Pasture," pp. 127–28. For a highly sophisticated investigation of alternative systems of sustainable commercial development of rainforest ecosystems, see Joseph Tosi and Robert Voertman, "Some Environmental Factors in the Economic Development of the Tropics," *Economic Geography* 40, no. 3 (July 1964): 189–205.

103. See Joseph Collins with Frances Moore Lappé, Nick Allen and Paul Rice, *Nicaragua: What Difference Could a Revolution Make?*, 2nd ed. (San Francisco: Institute for Food and Development Policy, 1985); and Joshua Karliner and Daniel Faber, *Nicaragua: An Environmental Perspective*, Green Paper no. 1 (San Francisco: Environmental Project On Central America, 1986).

5: *The Nicaraguan Revolution and the Liberation of Nature*

1. See Ernesto Cardenal, "New Ecology," in *From Nicaragua With Love* (San Francisco: City Light Books, 1986).

2. For a concise historical account of the Nicaraguan revolution, see John A. Booth, *The End of the Beginning: The Nicaraguan Revolution*, Second Edition (Boulder: Westview Press, 1985).

3. For a discussion, see Bill Gibson, "A Structural Overview of the Nicaraguan Economy," in Rose Spalding (ed.), *The Political Economy of Revolutionary Nicaragua* (Boston: Allen & Unwin, 1987), pp. 15–43.

4. See Joseph Collins, with Frances Moore Lappé, Nick Allen and Paul Rice, *What Difference Can A Revolution Make?*, 2nd ed. (San Francisco: Institute for Food and Development Policy, 1985), p. 2.

5. See Health PAC Bulletin, "Health Care and Revolution" special double issue, 13–14, no. 6 (1985): 1.

6. Booth, *The End of the Beginning*, pp. 102–03.

7. See George Black, *Triumph of the People: The Sandinista Revolution in Nicaragua* (London: Zed Press, 1981), p. 59; and Douglas L. Murray, "Pesticides, Politics and the Nicaraguan Revolution," *Policy Studies Review* (November 1984).

8. See L.A. Falcon and Rainer Daxl, "Informe al Gobierno de Nicaragua Sobre Control Integrado de Plagas de Algodonero," (Managua: Organización de la Naciónes Unidas para la Agricultural y la Alimentación; Programa de las Naciónes Unidas para el Desarrollo, 1977).

9. See Food and Agriculture Organization of the United Nations (FAO), "The Development of Integrated Pest Control in Agriculture: Formulation of a Co-operative Global Programme; Report on Ad Hoc Session," 15–25 October 1974, appendix B (Rome, 1975).

10. See IRENA, *Planificación de Cuencas Hidrográficas, Plan de Ordenamiento y Manejo*, vol. III, (Managua: Instituto Nicaragüense de Recursos Naturales y del Ambiente, 1983), p. 170.

11. See Denis Corrales Rodríguez, *Impacto Ecológico Sobre los Recursos Naturales Renovables de Centroamerica: Caso Particular de Nicaragua* (Managua: Instituto Nicaragüense de Recursos Naturales y del Ambiente, 1983), p. 70.

12. For a concise summary, see Joshua Karliner and Daniel Faber, with Robert Rice, *Nicaragua: An Environmental Perspective*, Green Paper no. 1 (San Francisco: Environmental Project On Central America, 1986).

13. See Sergio Ramírez Mercado, "Discurso Inagural del II Seminario Nacional de Recursos Naturales y del Ambiente," in *Forjando Una Política Ambiental* (Managua: Instituto Nicaragüense de Recursos Naturales y del Ambiente, 1984), p. 36.

14. Ibid.

15. Quotation from the Organic Law of IRENA, which was issued in October 1979. See Ange Wieberdink and Arjen van Ketel, "Institutionalization of an Environmental Programme in a Third World Country: The Establishment of an Environmental Institute in Nicaragua," *Development and Change* 19 (1988): 143.

16. Ibid., pp. 144–45.

17. For instance, see Charles Piller, "Industry and Health in Nicaragua: War, Technical Aid and Progress," *Science for the People* 17, no. 6 (November/December 1985): 24–28.

18. See also Egbert W. Pfeiffer, "Nicaragua's Environmental Problems, Policies, and Programmes," *Environmental Conservation* 13, no. 2 (Summer 1986): 137–42.

19. Wieberdink and van Ketel, "Institutionalization," p. 146.

20. See John Weeks, "The Mixed Economy in Nicaragua: The Economic Battlefield," in Spalding (ed.), *The Political Economy of Revolutionary Nicaragua*, pp. 43–60.

21. See Michael Zalkin, "Nicaragua: The Peasantry, Grain Policy, and the State," *Latin American Perspectives* 15, no. 2 (Fall 1988): 72–73.

22. Collins, Lappé, Allen, and Rice, *What Difference Can a Revolution Make?*, pp. 88–89.

23. For a discussion of the Sandinista agrarian reform from 1979 to 1985, see Eduardo Baumeister, "The Structure of Nicaraguan Agriculture and the Sandinista Agrarian Reform," in Richard Harris and Carlos Vilas (eds.), *Nicaragua: A Revolution Under Siege* (London: Zed Press, 1985) pp. 10–35.

24. The beneficiaries and their families made up one-third of Nicaragua's campesinos. See Collins, Lappé, Allen, and Rice, *What Difference*, p. 151.

25. For an elaborate discussion, see ibid.

26. See Zalkin, "Nicaragua," pp. 72–75; Collins, Lappé, Allen and Rice, *What Difference*, p. 138; and Carlos Vilas, "What Went Wrong," *NACLA: Report on the Americas* 24, no. 1 (June 1990): 10–18.

27. Zalkin, "Nicaragua," pp. 73–83.

28. Ibid., p. 74; and Ilja Luciak, "National Unity and Popular Hegemony: the Dialectics of *Sandinista* Agrarian Reform Policies, 1979–1986," *Journal of Latin American Studies* 19 (May 1987): 113–40.

29. See Lorenzo Cardenal and Ann Larsen, with Joshua Karliner and Jane McAlevey, "The Nicaraguan Environment from Sandinismo to UNO," unpublished report (San Francisco: EPOCA, 1990), pp. 11–12; and John Vandemeer, "Breaking New Ground: Agriculture and Environment in Nicaragua," *Nicaraguan Perspectives* 16 (Winter 1988): 28–33.

30. See USAID-Nicaragua I, *Environmental Profile of Nicaragua*, prepared by Steven L. Hilty (Tucson: Arid Lands Information Center, University of Arizona, 1981), pp. 56–57; and Ariane van Buren, "An Analysis of the Commercial Woodfuel System in Nicaragua" (Ph.D. diss. [draft], University of Sussex, 1988).

31. See IRENA, *Proyecto Héroes y Mártires de Veracruz Nicaragua, C.A.: Resumen Ejecutivo* (Managua: Instituto Nicaragüense de Recursos Naturales y del Ambiente, 1988), pp. 1–21.

32. See David Siegel, "The Epidemiology of Aggression," *Nicaraguan Perspectives* no. 10 (Spring-Summer 1985): 22; Paula Braveman and David Siegel, "Nicaragua: A Health System Developing Under Conditions of War," *International Journal of Health Services* 17, no. 1 (1987): 169–78; and Paula Braveman and Milton Roemer, "Health Personnel Training in the Nicaraguan Health System," *International Journal of Health Services* 15, no. 4 (1985): 699.

33. For a brief discussion, see Dave Henson, "Ten Years of Revolutionary Accomplishment," *EPOCA Update*, Spring 1990, pp. 8–11.

34. Wieberdink and van Ketel,"Institutionalization," p. 148.

35. For example, see New World Agriculture Group, "Summaries of Programs in Nicaragua" (January 1988), pp. 1–10; and Bruce Horwith, "A

Role for Intercropping in Modern Agriculture," *Bioscience* 35, no. 5 (May 1985): 286–91.

36. See IRENA, *III Seminario Nacional de Recursos Naturales y del Ambiente* (Managua: Instituto Nicaragüense de Recursos Naturales y de Ambiente, 1982), p. 20.

37. For an in-depth discussion, see Ulf Rasmusson, "Agricultural Development and Rain Forest Conservation in Nicaragua," Institute of Economic Geography, Stockholm School of Economics (1986), p. 9; and James D. Nations and Daniel I. Komer, "Tropical Rainforests in Post-Revolution Nicaragua," unpublished manuscript (Austin, TX: Center for Human Ecology, 1983).

38. IRENA, *Proyecto Heroes*, pp. 1–22.

39. Ibid., p. 11.

40. Karliner, Faber, and Rice, *Nicaragua* , p. 4.

41. See Joshua Karliner, "Make Parks, Not War," *The Amicus Journal*, Fall 1987, pp. 8–13.

42. See Inter-American Development Bank, "Nicaragua: Informe Presentado por la Delegación del País," in *The Forest Sector: Country Reports, Financiamiento del Desarrollo Forestal en America Latina* (Washington, D.C.: IADB, June 1982), p. 13.

43. See John Mohawk and Denis Shelton, "Revolutionary Contradictions: Miskitos and Sandinistas in Nicaragua," in *Native Peoples in Struggle* (Ottawa: Anthropology Resource Center, ERIN, 1982), p. 30.

44. For a discussion, see Martin Diskin, "The Manipulation of Indigenous Struggles," in Thomas W. Walker (ed.), *Reagan Versus the Sandinistas: The Undeclared War on Nicaragua* (Boulder: Westview Press, 1987), pp. 80–96; and Roxanne Dunbar-Ortiz, "Indigenous Rights and Regional Autonomy in Revolutionary Nicaragua," *Latin American Perspectives* 14, no. 1 (Winter 1987): 43–66.

45. Karliner, Faber, and Rice, *Nicaragua*, p. 5.

46. See Bernard Nietschmann, *Between Land and Water: The Subsistence Ecology of the Miskito Indians in Eastern Nicaragua* (New York: Seminar, 1973), pp. 177–99; and Stephen Cornelius, "Status of Sea Turtles Along the Pacific Coast of Middle America," in K.A. Bjorndal (ed.), *Biology and Conservation of Sea Turtles* (Washington, DC: Smithsonian Institute Press, 1981), pp. 211–19.

47. See Denis Corrales Rodríguez, *Impacto Ecologico Sobre los Recursos Naturales Renovables de Centroamerica: Caso Particular de Nicaragua* (Managua: IRENA, 1983), pp. 42–120.

48. See David Trexler, "Report from the Turtle Brigade," *Earth Island Journal*, Winter 1988–1989, pp. 44–45, and Todd Steiner, "Between Ecology

and Economics: Protecting Nicaragua's Sea Turtles," *Nicaraguan Perspectives* no. 16 (Winter 1988): 7–39.

49. See Ben Wisner, "Class Relations, Center-Periphery Relations and the Rural Energy Crisis," paper presented at the *Second International Symposium on Appropriate Technology*, Denver, CO (October, 1980).

50. See Mikos Fabersunne, Barbara Atkinson, and James Manwell, "Renewable Energy Technologies in Nicaragua: A Balanced Strategy for Energy Independence," presented at the *UPADI XVIII–III Congress on Energy*, Guatemala City (25–28 August 1986), pp. 5–6.

51. See Ariane van Buren, "End of Project Summary: Wood Fuel Commercialization Project," Report to Funder (Stockholm: Swedish International Development Authority, Agriculture Division, Environmental Fund, October 1984), p. 2.

52. See Peter Downs, "Towards a People's Science: The Innovators Movement in Nicaragua," *Science for the People* 15, no. 6 (November-December 1983), pp. 20–24.

53. See Barbara Atkinson, "Remembering Ben," *Earth Island Journal*, Summer 1987, p. 25. See also Benjamin Linder, "The El Cuá Project," and "Last Letters Home," *Earth Island Journal*, Summer 1987, pp. 26–27.

54. Fabersunne, Atkinson, and Manwell, "Renewable Energy Technologies," p. 11.

55. For a discussion of alternative energy projects in Nicaragua, see Barbara Atkinson, "Nicaragua: Making the Switch," *SunWorld* 9, no. 3 (1985): 66–87.

56. For a discussion, see Andy Feeney, "Revolutionary Sandinistas Back Wide Range of Renewables," *Renewable Energy News* 6, no. 12 (1984): 1–12; Tim Kuhn, "On the Road to Energy Self Sufficiency," *Science for the People* 15, no. 6 (1983): 25–33; and Close Up Section, "Energy in Nicaragua: The Problems and the Prospects," *Envio* 7, no. 79 (January 1988): 17–26.

57. Atkinson, "Making the Switch," p. 68.

58. Cardenal, Larsen, Karliner, and McAlevey, "The Nicaraguan Environment," p. 24.

59. Atkinson, "Making the Switch," p. 68.

60. Fabersunne, Atkinson, and Manwell, "Renewable Energy Technologies," p. 7.

61. For a discussion of the high energy potential for this type of project, see Jawaharlall Baguant, "Electricity From the Sugar Cane Industry in Nicaragua," *Interciencia* 6, no. 2 (March/April 1981): 77–80.

62. Atkinson, "Making the Switch," p. 68.

63. See James Manwell, Barbara Atkinson, and Mikos Fabersunne, "Renewable Energy Technologies in Nicaragua and Their Relation to Economic

Development," presented at the *12th National Passive Solar Conference*, Portland Oregon (July 1987), pp. 1–5.

64. Corrales, *Impacto Ecológico*, p. 90.

65. See IRENA, "Action Plan for the Recovery, Protection and Management of Lake Xolotlán" (Managua: Instituto Nicaragüense de Recursos Naturales y del Ambiente, 1982), pp. 1–58.

66. See IRENA, *Planificación de Cuencas Hidrográficas: Plan de Ordenamiento y Manejo* 3 (Managua: Instituto Nicaragüense de Recursos Naturales y del Ambiente, 1983), pp. 159–72; and Robert Harriss and Christoph Hohenemser, "Mercury: Measuring and Managing the Risk," *Environment* 20, no. 9 (November 1978): 25–36.

67. See Amin Hassan, Eliana Velasquez, Roberto Belmar, Molly Coye, Ernest Drucker, Phillip J. Landrigan, David Michaels, and Kevin B. Sidel, "Mercury Poisoning in Nicaragua: A Case Study of the Export of Environmental and Occupational Health Hazards by a Multinational Corporation," *International Journal of Health Services* 11, no. 2 (1981): 221–26; and David Michaels, Clara Barrera, and Manuel G. Gachara, "Occupational Health and the Economic Development of Latin America," in Jane H. Ives (ed.), *The Export of Hazard: Transnational Corporations and Environmental Control Issues* (Boston: Routledge and Kegan Paul, 1985), pp. 94–114.

68. Hassan et al., "Mercury Poisoning," p. 224.

69. See also Andrew Feeney, "Breaking the Circle of Poison," *Environmental Action* 15, no. 8 (April 1984): 16–20.

70. See Annie Street, "El Caso Pennwalt: Mercury Pollution in Nicaragua," *Business and Society Review*, Winter 1982, pp. 21–23.

71. See David Kowalewski, "Pennwalt—Under Pressure—Cleans Up Mercury Contamination," *Multinational Monitor*, April 1983, p. 8; and Annie Street, "Nicaraguans Cite Pennwalt: U.S. Company has Poisoned its Workers, and Lake Managua," *Multinational Monitor*, May 1981, pp. 25–30.

72. Cardenal, Larsen, Karliner, and McAlevey, "The Nicaraguan Environment," pp. 24–26.

73. Karliner, Faber, and Rice, *Nicaragua*, pp. 5–6.

74. See Sean L. Swezey, Douglas L. Murray, and Rainer G. Daxl, "Nicaragua's Revolution in Pesticide Policy," *Environment* 28, no. 1 (January-February 1986): 6–36.

75. Ibid., pp. 6–36; and Lori Ann Thrupp, "Pesticides and Policies: Approaches to Pest-Control Dilemmas in Nicaragua and Costa Rica," *Latin American Perspectives* 15, no. 4 (Fall 1988): 53–56.

76. See Jim Brophy, "Environmental Health and Revolution in Nicaragua," *Radical America* 17, no. 2–3 (March/June 1983): 81–87.

77. See Douglas L. Murray, "Social Problem-Solving in a Revolutionary Setting: Nicaragua's Pesticide Policy Reforms," *Policy Studies Review* 4 (November 1984): 219–29; and Andrew Feeney, "Breaking the Circle of Poison," *Environmental Action* 15, no. 8 (April 1984): 16–20; and Thrupp, "Pesticides and Policies," pp. 56–58.

78. Murray, "Social Problem-Solving," pp. 219–29; and Thrupp, "Pesticides and Policies," p. 58.

79. See Sean Swezey and Daniel Faber, "Disarticulated Accumulation, Agroexport, and Ecological Crisis in Nicaragua: The Case of Cotton," *Capitalism, Nature, Socialism: A Journal of Socialist Ecology* 1 (Fall 1988): 64.

80. See Sean L. Swezey and Rainer Daxl, "The IPM Revolution in Nicaragua: Breaking the Circle of Poison," *Science for the People* 15, no. 6 (November-December 1983): 8–13.

81. Swezey and Faber, "Disarticulated Accumulation," p. 64.

82. Ibid., p. 66.

83. See also Sean L. Swezey and Rainer G. Daxl, "Area-Wide Suppression of Boll Weevil (Coleoptera: Curculionidae) Populations in Nicaragua," *Crop Protection* 7 (June 1988): 168–76.

84. Swezey and Faber, "Disarticulated Accumulation," p. 66.

85. For a discussion of the environmental impacts of the contra war, see Karliner, Faber, and Rice, *Nicaragua*, pp. 6–7; and Robert Rice and Joshua Karliner, *Militarization: The Environmental Impact*, Green Paper no. 3 (San Francisco: Environmental Project On Central America, 1986), pp. 1–8.

86. See Tony Anderson, "Reagan Embitters Nicaragua by Cutting Sugar Imports," *Multinational Monitor*, June 1983, pp. 5–6.

87. For a discussion, see Dick Russell, "Nicaragua: Saving the Environment from War, Waste and Want," *In These Times*, 19 July–1 August 1989, pp. 10–11; and David Chatfield, "A Nicaragua Journal," *Not Man Apart*, September 1985, p. 6.

88. See Reed Brody, *Contra Terror in Nicaragua* (Boston: South End Press, 1985), pp. 55–58.

89. See also Robert Rice, "A Casualty of War: The Nicaraguan Environment," *Technology Review*, May/June 1989, pp. 63–71.

90. Swezey, Murray, and Daxl, "Nicaragua's Revolution," p. 33.

91. See Rural Advancement Fund International, "Saving Seeds: Sowing Revolution," *International Genetic Resource Programme Report*, October 1984, pp. 1–4; and Bill Weinberg, "Bad Seeds in Nicaragua," *The Nation*, 10 July 1989, pp. 50–52. For a discussion of international capital's control over the global seed market, and the dire implications that poses for developing countries, see Jack Kloppenburg, Jr. and Daniel Lee Klein-

man, "Seed Wars: Common Heritage, Private Property, and Political Strategy," *Socialist Review*, 17, no. 5 (September-October 1987): 7–41; Martin Kenney and Frederick Buttel, "Biotechnology: Prospects and Dilemmas for Third World Development," *Development and Change*, 16 (1985): 61–91; and Cary Fowler, "Plant Patenting: Sowing the Seeds of Destruction," *Science for the People*, September/October 1980, pp. 8–10.

92. Thrupp, "Pesticides and Policies," pp. 37–70; and Swezey, Murray, and Daxl, "Nicaragua's Revolution," p. 33.

93. Swezey and Faber, "Disarticulated Accumulation," p. 68.

94. See Rob McConnell, "An Epidemic of Furadan and Methamidiphos Poisoning in the Cultivation of Corn: Northern Pacific Nicaragua," unpublished manuscript (1989).

95. See John Vandemeer, "Breaking New Ground: Agriculture and the Environment in Nicaragua," *Nicaraguan Perspectives* 16 (Winter 1988): 28–33.

96. See Richard Harris, "The Revolutionary Transformation of Nicaragua," *Latin American Perspectives* 14, no. 1 (Winter 1987): 3–18; and Central American Historical Institute, "Revolutionizing Health: A Study in Complexity," *Envio* 7, no. 80 (February-March 1988): 22–38.

97. Cardenal et al., "The Nicaraguan Environment," pp. 31–33; and Roberto Chavez, "Urban Planning in Nicaragua: The First Five Years," *Latin American Perspectives*, 14, no. 2 (Spring 1987): 226–36.

98. Wieberdink and van Ketel, "Institutionalization," pp. 144–45.

99. Ibid., p. 150.

100. Karliner, "Make Parks, Not War," p. 12.

101. See Karliner, "Forging a New Development Model: Costa Rica, Nicaragua Sign Agreement for Peace Park," *EPOCA Update*, Summer 1988, p. 1.

102. See *EPOCA Update*, Summer 1987, p. 6; and Joshua Karliner, "Ortega Cancels Planned Timber Sale," *Earth Island Journal*, Summer 1987, p. 29.

103. Wieberdink and van Ketel, "Institutionalization," p. 152.

104. Joshua Karliner, "Peace Plans and the Central American War," *Earth Island Journal* 2, no. 4 (Fall 1987): 36.

105. See Nathaniel Wheelwright, "In Nicaragua, War Crippled Conservation," *Christian Science Monitor*, 18 July 1990, p. 18.

106. Vilas, "What Went Wrong," pp. 10–18.

107. For a discussion of its findings, see Katherine Yih, "A Rainforest Grows Back: Assessing the Impact of Hurricane Joan," *Oxfam America News*, Summer 1989, p. 5.

108. Cardenal and Larsen, "The Nicaraguan Environment," p. 21.

109. Vilas, "What Went Wrong," pp. 10–18; and George Vickers, "A Spider's Web," *NACLA: Report on the Americas* 24, no. 1 (June 1990): 19–27.

110. Vilas, "What Went Wrong," pp. 10–18; and Vickers, "A Spider's Web," pp. 19–27.

111. For a discussion, see Instituto Histórico Centroamericano, "Nicaragua: From a Mixed-Up Economy Toward a Socialist Mixed Economy," *Envio* 8, no. 94 (May 1989): 33–54.

112. See Gary Ruchwarger, "The Sandinista Mass Organizations and the Revolutionary Process," in Richard Harris and Carlos Vilas (eds.), *Nicaragua: A Revolution Under Siege* (London: Zed Press, 1985), pp. 88–119.

113. For an earlier evaluation, see Richard L. Harris, "Evaluating Nicaragua's Agrarian Reform: Conflicting Perspectives on the Difference a Revolution Can Make," *Latin American Perspectives* 14, no. 1 (Winter 1987): 101–15; and Carmen Diana Deere, Peter Marchetti, and Nola Reinhardt, "The Peasantry and the Development of Sandinista Agrarian Policy, 1979–1984," *Latin American Research Review* 20, no. 3 (1985): 75–109.

114. Zalkin, "Nicaragua: The Peasantry, Grain Policy, and the State," p. 74.

115. See John Miller and Joe Ricciardi, "Nicaragua's Other War: The Sandinistas Tackle the Economy," *Dollars and Sense* no. 143 (January-February 1989): 16–22.

116. For a discussion, see Laura J. Enríquez, *Harvesting Change: Labor and Agrarian Reform in Nicaragua, 1979–1990* (Chapel Hill: University of North Carolina, 1991); and Hermine Weijland, Jan de Groot and Rudolf Buitelaar, "Agrarian Transformation and the Rural Labour Market: The Case of Nicaragua," *Development and Change* 19 (1988): 115–38.

117. See Dave Henson, "Elections in Nicaragua: The Environmental Impact," *EPOCA Update*, Spring 1990, pp. 1–5.

118. Enríquez, *Harvesting Change*, pp. 175–76.

119. Henson, "Elections in Nicaragua," p. 6.

6: War Against Nature: Militarization and the Impacts of U.S. Policy

1. Cited in Jim Handy, *Gift of the Devil: A History of Guatemala* (Boston: South End Press, 1984), p. 260.

2. For a discussion, see Daniel Faber, with Joshua Karliner and Robert Rice, *Central America: Roots of Environmental Destruction*, Green Paper no. 2 (San Francisco: Environmental Project On Central America, 1986).

3. See Joshua Karliner, "Central America's Other War," *World Policy Journal*, Fall 1989, pp. 787–810.

4. See Jenny Pearce, *Promised Land: Peasant Rebellion in Chalatenango, El Salvador* (London: Latin America Bureau, 1986), pp. 164–74; and James

Painter, *Guatemala: False Hope, False Freedom* (London: Latin America Bureau, 1987), p. 16.

5. See Charles D. Brockett, *Land, Power, and Poverty: Agrarian Transformation and Political Conflict in Central America* (Boston: Unwin Hyman, 1988), p. 153.

6. See James Painter, *Guatemala: False Hope, False Freedom* (London: Latin America Bureau, 1987), pp. 2–23.

7. See Jan L. Flora and Edelberto Torres-Rivas, "Sociology of Developing Societies: Historical Bases of Insurgency in Central America," in Jan Flora and Edelberto Torres-Rivas (eds.), *Central America: Sociology of Developing Countries* (New York: Monthly Review Press, 1989), p.48.

8. See Daniel Faber, "Imperialism, Revolution, and the Ecological Crisis of Central America," *Latin American Perspectives* 19, no. 1 (Winter 1992): 17–44.

9. Brockett, *Land, Power, and Poverty*, pp. 130–34.

10. See Mitchell A. Seligson, *Peasants of Costa Rica and the Development of Agrarian Capitalism* (Madison: University of Wisconsin Press, 1980), p. 34; and Flora and Torres-Rivas, "Historical Bases," p. 50.

11. Brockett, *Land, Power, and Poverty*, p. 140.

12. For an excellent history, see John A. Booth, *The End of the Beginning: The Nicaraguan Revolution* (Boulder: Westview Press, 1985).

13. See Martin Diskin, *Trouble in Our Own Backyard* (New York: Pantheon Books, 1983).

14. For a discussion of national security doctrine and the rationale for U.S. interventionism in Central America and the third world, see Saul Landau, *The Dangerous Doctrine: National Security and U.S. Foreign Policy* (Boulder: Westview Press, 1988).

15. See Tom Barry and Deb Preusch, *The Soft War* (New York: Grove Press, 1988), p. 16.

16. See Deborah Barry, Raúl Vergara, and José Rodolfo Castro, "Low Intensity Warfare: The Counterinsurgency Strategy for Central America," in Nora Hamilton, Jeffrey A. Frieden, Linda Fuller, and Manuel Pastor, Jr. (eds.), *Crisis in Central America: Regional Dynamics and U.S. Policy in the 1980s* (Boulder: Westview Press, 1988), pp. 77–96.

17. See Daniel Faber, "Imperialism, Revolution, and the Ecological Crisis of Central America," *Latin American Perspectives* 19, no. 1 (Winter 1992): 17–44.

18. See Nora Hamilton and Manuel Pastor, Jr., "Introduction," in Nora Hamilton, Jeffrey Frieden, Linda Fuller, Manuel Pastor, Jr., (eds.), *Crisis in Central America: Regional Dynamics and U.S. Policy in the 1980s* (Boulder: Westview Press, 1988), p. 1.

19. See Joshua Karliner and Robert Rice, *Militarization: The Environmental*

Impact, Green Paper no. 3 (San Francisco: Environmental Project On Central America, 1986), p. 2.

20. See Tom Barry, *Central America Inside Out: The Essential Guide to Its Societies, Politics, and Economies* (New York: Grove Weidenfeld, 1991), p. 28.

21. See Jenny Pearce, *Under the Eagle: U.S. Intervention in Central America and the Caribbean* (Boston: South End Press), p. 52.

22. See Holly Sklar, "Born-Again War: The Low Intensity Mystique," *NACLA: Report on the Americas*, 21, no. 2 (March-April 1987): 9–11.

23. See Col. John D. Waghelstein, "Low-Intensity Conflict in the Post-Vietnam Period," transcript of presentation at American Enterprise Institute (Washington, D.C., January 17, 1985), p. 1.

24. See Tom Barry, *Low Intensity Conflict: The New Battle Field in Central America* (Albuquerque: Central America Resource Center, 1986); and "The Real War," *NACLA: Report on the Americas*, April/May 1986, pp. 17–48.

25. Barry, *Central America Inside Out*, pp. 332–33.

26. Ibid., p. 299.

27. See *Honduras Update*, March 1984.

28. See Morris J. Blachman, William M. LeoGrande, and Kenneth Sharpe, *Confronting Revolution: Security Through Diplomacy in Central America* (New York: Pantheon Books, 1986), pp. 129–52.

29. Barry, *Central America Inside Out*, pp. 320–28.

30. Karliner and Rice, *Militarization*, p. 5.

31. See D. Huss, "Reagan Rattles Saber, Wants Contra Funding," *Guardian* (New York), 12 March 1986, p. 14.

32. See Bill Hall and Joshua Karliner, "A Forgotten War: The Assault on Central America's Environment," *Greenpeace* 12, no. 3 (October-December 1987): 11.

33. See Florence Gardner, "U.S. Environmental Leaders Tour Central America," *Earth Island Journal* 2, no. 3 (Summer 1987): 30–31.

34. See Agencia Nuevo Nicaragua, 2 May 1986.

35. See James Nations and Daniel Komer, "International Action Halts Road Through Honduras Rainforest," *Ambio* 12, no. 2 (1983): 124–25.

36. See Jane F. McAlevey, "Honduras: Multi-Nationals, Military and Ecological Crisis," *EPOCA Update*, Spring 1990, pp. 5–13.

37. McAlevey, "Honduras," p. 12.

38. See Raymond Bonner, *Weakness and Deceit: U.S. Policy and El Salvador* (New York: Times Books, 1984).

39. See Michael McClintock, *The American Connection: State Terror and Popular Resistance in El Salvador*, vol. 1 (London: Zed Books, 1985); and Allan Nairn, "Behind the Death Squads," *The Progressive* (May 1984).

40. See Amnesty International, *El Salvador's Death Squads: A Government Strategy* (London: Amnesty International Publications, 1988), p. 9.
41. Barry and Preusch, *The Soft War*, p. 202; and Barry, Vergara, and Castro, "Low Intensity Warfare," p. 87.
42. It has been estimated that more than one-third of the population has been displaced by the war and 1986 earthquake. See Morris J. Blachman and Kenneth E. Sharpe, "Things Fall Apart: Trouble Ahead in El Salvador," *World Policy Journal*, Winter 1988, p. 111.
43. See Ricardo Stein, "Civil War, Reform, and Reaction in El Salvador," in Hamilton et al., eds., *Crisis in Central America*, pp. 193–205; and Gar Smith, "The Invisible War," *Not Man Apart* (July/August 1985).
44. Blachman and Sharpe, "Things Fall Apart," p. 111; and Arms Control and Foreign Policy Caucus of the U.S. Congress, *Bankrolling Failure: U.S. Policy in El Salvador and the Urgent Need for Reform* (Washington, DC: U.S. Congress, November 1987).
45. See Michael Klare and Peter Kornbluh, *Low Intensity Warfare* (New York: Pantheon, 1988), p. 112.
46. See John MacLean, *Prolonging the Agony: The Human Cost of Low Intensity Conflict* (London: El Salvador Committee for Human Rights, 1987), p. 11; and Jenny Pearce, *Promised Land: Peasant Rebellion in Chalatenango, El Salvador* (London: Latin America Bureau, 1986).
47. See *Soldier of Fortune Magazine* (June 1984).
48. See James Stephens, "El Salvador: Environment and War," draft manuscript, American Friends Service Committee Report (February 1989), p. 13.
49. Smith, "The Invisible War"; and T. Redmond, "Too Hot to Handle: Ten Major Stories the Nation's Media Ignored in 1985," *San Francisco Bay Guardian*, 1 June 1986, pp. 9–12.
50. Cited in Stephens, "El Savador: Environment and War," p. 14.
51. Smith, "Invisible War," p. 12.
52. Cited in ibid., p. 13.
53. For a discussion of the ecological impacts of these weapons, see María del Carmen Rojas Canales, *Efectos Ecológicos de la Guerra en El Salvador* (Mexico City: UNAM, 1983), p. 5.
54. See Oscar Antonio Pérez, "El Silencioso Dolor de una Guerra Escandalosa," *Nueva Sociedad* no. 87 (1983).
55. See *Central America Report* (November/December, 1984); and Rojas Canales, *Effectos Ecologicos*.
56. Smith, "Invisible War."
57. See *Diagnóstico de la Dequia 1987/1988 y su Impacto Económico-Social en El Salvador* (San Salvador: Consultores Alternativas Regionales Para El Desarrollo, July 1988), pp. 11–12.

58. See Bill Hall and Daniel Faber, *El Salvador: Ecology of Conflict*, Green Paper no. 4 (San Francisco: Environmental Project On Central America, 1989), pp. 1–2.

59. Ibid., p. 9.

60. Based on first hand field research and interviews with Salvadoran environmentalists in ibid., p. 8.

61. Smith, "Invisible War."

62. See E.R.F. Sheehan, "The Clean War," *New York Review of Books* (26 June 1986), pp. 25–30; and Karliner and Rice, *Militarization,* p. 4.

63. Stephens, "El Salvador: Environment and War," p.16.

64. See José Ignacio Martínez Arnaíz, *Ecología* (San Salvador: Universidad Centroamericana, 1987), p. 172.

65. Stephens, "El Salvador," p. 18.

66. See Hector Armando Marroquín Arévalo, "Impacto de la Guerra en el Hombre, la Sociedad y Los Recursos Naturales de El Salvador," lecture prepared for the Universidad Centroamericana José Simeon Canas (San Salvador), 25 August 1988, pp. 28–32, cited in Stephens, "El Salvador," p. 18.

67. Hall and Faber, *El Salvador: Ecology of Conflict,* p. 9.

68. Rojas Canales, *Effectos Ecologicos.*

69. Rice and Karliner, *Militarization,* p. 4.

70. See Pamela Constable, "Baker Hails El Salvador Accord, Pledges Aid," *Boston Globe,* 18 January 1992, pp. 1–4.

71. See Arms Control and Foreign Policy Caucus of the U.S. Congress, *Bankrolling Failure,* pp. 75–84.

72. See Kevin Danaher, Phillip Berryman and Medea Benjamin, *Help or Hindrance?: U.S. Economic Aid in Central America* (San Francisco: Institute for Food and Development Policy, 1987), p. 26.

73. See Barry and Preusch, *The Soft War;* and Danaher, Berryman, and Benjamin, *Help or Hindrance?;* and Colin Danby, *Stabilization and Transformation: Bilateral U.S. Economic Aid in Central America,* draft background paper (March 1989).

74. See Hall and Faber, *El Salvador,* p. 6; Danby, *Stabilization and Transformation;* and PACCA, *Changing Course: Blueprint for Peace in Central America and the Caribbean* (Washington, DC: Institute for Policy Studies, 1984), pp. 75–84.

75. See Phillip Wheaton, *Agrarian Reform in El Salvador: A Program of Rural Pacification* (Washington, DC: EPICA Task Force, November 1980); and *Boletín Internacional del Socorro Jurídico del Arzobispado de San Salvador,* no. 40 (15 May 1982): 3–6.

76. See Lawrence Simon et al., *El Salvador Land Reform 1980–81: Impact Audit* (Boston: Oxfam America, 1981), p. 19.

77. See USAID Inspector General (Latin America), *Agrarian Reform in El Salvador: A Report on its Status* (1984), cited in Barry and Preusch, *The Soft War*, p. 152.

78. See George Black, *Garrison Guatemala* (New York: Monthly Review Press, 1984).

79. See Gabriel Aguilera Peralta, "The Hidden War: Guatemala's Counter-insurgency Campaign," in Nora Hamilton, Jeffrey A. Frieden, Linda Fuller, and Manuel Pastor, Jr. (eds.), *Crisis in Central America: Regional Dynamics and U.S. Policy in the 1980s* (Boulder: Westview Press, 1988), pp. 153–72.

80. See Centro Exterior de Reportes Informativos sobre Guatemala (CERI-GUA), *Weekly Briefs*, 11 June 1990.

81. See Amnesty International, *Guatemala: Human Rights Violations Under the Civilian Government* (New York: Amnesty International Publications, June 1989), p. 5.

82. See Florence Gardner, with Yaakov Garb and Marta Williams, *Guatemala: A Political Ecology*, Green Paper no. 5 (San Francisco: Environmental Project On Central America, 1990), p. 8; and Kenneth Freed, "U.S. Is Taking a New Tack in Guatemala," *Los Angeles Times*, 7 May 1990, pp. A7–A8.

83. See Ken Anderson and Jean-Marie Simon, "Permanent Counter-insurgency in Guatemala," *Telos* no. 73 (Fall 1987): 30–31.

84. For a critique of the political and strategic failures of the Guatemalan revolutionary movement, see Peralta, "The Hidden War," p. 158.

85. See Beatriz Manz, *Refugees of a Hidden War: The Aftermath of the Counter-insurgency in Guatemala* (New York: State University of New York Press, 1988).

86. See Americas Watch, *Human Rights in Guatemala: No Neutrals Allowed* (New York: 1982).

87. See Coordinating Commission of the Communities of Population in Resistance of the Sierra, "Declaration of the First General Assembly of the Communities of Population in Resistance of the Sierra to the Government and the People of Guatemala, and to the Government and Peoples of the World" (March 27, 1990), p. 7.

88. For a discussion, see Naomi Roht-Arriaza, "Guatemala: Politics of Destruction," *Central America Reporter*, September/October 1991, p. 6.

89. See Guatemalan Church in Exile (IGE), *Security and Development in Guatemala* (April 1989), p. 41.

90. See Jim Burchfield, "Natural Resources Under Siege: The Environmental Costs of Counterinsurgency," *OSGUA Newsletter* (Chicago), Spring 1989; Guatemala News and Information Bureau, "Scorched Earth: Eco-

logical Effects on Indigenous Communities," *Guatemala* 5, no. 2 (1984); and Karliner and Rice, *Militarization*, p. 5.

91. Gardner, Garb, and Williams, *Guatemala: A Political Ecology*, p. 8.
92. See USAID-Guatemala I, *Draft Environmental Profile on Guatemala* (Athens: Institute of Ecology, University of Georgia, 1981), p. 18.
93. Ibid.
94. Barry, *Central America Inside Out*, p. 244.
95. Manz, *Refugees of a Hidden War*, p. 12.
96. Barry, *Central America Inside Out*, pp. 270–75.
97. See CERI-GUA, *Special Service* (March 1990); Gardner, Garb, and Williams, *Guatemala*; and Barry, *Central America Inside Out*, pp. 269–75.
98. For a discussion of the economic and political privileges of the Guatemalan military, see Carol A. Smith, "The Militarization of Civil Society in Guatemala: Economic Reorganization as a Continuation of War," *Latin American Perspectives* 17, no. 4 (Fall 1990): 8–41.
99. See Special Report, "An Appeal from the Guatemalan Human Rights Commission: The Drug War and the Environment," *Earth Island Journal* 3, no. 3 (Summer 1988): 32.
100. See Kenneth Freed, "U.S. Is Taking New Tack," p. A7.
101. See Karen Parker, *Fumigation Programs in Guatemala* (San Francisco: Association of Humanitarian Lawyers, 1989).
102. See Gardner, Garb, and Williams, *Guatemala*, p. 13; Environmental Protection Agency, "Decision and Emergency Order Suspending Registration for Certain Uses of 2-(2,4,5-Trichlorophenoxy) Propionic Acid (Silvex)," Office Pesticide Programs (February 1979); S. Quee Hee and R.G. Sutherland, "The Phenoxy Alkanoic" (CRC Press, 1981); and Barry, *Central America Inside Out*, p. 266.
103. CERI-GUA, *Special Service* (March 1990).
104. Gardner, Garb, and Williams, *Guatemala*, p. 13.
105. See Jim Handy, "Insurgency and Counter-insurgency in Guatemala," in Jan L. Flora and Edelberto Torres-Rivas, eds., *Central America: Sociology of "Developing Societies"* (New York: Monthly Review Press, 1989), pp. 112–39.
106. Anderson and Simon, "Permanent Counterinsurgency in Guatemala," pp. 30–31.
107. See Patricia K. Hall, "Military Rule Threatens Guatemala's Highland Maya Indians," *Cultural Survival* 10, no. 2 (1986): 48–52.
108. Cited in Gardner, Garb, and Williams, *Guatemala*, p. 9.
109. Anderson and Simon, "Permanent Counterinsurgency," p. 32; and Smith, "Invisible War," pp. 18–23.
110. Anderson and Simon, "Permanent Counterinsurgency," pp. 9–46.
111. Barry, *Central America Inside Out*, pp. 268–79.

112. Peralta, "The Hidden War," p. 168.
113. Ibid., p. 178.
114. Ibid., p. 168.

Conclusion: *The Struggle for Social and Ecological Justice*

1. See Daniel Faber, "The Ecological Crisis of Latin America: A Theoretical Introduction," *Latin American Perspectives* 19, no. 1 (Winter 1992): 3–16; and other articles in this special issue of *LAP*.
2. See Daniel Faber, with Josh Karliner and Robert Rice, *Central America: Roots of Environmental Destruction*, Green Paper no. 2 (San Francisco: Environmental Project On Central America, 1986), pp. 1–7.
3. See Tom Barry, *Central America Inside Out* (New York: Grove Weidenfeld, 1991), p. 20.
4. See Daniel Faber and James O'Connor, "The Struggle for Nature: Environmental Crises and the Crisis of Environmentalism in the United States," *Capitalism, Nature, Socialism*, no. 2 (Summer 1989): 27; and Barry I. Castleman and Vicente Navarro, "International Mobility of Hazardous Products, Industries, and Wastes," *International Journal of Health Services* 17, no. 4 (1987).
5. Faber and O'Connor, "The Struggle for Nature," p. 27.
6. See Pip Hinman, "Nicaragua: Strong Campaign Saves Wilderness," *Venceremos!: Magazine of Latin American & Caribbean Solidarity* (Australia), no. 41 (Autumn 1992): 5.
7. See Glen Martin and John Otis, "Big Plans to Log a Virgin Rain Forest: Years of Warfare Spared the Land in Honduras and Nicaragua," *San Francisco Chronicle*, 19 December 1991, p. A14.
8. See Alan A. Block and Frank R. Scarpitti, *Poisoning for Profit: The Mafia and Toxic Waste in America* (New York: William Morrow, 1982).
9. See Bill Hall and Joshua Karliner, "A Forgotten War: The Assault on Central America's Environment," *Greenpeace* 12, no. 4 (October-December 1987): 11–15.
10. See Bill Hall and Joshua Karliner, "Garbage Imperialism," *EPOCA Update*, Summer 1988, p. 4.
11. Ibid.
12. Ibid., p.5.
13. See Jim Vallette and Heather Spalding, *The International Trade in Wastes: A Greenpeace Inventory* (Washington, DC: Greenpeace USA, 1990).
14. For a discussion, see Mark Dowie, "The Dumping of Hazardous Products on Foreign Markets," in Stuart L. Hills (ed.), *Corporate Violence: Injury and Death for Profit* (New York: Rowman and Littlefield, 1987), pp. 46–59; and Tomás Mac Sheoin, "The Export of Hazardous Products

and Industries: A Bibliography," *International Journal of Health Services* 17, no. 2 (1987): 343–64.

15. See Elie Sasson, "Pressure Mounts to Halt Pesticide Exports: The Pesticide Export Reform Act of 1990," *EPOCA Update*, Summer 1990, pp. 13–14.

16. See Lori Ann Thrupp, "The Political Ecology of Pesticide Use in Developing Countries: Dilemmas in the Banana Sector of Costa Rica" (Ph.D. diss., University of Sussex, 1988), pp. 157–263.

17. See Douglas Murray, "Recurring Contradictions in Agrarian Development: Pesticide Problems in Caribbean Basin Non-Traditional Agriculture," *World Development* 20, no. 4 (April 1992): 597–608.

18. For a brief overview of the pesticide crisis in Central America, see Daniel Faber, "A Sea of Poison," *NACLA: Report On the Americas* 25, no. 2 (September 1991): 36.

19. Dowie, "The Dumping," p. 53.

20. Barry, *Central America Inside Out*, p. 15.

21. Ibid.

22. See Douglas Murray, "Export Agriculture, Ecological Disruption, and Social Inequity: Some Effects of Pesticides in Southern Honduras," *Agriculture and Human Values* 8, no. 4 (Fall 1991): 10–29; and Susan C. Stonich, "The Promotion of Non-traditional Agricultural Exports in Honduras: Issues of Equity, Environment and Natural Resource Management," *Development and Change* 22, no. 4 (October 1991). See also Denise L. Stanley, "Communal Forest Management: The Honduran Resin Tappers" (same issue), for another interesting article on environmental issues in Honduras.

23. For a discussion of the social impacts of nontraditional agriculture, see Peter Rosset, "Sustainability, Economy of Scale, and Social Instability: The Achilles Heel of Non-Traditional Agriculture?," *Agriculture and Human Values* 8, no. 4 (Fall 1991): 30–37.

24. See Josh Karliner, "Central America's Other War: The Environment Under Siege," *World Policy Journal*, Fall 1989, p. 802.

25. See Brad Erickson, "Are Debt-for-Nature Swaps the Answer?," *EPOCA Update*, Summer 1990, pp. 2–5.

INDEX